Knowledge Transfer for Quality Education

KNOWLEDGE TRANSFER FOR QUALITY EDUCATION

Rajarshi Roy

SHIPRA

Rs. 1500

ISBN: 978-81-7541-862-2

First Published in India in 2016

Knowledge Transfer for Quality Education

Published by:

SHIPRA PUBLICATIONS
LG 18-19, Pankaj Central Market,
I.P. Ext., Patparganj, Delhi 110092, India
Ph.: 011- 2223 5152, 2223 6152
Email: info@shiprapublication.com
www.shiprapublication.com

Dedicated to
Prof. Subhrangshu Kumar Sarkar

Foreword

The knowledge transfer for quality education involving techniques and methods is indeed a critical area in educational research and training, especially in Teacher Education, for the simple reason that the educators have to be adequately equipped in the art and science of teaching as well as in training the teachers for relevant levels, to which the curriculum at the masters level needs to be appropriately focused on the objective and purposes of education. The inputs are to be drawn from the changing global, national and regional scenarios and the social and cultural background of the teachers and the learners are also to be taken into account in designing relevant curricula, particularly in areas like psycho-pedagogy and applications thereof. The Indian paradigm by the logic of its history and geography has to be inclusive of the neighbouring SAARC nations, and the changing perception of the role of education *vis-á-vis* globalization deserves appreciation without compromising the basic principles and ethical values of education. It is true that the curricula in higher education have been significantly improvised over the years to meet the challenges of changing times, but it is equally important that the reading references and study materials should also be regularly updated by the experts and many more books should be authored by scholars alongside improvisation of various curricula, irrespective of disciplines. The academia across nations is seemingly alive to these requirements and new publications are always striking the shelves.

Rajarshi Roy's *Knowledge Transfer for Quality Education* has been well structured to cover the basics of educational theories, technology and training, like teacher, pedagogy-system and curriculum; instruction; learning style, motivation and communication; skill-sets for teaching and instructional media; measurement, evaluation and measuring devices, and psycho-pedagogy and teaching, in conformity with the stated objective of his work to meet the requirement of the students of Education at the post-graduate level and of the teacher-trainers for the varied levels of the teaching profession. The book is indeed expected to enable the serious readers in the field of education to assimilate the concepts, facts, procedures and principles guiding the theoretical and operational dimensions of education and at the same time, to adequately empower the teachers to effectively respond to the call of their profession to become skilful communicators in the classroom ambiances.

I have closely known the author as a serious teacher and researcher since the time he joined the faculty of Education at the Assam University, Silchar, in 1997. What impressed me most is his student-friendly approach to find and/or create quality readings for them and his capacity to motivate the students to sincerely study such materials. He has grown in scholarship and in his profession over the years, but this student-friendly approach as well his concern for the development of the socially disadvantaged is consistently maintained in his host of publications, some of which I had the opportunity to read. I am sure his *Knowledge Transfer for Quality Education* will also be found useful to those for whom it is written.

Shillong
18 May, 2016

J.B. Bhattacharjee
Founder Vice Chancellor, Assam University, Silchar
Former Vice Chancellor, North Eastern Hill University

Preface

The present volume, *Knowledge Transfer for Quality Education* is an humble attempt in the arena of Psychopedagogy, which is expected to cater to some specific needs of the students of Education at post graduate level, including M.Ed. and M.A./ M.Sc. (Education) as also the trainers who deal with discharging the responsibility to train the teachers at varied levels within the gamut of education.

The volume is divided into six sections, namely

I. Teacher, Pedagogy-System and Curriculum;
II. Instruction;
III. Learning Styles, Motivation and Communication;
IV. Skill-sets for Teaching and Instructional Media;
V. Measurement, Evaluation and Measuring Devices; and
VI. Psychopedagogy and Teaching.

The first section, titled, *Teacher, Pedagogy System and Curriculum* accords three chapters, namely 'The Teacher', 'Learning: Psychology and Principles' and 'Glimpse of Pedagogy and Curriculum'. The first chapter deals with the pertinent issues like Teacher and associated changed roles, manpower characteristics in the changing scenario in India and neighbouring SAARC countries and changed educational perspectives and role of teacher in the rapidly changing paradigm along with their necessary traits to enhance effectiveness and ethical vitalities and values amidst of marketization of education, suggesting the expected value components and obligations. In consonance, the second chapter emphasizes over the behavioural, developmental and perceptual approaches of learning, along with associated dominant theories and their applications. The third chapter focuses on systems thinking in teaching and learning along with its levels, instruction, it's schemata and curricular issues.

The second section, titled, *Instruction* is a cloud of Instructional objectives, Instructional strategies and methods and Instructional planning, with specific focus over the basics of Instruction, Instructional objectives and strategies to formulate objectives at different domains of learning and their linkage with evaluation. Overall instructional strategies, tactics and methods are dealt in length in this section, which is followed by classroom instructional plan. The section is supplemented with some standard instructional plan.

The third section deals with the pivotal issues like Learning-styles, motivation and communication for better dissemination of education to ensure the quality of education. Up till date, most of the curricula in Education at Post Graduate level have not recognised the need to accord learning-style, unlike the developed nations. Various models of learning-styles are expected to fulfill the need of the present generation students of Education. The immediate next chapter themes to equip the readers into efficient motivator for quality education by enabling them to turn into good communicator, both from theoretical and practical aspects.

Fourth section of the volume is dedicated towards the instructional and visual media designing along with 'skill' component of teaching.

The section five deals with the basics and bases of Measurement, Evaluation and Allied Devices to evaluate achievement of students and trainees in differing domains of learning and also extending an exposure to different devices to do so. Types and characteristics and questions are also naturally come into central position of discussion in context, giving proper emphasis over 'skill-evaluation' too.

The last section of the volume is titled as *Psychopedagogy and Teaching*. The section accord three chapters namely Interface of psychology, Education and guidance, followed by Psychopedagogy for guiding adolescent students and Psychopedagogical tests and inventories in carrier guidance vis-à-vis Emotional Intelligence.

The volume is prepared in such a way that while at one hand, serious reader from the field of Education will be able to link-up the concepts, facts, procedures and principles guiding the theoretical and practical dimensions of Education, on the other hand, the casual readers are also expected to be benefitted to become efficient in the teaching profession.

Since the volume is an outcome of theoretical knowledge supplemented with the experience across decades, which ramified the views of the author and in course influenced the knowledge base, hence it is expected that the volume will help in supplement the thought process of the readers.

The author will be pleased to be communicated in the email address <dr_r_roy@yahoo.com> for any query, clarification and comments relating to any issue of the volume.

Contents

SECTION E
Measurement, Evaluation and Measuring Devices

SECTION F
Psychopedagogy and Teaching

SECTION A

Teacher, Pedagogy-System and Curriculum

1
The Teacher

A changing world requires a changing style of education. Young people who are being prepared for entry into the adult responsibilities of teaching are to be equipped with skill-sets that are quite different from those which sufficed for their predecessors. Senior teachers find it increasingly necessary to brush-up their knowledge and skill bases so that they can perform successfully in a changing environment. With the changing time the traditional roles and attributes of a teacher of any institution has changed substantially over the past few decades. Such changes have been accentuated particularly since the time the country's economy was opened up in the early 1995. With the process of liberalisation gathering momentum, perceptible changes have been taking place in the various fields of activities.

With the opening up of the then new-economy the multinational companies were allowed to invest and do business in this country. Their high quality products and services backed up with modern technology and management efficiency forced our domestic business houses to:

(i) Update their technologies, machineries, management perspective and

(ii) Face the challenges thrown up by liberalisation by developing their manpower on the lines of the market requirements. Effect of such changes has also been felt in the special types of educational sector. In an environment defined by buzz words such as *quality*, *competition* and universalisation of the education, the system dealing with education also needed to face the challenges at the door steps and achieved desired quality and efficiency in the entire gamut of activities. It has been realised by all that without being responsive to the social changes, and market needs, it would be difficult to survive in the present times.

Teacher as a Change Agent

Changes in the international business environment possess its impact and effect on the domestic educo-social and educo-industrial scenario. This in turn has an effect on the education sector in general and the specialised education sector in particular. With the adoption of new technologies, new business initiatives, systems standardisation for quality in the industries in place, the need for technically equipped manpower with wider spectrum of knowledge and skill-sets have become a necessity.

At the institutional level such changes are primarily addressed through updating the *curricula*, introducing courses in the emerging areas, modernising classrooms, laboratories and workshops and developing effective teaching-learning systems, teaching-learning strategies and teaching-learning tactics.

However, all efforts would have no meaning if the system fails to provide adequate number of qualified and discerning teachers who would inculcate knowledge and impart training to the students and help them to face the challenges of the world of work. The quality of teacher, therefore, is of prime importance to not only the planners and administrators of education but also to the students.

It is the teacher who acts as an *'interface'* between the students and the world of work, and therefore should be viewed as a change-agent in the educational process. It follows that the teacher himself would have to keep on learning, update his own knowledge and skill-bases, internalise new knowledge, new values generated by the changing times and pass on the same to his pupil.

Role of a Teacher

Education is a tri-polar process. At one end is the 'educator' i.e. the **teacher**, at the other is the 'receiver' his **pupil** and in between is the **content** i.e. what is being taught.

While engaged in the process of educating, the lecturer, or today's assistant professors or a teacher not only transmits some curricular contents but also 'transfers' his own personality to certain extent.

In general, this transference of personality is unintended. But there is little doubt that it takes peace in this way or that way. Apart from the subject-matter or topic, or 'content', the teacher also tries to implant the best in him/her on the students, help him/her imbibe essential value system, skill-sets of social relation, fellow feeling, compassion and so on, in order to make him/her a better human being who can suitably fit into the socio-cultural milieu of the country and contribute positively in developmental activities.

A teacher, therefore, primarily plays the role of an educator which actually encompasses other important 'roles' as well. As an educator, he communicates important knowledge in the form of concepts, facts, procedures and principles to his/her students. S/he helps students to 'understand' concepts, ideas that are new to them. This is the primary and most important role, a teacher plays. However, apart from subject knowledge, a teacher also, directly or indirectly inculcates essential values to his students with the hope that his students will not only be knowledgeable and skilled in the area of specialisation but also be a 'good human being'. Such inculcation it has been mentioned, may be deliberate *(direct classroom teaching of dos and don'ts for example)* or indirect by transmitting essential message through his own life style, ethos, beliefs and behaviour.

A teacher supposedly should have 'close contact' with the students throughout the period of study and guide them through various phases of development. S/he, often at times, would suggest and guide them through their selection of subjects, career and different other situations in which it becomes difficult for the students to make a choice. Therefore, it indicates that, a teacher besides being an educator also plays '*parental role*', or of a counselor. These are no less important. A teacher is in a sense is also a 'philosopher-guide' for the students. There 'role-plays' are apparent throughout a student's study years—right from the schools through the college and possibly beyond it. As a matter of fact, the role of a counselor becomes important for a teacher at a higher level of education in the college or university. However it may be pointed out that teachers' role and their various dimensions are not constant factors – they may be changed, be modified as and when required, as the society develops and progresses.

Manpower Characteristics in a Changing Scenario

Industries adopt new technologies, develop new ways of doing things, and modify management techniques and so on. As a result, there are continuous modifications in the job requirement of the changing manpower—new competencies are sought for. As a consequence, the teaching-learning systems in the institutions are also modified so as to develop and offer trained and skilled manpower equipped with new competencies. Not only the studios, classrooms, laboratories and workshops are modernised, the manpower at its disposal, particularly the faculty is retrained to address the new requirements.

In such a complex situation the teachers' roles are modified too: new dimensions are added to his already defined job-function. In order to understand the changing pattern of teachers' roles and competencies, it will be helpful to note some of the changing characteristics of the changed manpower requirements in the 'education-industries'. This is an important aspect because unless the teachers and trainers are geared up for the required changes, it would be difficult for them to prepare their students on the lines of industries' requirement. A short list is presented below according to 'a few' desirable characteristics of graduates at present:

- In-depth knowledge in the area(s) of specialisation
- Problem solving skill
- Knowledge in 'work field strategies'
- Knowledge in 'management principles'
- Good communication-skill
- Willingness to keep on learning
- Ability to work in team-situation
- Positive frame of mind
- Working knowledge on global perspective in work-activities
- Working knowledge in environmental impact due to changing activities
- An orientation towards quality management and standards
- An orientation towards quality tools
- Working knowledge in occupational safety
- Concern for fellow workers
- Leadership qualities.

It may be appreciated that, the list above, which is not exhaustive at all, but depicts a few, unfailingly indicates that special academic activities over and above classroom teaching in subject matter only, are required to be undertaken to inculcate these characteristics in the students to go beyond.

Changes in Education Perspectives

In the higher education sector, as much, some important change have also been seen primarily to cope-up with the new challenges of the changing scenario. Higher education experts have identified a number of broad areas in which immediate attention would be required. Some of those areas of initiatives are:

- Driving out the obsolescence in studios, classrooms, laboratories and work environment
- Retraining of personnel
- Modernising existing curricula
- Access to information through internet

- Developing systemic and logical institutional management
- Promoting quality educational services
- Exploring possibilities of external finding (to lessen burden on state funding).

National Educational Policy (1986) also reflects similar concerns and recommends various initiatives at the institution level. Some of them are:

- Introduction of new technology-based/enabled programmes.
- Conduction of special programmes for specific gender groups, such as women and trans-genders
- Conduction of continuing education programmes.
- Modernisation of laboratories and workshops.
- Development of linkage with industries.
- Development of management reformation systems and the like.

Thus it may be said that in order to implement all these, institutions will have to:

- Develop new strategies for effective teaching-learning systems, with, or focus on, needs of the world of work
- Assure quality in institutional services
- Develop capabilities of the faculty and
- Improve the efficiency of the institutional management system.

It cannot be overemphasised that faculty members being at the fulcrum of institutional activities play a pivotal role in developing the overall quality and efficiency of the institutions.

Role of Teacher in a Changing Scenario

In the light of the above specifications, it would be helpful to take a close look at the roles of a teacher of an advanced institute or a department of a university. The list below containing a host of role of advanced teacher is a suggestive one and contains basic roles over and above 'new' roles that have become necessary at present:

- Class room/record-room/archive/studio/laboratory instruction
- Guiding graduate projects in tune with changed curricula
- Participating in curricula revision and development exercises
- Students' assessment
- Developing and procuring learning resources
- Developing and procuring instructional materials
- Developing and procuring record-room/archive/studio/laboratory manuals

- Actively participating in respective industry/stakeholder -institute interaction activities
- Participating in entrepreneurship developments programmes
- Developing and conducting continuing education programmes.
- Organising appropriate training for students
- Participating in institutional developmental activities, promotional/ image building activities.
- Self- developmental initiatives
- Participating in community development and outreach programmes.
- Understanding and participating in students counseling activities.
- Undertaking research and consultancy activities
- Actively participating in quality and environmental awareness building activities
- Organising seminars/workshops/entrepreneurship development programmes
- Organising special classes to develop social relation skill among students.

The list given above is again, not an exhaustive one. The teacher themselves may add more to the list. But, the thing should be remembered that, the focus of any or a set of activities would have to be directed towards achieving educational objectives and desired quality.

Effectiveness of a Teacher

Teaching activity essentially boils down to communicating effectively the concepts, fact, procedures, principles and ideas to the learner and expect some kind of behavioural changes to take place in them. Teaching should be viewed as a live performance in a classroom or in any other learning situations. It is difficult to imagine that all members of the profession would prove equally effective as teachers in any particular learning situation. A teacher's effectiveness has been discussed at length by many authors. Some have seen it from the point of view of curricular achievement only; some of them have brought in development of basic skill-sets, understanding, work-habits, desirable attitude, and value-judgment of student to explain teachers' effectiveness.

On the other hand, some other researchers defined teachers' effectiveness as a relationship between the characteristics of teachers, teaching acts, with their effects on the educational outcomes of classroom teaching, while certain others researchers discussed teachers' effectiveness in terms of certain qualities, such as sense of humor, understanding of students problems, clearly explaining the concepts and the like.

Attempts have been made by many scholars such as to evaluate teachers' effectiveness in terms of various factors like—classroom management, instructional skills, professional preparation, ability to work with others, competencies, leadership, personal and essential adjustments.

Later, categories of teaching effectiveness were also suggested some of which are listed as:

- Physical fitness (such as, good health, drive etc.)
- Personal fitness (such as, attractiveness, cooperation, considerateness, ethics, reliability etc.)
- General skill-sets (such as, communication, human relation, verbal skills etc.)
- Cognitive abilities (such as, intelligence, problem solving, aptitude etc.)
- Affective ability (such as, motivation, interest, attitude etc.)
- Professional Confidence (such as, knowledge, skill, personal characteristics etc.).

Interestingly, one of the studies made as back as in 1930s on qualities of 'good' and 'bad' teachers concluded that:

- Good teachers if compared with poor teachers are characterised by qualities of vigorousness, enthusiasm, happiness, and pleasantness and humorous.
- Good teachers differ from poor teachers in respect of use of illustrative materials, knowledge in subject matter, good delivery, manner of conversation, use of pupils' experiences, socialisation in class, techniques of asking questions etc.

Teacher's Traits

It has been already mentioned that effective teaching is all about putting across concepts, facts, procedures and principles as also ideas to the learners clearly and consequently expecting a desired behavioural change.

Research in the field, as mentioned above, shows that effectiveness of a teacher, does not depend upon any single factor. On the contrary, effectiveness of a teacher be in general education or in specialised education depends upon a plethora of characteristics that can suitably be called as traits.

Without discounting on modern day technique of web-based distant mode of teaching, in majority of cases teaching happens to be a live performance involving the teacher and his students in 'contact' mode. It may therefore be expected that effectiveness of a teacher *vis-à-vis* satisfaction of the students will depend upon more than one factor- a great chunk of which can be attributed to teachers' personality and other characteristics. Had it not been the case, then recorded lectures, computer/television based teaching would have long replaced contact mode of teaching. It follows that in a contact mode of teaching-learning situation, the teacher remains at the helm of affairs delivering in real time, managing, controlling the entire class room having scores of student ogling at him and observing minutely his behaviour, his posture, body language and so on—that is to say every bits of his performance. Therefore, to impress upon the students and to increase the effectiveness of the learning session, s/he will have to consciously control a number of things that include not only the behaviour, body language, attitude, subject matter competence, communication, eye-contact, acknowledging students' responses and many such things.

In a study (Singh, 1992), which aimed to identify and correlate teachers' traits with teaching effectiveness, the respondents identified more than 25 traits to describe a competent teacher. The identified traits were a combination of traits under cognitive, psycho-motor and affective domains. A selection of the identified traits from the work is given below:

- Knowledge of subject matter.
- Readiness to remove students' difficulties.
- Knowledge of teaching methodology.
- Understanding the pupils.
- Sympathy and cooperation with the pupils.
- Impartiality with students.
- Punctuality and regularity.
- Self-confidence.
- Cheerful appearance.

Traits of an effective teacher as specified above are applicable to all sections of the teachers belonging to different types of institutions. In a recent study, conducted by the author a couple of years back, responses received against a simple question *'What do you think should be the characteristics of a successful teacher?'* from young teachers who are new to the 'certain specialised educational system' in the states of Orissa, Jharkhand, Bihar, West Bengal, A and N island and Northeastern states, indicated that a successful teacher in institution should have a generous combination of various traits and competencies.

Analysis of the responses indicates that their perception corroborates with the finding of the researcher as desired above. According to the respondents a successful teachers should—

- Have through knowledge of his subject of specialisation

- Be able to develop a modern approach in teaching
- Use instructional aids in teaching learning sessions
- Be able to understand students
- Have ability to express his ideas clearly
- Be able to manage the class competently
- Be able to judiciously plan *a* lesson
- Be able to explain theories with suitable examples
- Give more assignments to the students (preferably referring to practical' problems)
- Be able to justify practical relevance of topics under reference
- Be able to motivate students
- Develop an interface with students for better understanding and feedback
- Be open to being assessed by students
- Have good communication capability, modulation of voice, good voice
- Offer extra assistance to poorer students
- Develop a positive attitude towards students
- Be punctual
- Be a good listener
- Maintain a distance without being unfriendly/unapproachable to the students
- Have a helping attitude
- Be responsive
- Be accountable
- Be honest
- Be sincere
- Be impartial
- Be polite
- Be confident
- Be cooperative and finally, simple.

However, there may be a need to modify the general set of identified traits and competences for specific cases. For example, a teacher in a management Institute, apart from general set of identified traits, would be expected to be competent enough to pick up Management based programmes for his students' project work. There are quite a few examples of traits that would be expected of a management Institute teacher such as: inclination and capability to undertake research work, correlating 'concepts' with reality by setting effective examples, develop and announces about technological development taking place in the industries, competency in using teaching aids in learning sessions, capability to effective examples, develop an awareness about management-developments taking place in the market, competency in using modern teaching aids in learning sessions, ability to effectively guide students in choosing career and so on. It would be quite logical to derive traits as applicable to a college or university teacher from the identified roles of teachers supposed to play as stated above.

TEACHER AND ETHICAL ASPECTS

Teaching is a noble and respected profession and has wide acceptance in the society. It follows that a teacher should have some obligation towards his students, society and profession largely based on prevailing and changing ethics and value system. General preparation is that, whatever be the nature of the institutes, a teacher must have high degree of honesty, cherish an acceptable value-pattern and maintain certain specific professional ethics. Some of the traits identified with teachers clearly indicate that this is true. Strictly speaking, with fast changing social-ethos and with the onslaught of consumerism, some of the traditional values and professional ethics have been eroded. This is indeed unfortunate but a fact.

Ethics

Ethics is basically concerned with human character and conduct relating to duties. We hear a lot about this term but to the persons working in the organisation it looks like some high sounding philosophical propositions and they confuse it with religion because religion talks about moral and ethics too is moral.

In the workplace (all sorts of workplaces including educational institutions) people tend to feel that ethics, commitment, and allied positive adjectives are for others to maintain and to follow and one can remain a law unto himself away from others. We expect others to change without changing ourselves! However all will tend to agree that there are some finer human qualities that need to be pursued for one's more fulfilling personal as well as working life. Let us analyse some of the simpler aspects which can create the right atmosphere and right culture if practiced by all without exception. It may be noted that issues discussed below need nobody's approval to practice. These depend only on one's own will to change and approval to practice. In an institution, every member must have respect for the basic values practiced in the organisation. The question of value assumes importance since every institution has certain social responsibility also.

Importance of Value Systems

A value system is important because it provides a perspective for the members of the institution. Different institution nurture some core values expressed through words such as—*equity, empowerment, transparency, care for quality and environment and so on.* Institutional vision statements and mission statements also refer to these core values. Therefore, we may say that a value system is necessary because it:

- Provides the ideological mooring for the working of the Institution
- Provides greater clarity for both day to day working as well as for the long term activities
- Bridges the gap between size and adaptability
- Increases flexibility and reduces the need for rules and procedures
- Creates a sense of ownership and pride resulting higher degree of motivation.

Simple Principles

There are some simple principles if followed in our day to day working life by one and all (including teachers) then it can contribute to building a proper work-culture in an educational institution or for that matter in any kind of organisation:

Principle 1 : Maintain punctuality
Principle 2 : Do not speak ill of others
Principle 3 : Avoid wastages
Principle 4 : Avoid pilferage
Principle 5 : Do not discriminate
Principle 6 : Acknowledge dignity of labour
Principle 7 : Maintain professional approach to work
Principle 8 : Do not do to others what you would not like them to do to you
Principle 9 : Practice what you preach

Ethical and Value Components of a Teacher's Traits

For a teacher, ethics and value system assume high importance. Analysis of teacher' traits indicate that this indeed is true. It is expected that a teacher should:

- Be honest.
- Be accountable.
- Have the courage to accept being evaluated by the students.
- Be impartial in judgment/evaluation of students.

- Be sincere.
- Be polite.
- Be cooperative.

It may be pointed out that, a teacher being a member of his Institution has two distinct aspects as an employee does have.

Firstly, as a teacher doing the teaching and guiding functions and, secondly, as an employee, discharging other duties as and when assigned. Therefore, his responsibilities as a professional become doubly important having being judged by his students as also by his superiors and colleagues.

Teacher's Obligations

In the light of above mentioned points, we can briefly identify the obligations a teacher should have towards his students, the community and him/herself:

i) Obligation Towards Students

- A teacher should deal with students with deep sense of moral obligation in order to extract the potentials inherent in the students.
- A teacher should not act vindictively and victimise any one individual nor would he exploit any student or group.
- S/he would encourage the students to become self-reliant.
- S/he should remain abreast of latest developments elsewhere and disseminate the same among the students.
- Make effort to inculcate strong rationale value-pattern in the students and especially train them in skill sets pertaining to social relations.

ii) Teachers' Obligation Towards Community

- A teacher should ensure that equal opportunity is extended to all the students irrespective of caste, creed, gender, psyche, physic, religion, socioeconomic status and other discriminating factors.
- S/he should have strong sense of civic responsibilities.
- S/he should be sensitive to community opinion.
- Propagate environmental concerns among students and colleagues.
- S/he should use organisational facilities with professional honesty.
- Should develop a healthy interface with the members of community as a part of confidence-building measures.

iii) Teachers' Obligation Towards Profession

It is expected that:

- A teacher should maintain and follow a code of ethical conduct as applied to his profession.

- S/he should accord just and proper treatment to others.
- S/he should faithfully perform duties and ensure that educational objectives are achieved.
- S/he should keep private and confidential information secret.
- Use every opportunity for his own professional growth.
- S/he should develop a culture of sharing responsibilities with colleagues.
- S/he should uphold organisational values and policies.

Should the teachers of the day and of future put an effort in the direction, it will result in a just and congenial educational atmosphere in the educational institutional spectrum of the nation.

2
Learning: Psychology and Principles

Learning is involved in almost anything that an individual does. Learning represents a broad behavioural arena that encompasses training, the acquisition of skills, education, management development or any other similar change or modification process. In Applied psychology, i.e., the study of behaviour, learning is defined as a relatively permanent change in behaviour as a result of practice or reinforced practice. To teach effectively, teachers should know how students learn. The theories of learning provide certain ideas as to how learning occurs and about teacher's role in the learning process. There are various theories but in this chapter we shall have a brief description of the 'cognitive theory of learning' and focus on the three most popular theories, each quite different from others.

The Behavioural Approach

The behavioural approach to learning is characterised by the view that visualises learner's learning as a result of teacher's behaviour. The classical behaviourists, such as Ivan Pavlov and J.B. Watson, attributed learning to the association or connection between stimulus and response. The behaviourists try to shape the learners' behaviour into a predetermined form using *conditioning* (repetition response), *reinforcement* (strengthening behaviour through supportive action) *extinction* (withdrawing reinforcement) and *transfer* (connecting behaviour with response). Thus, in this approach, the teacher delivers specific and structured lessons to students as an attempt to encourage *'desired patterns of behaviour'*.

The Developmental Approach

This approach emphasises on the needs and growth of students when planning learning experiences, through readiness, modeling, identification and imitation. According to this approach, learners are motivated by their desires to fulfill certain needs and drives associated with the developmental stages of growth, and teachers plan instruction according to these pre-determined predictable behaviour.

The Perceptual Approach

Learning results from a changing perception of reality. Here the teachers seek to alter the environment in ways that create positive learning experiences for learners, thus enabling them to broaden their perceptual approach to learning. This approach holds that learners can learn even without formal teaching.

The teacher's role is not to predetermine outcomes or predict desired changes but to provide a congenial environment in which all learners can grow to their fullest potential.

These three approaches to learning provide an idea as to how learning occurs. There are different ways of interpreting how learning takes place. The rapid advancement in this aspect and the educational goals involve higher level processes such as problem-solving, making inferences, applying concepts in new situations and the like.

The Cognitive Theory of Learning

This theory suggests that learning is an active, constructive and purposive process dependent on the mental activities of the learner. Learning is a highly active and complicated process, consisting of a closely related and even more complex series of mental processes and some psychological phenomena.

According to the cognitive theory of learning, the human mind is a 'mental executive' that makes comparisons and decisions. In learning this, mental executive constantly examines the information about the environment that the sense-organs bring to the learner. The executive then selects the important ones and compares it with previous experiences, and thereby weighs and judges it. This meaningful connection of new information with the old enables the learner to store it in the memory and then the learner is said to '*have learnt it*'.

Schema theory is a useful approach to cognitive learning. According to this theory, the organised, structured and abstract bodies of information (or schemata) that a learner brings to bear in learning new content, determine how the learning-task is interpreted and what the learner understands and acquires from the study. The theory assumes that what learners will learn is determined by their previous knowledge, i.e., what they already know. The learner's prior knowledge (existing schema) interacts with new situations to create psycho-pedagogical meaning. Comprehending, a new learning content and/or material involves constructing a correspondence between an existing schema and the elements of that material.

According to Rumelhart and Norman, learning implies a change in schemata. Such a change occurs in three ways:

i) ***Accretion***: It is merely putting new information into a schema we already have.

ii) ***Fine tuning***: This involves minor modifications in existing schemata, by deleting irrelevant aspects of a schema and adding-up new variables.

iii) ***Restructuring***: It is a major change in one's schema system. This is a gradual process and occurs as the new view is given higher status than the old one by the learner.

The cognitive view of learning has given rise to teaching strategies based on five closely related assumptions about how learning occurs. This involves:

- Linking new information to Prior Knowledge
- Restructuring background knowledge
- Learning how to learn, including how to connect cognitive processes and to monitor one's own performances
- Setting purposes with motivation in pursuit of a goal
- Organising knowledge so that learners repertoire of organisational plans for connecting and interpreting information.

Conceptual and Insightful Learning

This is a more complex process of learning. A sudden awareness of how a problem can be solved without any trial and error preceding it describes insightful learning. Problems create a disequilibrium, which generates tension and motivation to solve the problem in order to regain equilibrium. The learner moves initially according to natural laws in solving the problem but the solution occurs in a sudden flash of insight. This type of problem solving occurs after mental rehearsal or hypothesis testing, rather than through Trial and Error approach.

Learning through Observation

This is the most common and important form of human learning. Learning through observation or modeling or by imitation is not simply by mechanical copying but is actively judgmental and constructive. An individual keeps on learning throughout life by his/her experience. He/she stores the information gained, assesses its worth and finally adopts it partially or fully or even may reject it. Such observational learning is not always direct but can be symbolic through human language, spoken or written.

Observational learning comprises of four interrelated sub processes, viz. *Attention, Retention*, *Motor Reproduction* and *Motivational*.

Sensory abilities of learner, the distinctiveness of the model performer (teacher) and the past functional value of attention contribute to enhancing attention processes. The retention process emphasises upon the importance of human memory involving symbolic coding, cognitive organisation, symbolic rehearsal and motor rehearsal. Motor reproduction requires the learner's physical capabilities, availability of component responses, self-observation of reproductions and accuracy check. Motivational processes are interpreted as a sort of reinforcement which can even alter the level of observational learning by affecting who or what the observer will attend to and how actively s/he codes and rehearses the modeled behaviour.

Factors Affecting the Learning Process

Gagne (1974) suggests that the act of learning involves a chain of eight events, some internal to the learner and others external. These events, in their usual order of occurrence are listed below.

- ***Motivation*** (Expectancy of the learner)
- ***Apprehending*** (the learner perceives the material and distinguishes it from the other stimuli competing for his/her attention)
- ***Acquisition*** (the learner codes the knowledge, i.e., derives its sense and relates it to what he/she already knows)
- ***Retention*** (the learner stores the knowledge in short or long term memory)
- ***Recall*** (the learner retrieves the material from memory)
- ***Generalisation*** (the learner is transferred to new situation, thus allowing him/her to develop strategies for dealing with them)
- ***Performance*** (these strategies are put into practice)
- ***Feedback*** (the learner obtains knowledge of results)

According to Gagne, when there is a failure in learning, it takes place atleast one of these eight levels. Therefore, a teacher needs to know and ascertain where the lacuna exists.

There are several other factors that affect the learning process, to cite a few are:

- Motivation
- Stimulus and response
- Reinforcement
- Feedback or knowledge of results
- Participation and practice
- Transfer and application of knowledge

These factors have been discussed in detail in other sections of this module.

Role of a Teacher

The three theories of learning described earlier, differ considerably in their perceptions of teaching and learning, sources of learners' motivation and role of the classroom teacher.

Teacher should consider the different approaches and determine their own way as to how they will manipulate the different variables within the classroom. Say for example, if a student has difficulty in learning because of a negative self-image, the ***perceptual learning theorist*** would attempt to solve the problem by creating a series of 'confidence-building activities' for the student. These activities would allow the student to experience success, to gain a more enlarged and meaningful view of the learning process, and to become more capable of entering into learning experience.

As learners differ from one another in their techniques of observing, a teacher as a facilitator of learning has to consider such individual differences as the learning styles and strategies, memory, attention and motivation. The nature and structure of subject matter information also contributes to the learners' cognitive structure (schema).

A teacher has to be flexible enough to come down to the level of learners. The teacher must possess a way of thinking so as to make learning effective and for this s/he needs to have a proper planning. This plan must include *approaches, procedures, strategies, techniques* and *manipulation of other variables* of the learning environment. Teacher should focus on motivational aspects in addition to the instructional aspects. Innovative teaching techniques, objective assessment and communication, matching of function with aptitude and capability, freedom to the learner team-work, suitable designed changes in environment are some of the factors that can act as motivating tools in the learning process.

In sum, Learning is a process of transforming the state of a person's knowledge, attitude and performing-ability together with developing certain specific skill-sets. The content and procedures involved in learning are quite diverse and usually deals with a wider spectrum of perceptual, motor, verbal and conceptual domains of experience. However, like in any other process, there are certain basic parameters in learning that have to be carefully handled by a teacher to bring in a proper learning environment.

The different approaches and concepts of observational learning focus our attention on the new development in cognitive approach or to the understanding of teaching-learning process. Thus, we find that psychology of learning can contribute to our knowledge of learners' behaviour. From the discussion so far, we found that behaviour is a broader term, so we speak of it in terms of components called performances or responses. Hence, we can say that in psychology of learning we are more concerned with the conditions that determine changes in some measure of performance.

PRINCIPLES OF LEARNING

Learning theories were formalised during the thirties of the last century when the proponents of different schools attempted to build their own theories to explain the problems of learning. However, all cannot be satisfied by putting forward the theories. Here we can quote the definition of theory as observed by *Melvin H. Marx*. The theory is a 'provisional' explanatory proposition or a set of proportions, concerning some natural phenomena and consisting symbolic representation of

(1) The observed relationships among independent and dependent variables,
(2) The mechanisms of structures presumed to underline such relationships or
(3) Inferred relationships and underlying mechanisms intended to account for observed data in the absence of any direct empirical manifestation of the relationships.

Many theories have been put forward, which can be classified broadly into two groups. One group in order to establish psychology on strong scientific footings gave much stress on obvious behaviour and are called '*behaviourists*'.

Behaviourists contend that the microscopic element of stimulus leading to → Response (S→R) is the basis of all complex behaviour and higher mental activities can be explained as an aggregation or sequences of such S→R elements. This concept of course was a revolt against the old introspective and subjective methods applied in psychological investigations.

On the other hand a group of German psychologists who refused to accept the behaviourists, and concentrated over physiology, which appeared to be over simplification of the higher and complex mental phenomena. Their approach was holistic in nature and they put much importance on the 'organism' and its insight in the phenomena of learning.

We shall present the views of the two groups under the following categorisation

S→R Theories (without Reinforcement):

1.1 Conditioning of Pavlov (Classical conditioning)
1.2 Watson's Learning theories
1.3 Guthrie's learning theory

S→R Theories (with Reinforcement)

2.1 Thorndike's learning laws
2.2 Hull's theory of learning
2.3 Skinner's theory of operant conditioning

Cognitive Field Theory

3.1 Gestalt—theory of learning
3.2 Lewin's field—theory of learning
3.3 Tolman's Sign—Gestalt theory of learning

Classical Conditioning

Reflex actions are involuntary in animal beings. These are controlled by autonomic nervous system. It was found by I.V. Pavlov, a Noble Laureate Physiologist of Russia that on the very sight of food a dog started salivating. Even the sound of the footsteps of the Caretaker induced salivation in the dog. Pavlov classified reflex action into two classes, one the physiological reflex and the other as psychic reflex.

He conducted the following experiment on dogs. As Salivation on getting food is natural and unfailing, this food and the corresponding salivation were called UCS (Un-Conditioned Stimulus) and UCR (Un-Conditional Response) respectively. During experimentation the following model is followed:

Steps:

1. UCS (food material) → UCR (Salivation)
2. CS (conditioning stimulus—Sound of bell) + UCS (food material) → UCR (Salivation)
3. CS (Sound of bell only) → CR (Salivation)

Definition of Classical Conditioning): "This is a process in which a neutral stimulus (sound of bell) by pairing with a natural stimulus (food), acquires the characteristics of the natural stimulus".

In similar way, higher order conditioning is also possible according to the following model:

Steps:

1. UCS (food) ... → UCR (Saliva)
2. CS + UCS (bell) (food) ... → CR (Saliva)
3. $CS_1 + CS_2$ (bell) (light) ... → CR (Saliva)
4. CS_2 (light only) ... → CR (Saliva)

Here from it may be concluded that according to this theory the response originally made to the UCS becomes associated with the CS (conditioned stimulus) and what is learned is a CS→CR bond of some kind.

Pavlov's contribution was that he could explain learning in terms of physiological changes, by adopting an objective method of study. This conditioning has been accepted as the theoretical framework and practical technique of solving a variety of applied problems.

Applications of Classical Conditioning

Though it has no direct application to classroom learning, yet this principle can be used in the following areas of human learning:

1. Developing good habits.
2. Breaking of bad habits.
3. Eliminating conditioned fear, anxiety etc.
4. Application in Psychotherapy.
5. Developing Positive Attitude.
6. Training of animals.

J.B. Watson's Learning Theory

Watson's theory is known as **contiguity theory**, where he assigns no role of any intervening variable like a reinforce. In his opinion only contiguity is sufficient for establishing connection or bond between S→R (stimulus → Response). It is very simple because it denies any place for effect in learning.

Watson brought a revolution in the field of Psychology almost at the inception of the last century. People were already fed up with the traditional Psychology of consciousness and its method of introspection. He closed the gap between the study of animal and man. He defined Psychology as the study of *'overt'* or observable behaviour, which can be measured objectively. He had a strong conviction that behaviour can be explained in terms of stimulus response (S → R) connections in the brain.

Theory

Watson proposed that when a stimulus and response occur at the same time in close contiguity, (nearness) the connection between them is strengthened. The strength of connection between Stimulus→Response (S→R) depends upon the frequency of S→R repetitions. He did not recognise any effect of learning like Thorndike, but he emphasised the importance of frequency or exercise in learning. In Watson's opinion, Thorndike's law of effect was materialistic in nature.

Second law, that he proposed was of 'Recency'. The most recent response is strengthened more by its frequent occurrence than that of an earlier response. Conditioning was the basis for him. He convinced the psychologists that the real explanation of behaviour lies in nervous system. He popularised the theory of conditioning in America.

Guthrie's Theory of Learning

Guthrie was the most leading advocate of Stimulus→Response (S→R) theory of *Association by contiguity*. Contiguity according to him is 'A combination of stimuli which has accompanied a movement, will on its recurrence tend to be followed by that movement'.

Guthrie's Principles of Learning

i) Principle of conditioning
ii) Inhibitory conditioning, which means that responses are inhibited if any other response occurs
iii) Delayed conditioning is no conditioning
iv) Improvement in performance is the result of practice.

S→R Theory (with Reinforcement)

Thorndike, E.L. developed his theory years ahead of I.V. Pavlov and J.B. Watson. But here they are presented earlier only for categorical understanding. All learning according to Thorndike is the formation of bounds or connections between S→R, which depends on a number of variables that operate in the environment and on the organism. He conducted series of experiments under controlled conditions and has propounded the *basic laws of learning* and five supplementary *principles of learning*. Here the discussion will be restrict on the major three laws of learning for convenience.

Basic Laws of Learning

1. ***Law of Effect***: This states 'when a modifiable connection between a situation (stimulus) and a response is made and accompanied or followed by a satisfying state of affairs, that connection's strength is increased; when made and accompanied or followed by an annoying state of affairs, its strength is decreased'.

   Classroom Applications:

   The teacher can make use of this law in a teaching–learning situation:

   a) The classroom experience should be satisfactory and pleasant; teacher also must enjoy his teaching work.
   b) Learning experience must be meaningful and understandable in terms of the personal life of the learners.
   c) Learning experience and activities must be arranged in such a way that the learners may have some degree of confidence and success in their work.
   d) Activities should be organised in all order of increasing difficulty, so that the students may progress without failure.
   e) Materials for study should have novelty.
   f) Guidance, praise and encouragement should be properly used.

2. ***Law of Exercise***: This is divided into two parts:

   (a) *Law of Use*: 'When a modifiable connection between a situation and a response is made over a length of time, that connections strength is increased, all other things remaining constant'.

(b) *Law of Disuse*: 'Other things remaining the same when a modifiable connection between a situation and the response over a long period of time, that connections strength is decreased'.

Classroom Application:

i) More and more opportunities should be provided to repeat the knowledge the students get in a classroom.

ii) To maintain the connections for a longer period, review of the learned material is necessary.

iii) Drill is needed to strengthen the bounds.

3. ***Law of Readiness***: 'When any conduction unit is ready to conduct, for it to do so is satisfying and when it is not in readiness, for it to conduct is annoying. When a conduction unit is in readiness to conduct, for it not to do so is annoying'.

Classroom implications:

(i) Teacher must wait till the learner is ready to learn and should give those experiences, which help enhance readiness.

(ii) Aptitude tests may be used to verify readiness in different subjects.

Clark L. Hull

Another S→R reinforcement theorist **Hull** has many similarities in his theory of learning for example: It is based on:

i) Association theory of Stimulus→Response.
ii) Survival model of life.
iii) Biological needs and their fulfillment.
iv) Pavlovian conditioning.

Hull mentioned a few concepts like, Need, drive and also reinforcement in his own style. Mainly Hull's theory is called ***'Need-reduction theory of learning'***.

B.F. Skinner's Operant Conditioning

The term 'operant' emphasises the fact that the behaviour operates upon the environment to generate its own consequences. He described his own procedure as type 'R' conditioning, in which a response occurs spontaneously in the absence of any stimulation from outside.

In the process of operant conditioning several operations are involved. Some of them are:

i) Shaping of behaviour (includes, generalisation, chaining and habit competition)

ii) Extinction
iii) Spontaneous recovery and
iv) Concept of reinforcement

i) ***Shaping***: It refers to the judicious use of selective reinforcement to bring about certain desirable changes in the behaviour of an organism. It is a successive approximation to the desired behaviour.

a) *Generalisation* of experience is common in human being. This endowed ability enables us to use the acquired behaviour in case of a changed stimulus (environment).
Generalisation may be response generalisation or stimulus generalisation.

b) *Habit competition:* It is dominance of the correct habit over the competing habit. This is accomplished by reinforcing the correct habit alone.

c) *Chaining, the third principle in shaping* means, linking up the segment of reinforced behaviour to the subsequent behaviour towards achievement of final objective.

ii) ***Extinction***: It is simply withholding the reinforcer when appropriate behaviour response occurs. When it is repeated the particular response (correct) is found to be extinguished.

iii) ***Spontaneous Recovery***: It is found that after a lapse of time after extinction the response (correct) again reappears, and is similar to that which occurs in case of Pavlovian conditioning.

iv) ***Concept of Reinforcement*** is central to operant conditioning principle. Reinforcement is an environmental event, which enhances the probability of occurrence of a response, under same conditions. Reinforcement may be
(a) Positive,
(b) Negative. Also there is another concept of reinforcement, termed as
(c) Punishment, which is usually confused with negative reinforcement.

Application

Some short-falls in education system which can be rectified using Skinners concepts:

i) Usually behaviour is dominated by aversion stimuli like fear, anxiety and unpleasant experiences.
ii) Wide gap between response and reinforcement
iii) Absence of a programme of serial reinforcement.
iv) Objectives of education are vague.

(These may be rectified on the light of Skinnerian principles of learning).

Cognitive Field Theories

Gestalt Theory of Learning: Gestalt is a German word, which means some pattern, shape, form or a configuration. This theory is due to three German exponents in the field of psychology viz., *W. Kohler, K. Koffka* and *M. Wertheimer*, who rejected the simple stimulus→response connections as the explanation of behaviour. They introduced the concept of 'organism' between the S→R approaches developed by the behaviourists.

According to cognitive field theorists, teaching is a process of developing understanding or insight in the learner. Learning is the organisation of the percepts and purposes by the learner.

The Gestaltans vehemently criticised the behaviouristic view that everything we see or think is put together in tiny pieces like those of a jigsaw puzzle, instead they advocated that we perceive and think of a whole. They also assumed that the perception of tile world is of meaningful wholes and that is different form and something more than an accumulation of sensations, images or ideas.

Basic Principles of Perceptual Organisation

i) ***Figure-Ground Relationship***: Everything we perceive has a background.
ii) ***Principle of Pragnanz***: Our perceptual patterns always tend to be simple, regular and complete with no loose ends. The gaps are closed by tile perceiver.
iii) ***Law of Transposition***: Because the Gestaltans think that stimulus - patterns are isomorphic; they may undergo extensive changes without losing identity.
iv) ***Law of Similarity***: It suggests that similar words numbers and objects tend to associate in a group, and are easy to recall than 'dissimilar ones.
v) ***Law of Proximity***: It states that objects which are close in space and time tend to form a Gestalt.

Kurt Lwein's Learning Theory

Lwein's theory represents Sign-Gestalt theory of learning in contradiction to S→R theory of learning. He shares the insightful learning of the Gestaltans and holds that insight is a process of structuring or restructuring the perceived area. Perception is the main issue in Lwein's theory of learning. He has classified learning into the four categories as follows:

a) Learning is a change in the cognitive structure
b) Learning is a change in motivation, i.e., in valence and values.
c) Learning is acquisition of skill-sets
d) Learning is a change in-group belonging.

According to Lwein, level of aspiration is indicative of one's potentiality and influence of the group in which s/he belongs. Too high or too low level of aspiration discourages learning.

Tolman's Sign-Gestalt Theory of Learning

Tolman's theory is a combination of the advantages of S→R as well as the cognitive theories of learning. He was also influenced by McDougall and Sigmand Freud. His system is known as 'purposive behaviourism'. It is behaviourism in the sense that it rejected introspection and consciousness but accepted the scientific methods of behaviourism. He also rejected molecular approach and developed molar-theory. Molar behaviour is goal seeking and purposive.

He introduced the concepts of variables as, independent, dependent and intervening in nature. He expressed behaviour as, $\bar{B} = f(S.P.H.T.A)$, where

S = environmental stimuli,
P = Physiological Drives
H = Hereditary factors,
T = Previous training and
A = Maturity or Age, all being independent in nature.

Later he revised his list of independent variables and classified these as (i) Individual differences and (ii) Experimental independent variables.

Dependent Variables of Tolman Consists of

i) Active and selective behaviour
ii) Purposeful and goal directed behaviour
iii) Behaviour is S→R affair but not mechanistic
iv) Behaviour is molar and teachable. It is the function of the organism as a whole.

So far as intervening variables are concerned, he gave three types of variables, which are:

i) Need, i.e., system-physiological deprivation or drive situation.
ii) Belief, value and motives.
iii) Behaviour spaces.

Tolman's main contribution is that behaviour is purposeful and docile. He emphasised that what is learned is expectancy or the value of signs rather than stimulus response connections. Tolman attempted to combine the advantages of two families of learning theory and succeeded to certain extent.

Here the discussion centers round the learning principles of the two distinct schools of thought. A teacher should make a comparative study of the both. Some principles are more applicable to lower levels of learning, whereas some are more for higher types of learning. Moreover when we are aware of two extreme opinions, it is helpful for us to choose and select the demands of the situation. After all, a teacher's philosophy should be eclecticism. S/he should try to take the best of the things from different school of thoughts and make use of them for the benefit of the learners.

3
Glimpse of Pedagogy and Curriculum

System Thinking in Teaching-Learning

The term 'system' is traditionally defined, as *'a set of components or elements, interacting together and working as a functional unit towards a common goal'*. The input unit provides some process by which material or information or the like is entered into the system. The processor acts on the material or information to modify it in some way. The output unit consists of some procedure for discharging the results of the process from the system.

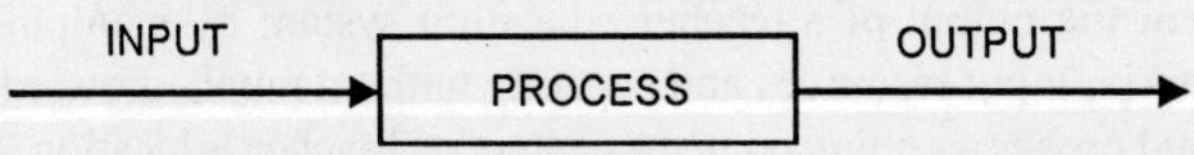

In a closed loop or cybernetic system the output is returned to the system and consequently affects future output of the system. (Cybernetic is derived from the Greek word *cybernetic*, meaning being to pilot or to govern).

Cybernetic systems are systems, which have some mechanism for controlling, or governing themselves. The room air conditioning system is a familiar example of such system. The output is cold air, which lowers the room temperature. The information about the room temperature is put back in the system through a thermostat, which compares it with a pre-set standard. When the temperature of the room is higher than the pre-set standard, the electrical current starts the compressor. When the room temperature is equal to the preset standard, the compressor shuts off. Output from a system, which is returned as input to control future output, is called feedback.

A cybernetic system is graphically represented as shown in figure below, including input, process and output and a feedback control loop.

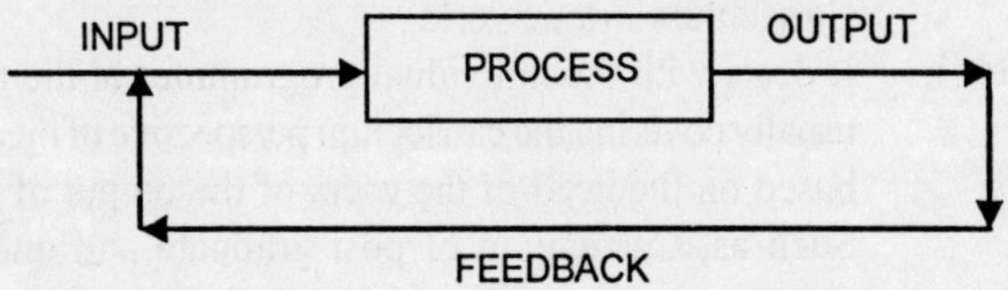

To a large extent, a system exists because someone has defined as such. Thus, for our practical purposes, a system exists because we have chosen to consider this. We have drawn the boundary that limits the extent of the system, thus defining the components, or subsystems that compose our *'system of interest'*. Once defined in this way, we can identify the principal connections between this system and its environment, the inputs from the environment to the system and the outputs from the system to the environment. The reason for existence of the system can be identified by examining its relationship to its environment, inputs and the outputs.

The first step in 'system analysis' is to define the system of interest, its boundaries and the chief inputs and outputs across these boundaries. Quantifying these inputs and outputs defines the purpose and to some extent the efficiency of the system.

Once we have defined the outputs and know the capability of our system, we usually have some means of controlling the output from outside the black-box. A listener may control the volume, colour and brightness of a television set without the knowledge about how a television functions.

Similarly, the Ministry of Education or Human Resource Development may control the output of a teacher education system by manipulating the output criteria, input resources and capacity without much knowledge of the instructional processes going on in the centers of Teacher Education. A teacher may control the learning of a student by observing the outputs (new capabilities or behaviours) and manipulating the inputs (type of information, type of task, frequency and repetition, duration of practice etc.) without any detailed knowledge of the internal learning processes that are going on inside the student. In all these cases, one is applying control by feedback.

Levels of Educational System

Depending on application, the educational systems may be classified in major four levels. These are:

Level I: It deals with the general aims based on Philosophy of Education at the macro level usually covering national perspectives to identify the type of programmes and their mode of offering on the basis of the futuristic needs of the country, such as National Policy of Education or National Curriculum Framework.

Level II: It deals with the individual programmes at the macro level usually covering the curriculum perspective of the programme based on the need of the users of the output of the system. Such as, Curriculum of post graduate and undergraduate Degree programmes in Educational Technology.

Level III: It deals with the individual courses (subject) or individual topic or a subtopic of the course at the micro level usually covering the actual teaching-learning perspectives based on the specified desired learning outcomes. For example, teaching a course on ICT in Education at 2nd semester class in Master of Education or teaching the topic on Education for Sustainable development.

Level IV: It deals with the individual learning of a course or a topic at the micro level usually covering the self-learning perspective e.g., Self-learning of principles of Educational Technology through Computer Assisted Instruction (CAI)

What is Teaching-Learning System?

The practicing teachers are usually involved most of the time at this Level III of the educational system. Following figure illustrates the system:

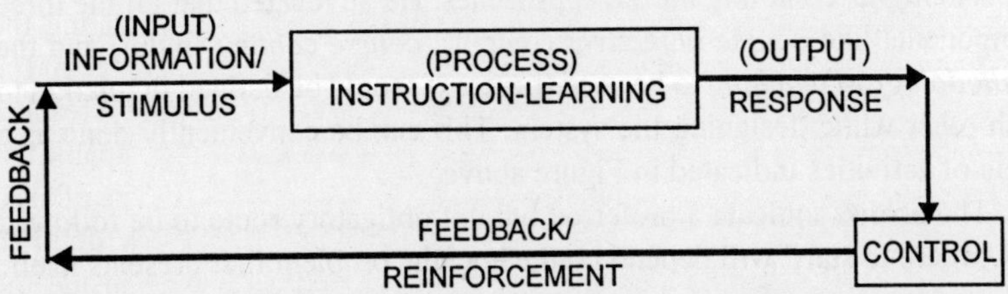

This model was first adopted by Professor B.F. Skinner from behavioural Psychology approach, suggesting that one can control and predict learning entirely by observation of behaviour and the relationships that exist between specific input, specific output and consequences which follow.

This output oriented approach was advocated by the behavioural objectives movement of the 1950s and 1960s leading to development of 'Taxonomy of Educational Objectives' commonly by Professor Benjamin Bloom in 1956 and development of *'Performance Objectives'* by *Mager* in 1961.

A process oriented approach was advocated by the gestalt psychologists as an alternative approach which focuses on the learning process and have led to the development of specific instructional models as *expository learning*, *exploratory learning* and the like. Jerome Bruner in 1966 adopted this approach focusing on the processes adopted for instruction. He suggested that the learner should be instructed in such a way that the ability to learn in future, without any instruction, is developed in him/her. According to him such skill-set as identifying relevant information for a given problem, interpreting it, classifying it in a useful way and discovering interrelations between new and previously learned content or information or in other words ***'learning to learn'*** ability emerged as the important output of the instructional process.

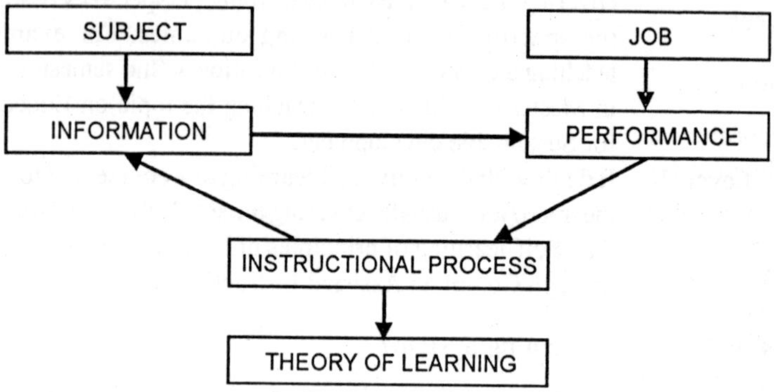

In the decade of 1970s a more balnced system view was advocated by *Robert Gagne* combinig all the approaches. He advocated that all the three components like *course objectives* (output), *course content* (input) and the *methodology of teaching* to be used (process) should be defined in relation to each other while designing the system. This can be conveniently done as a cycle of activities indicated in Figure above.

The arrows indicate a preferred but not obligatory route to be followed and 'where to start' will depend on the how the problem first presents itself.

Components of Teaching-Learning System Process

The process of the Teaching-Learning system comprises of two major components, namely the TEACHER and the LEARNER and interrelationships between two may be illustrated in the Figure below.

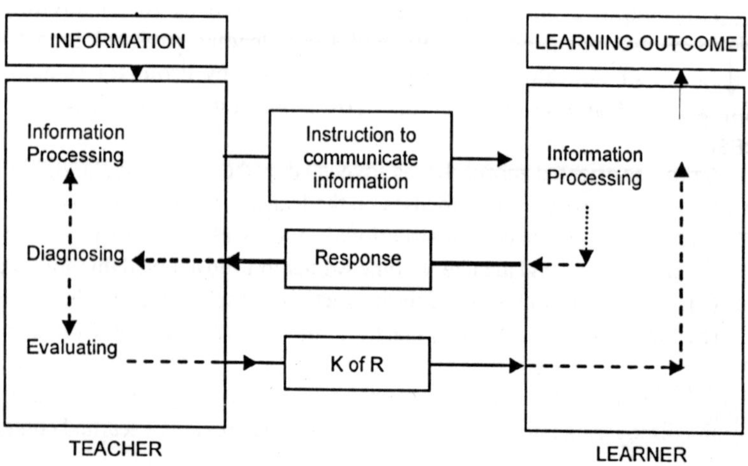

The internal processes taking place in the teacher is an instruction to communicate information and in the learner assimilation of the information received for learning and optimisation of both increases the complexity of the process of teaching-learning system.

What is Instruction?

According to *Merrill*, it is the 'process whereby the environment of an individual is *deliberately* manipulated to enable him to learn *to emit or engage in specified behaviours* under specified conditions or as responses to specified situations'. It is a subset of the classroom-teaching behaviours. Instruction is related to, but not synonymous with learning. Instruction takes place only when *a specified effort* has been made to modify the environment in such a way that *a specified learning outcome* occurs. The considerations those are central to our view of instruction as a special case of teaching are

(a) The 'specificability' of the behaviour to be learned as well as the conditions appropriate for that behaviour and
(b) The degree of control exercised over the environment to the end that these behaviours will be brought under the control of appropriate or relevant situations.

One important cluster of implication of this definition is suggested by the word 'deliberate', i.e. *the instruction is always a planned activity.*

According to *Ramiszwoski*, by 'instruction' we shall mean a *goal-directed* teaching process, which is more or less pre-planned. It is immaterial whether the goal has been established by the learner or the teacher rather than a pre-determined goal has been established is the most important aspect. The figure below shows a matrix for this definition:

DEFINITION OF INSTRUCTION

Blocks → ↓		SPECIFIC OBJECTIVES EXIST?	
		YES	NO
PRE-PLANNED STUDY RESOURCES EXIST?	YES	INSTRUCTION	Study tour, library study etc.
	NO	Projects, Apprenticeship etc.	Incidental Learning

It is immaterial whether

(a) The routes to the goal are unique or various,
(b) Whether they are prescribed by the instructor or chosen by the learner.

What is important is whether the pre-planning has taken place to establish and test-out viable routes or not.

It is thus the presence of precise goals or objectives (however arrived at) and the presence of careful pre-planning and testing out that shall be taken as the main characteristics of the term '***Instructional System***'.

Information Schema

The knowledge here refers to the information stored in the learners' mind. On the basis of system approach knowledge can be categorised as below:

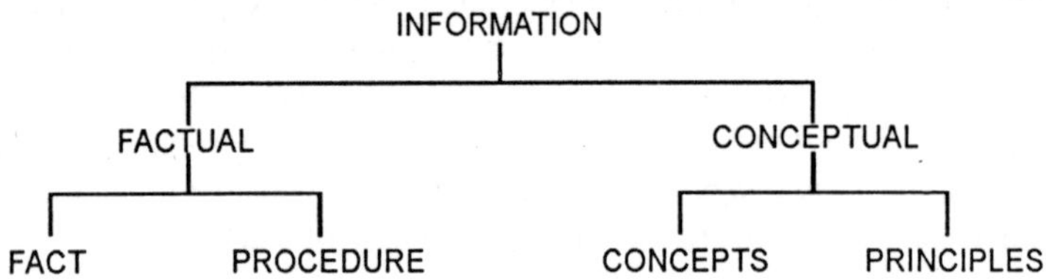

Facts: This category includes all information that can be gained by direct experience (concrete) or by means of symbolic language (defined). For example, movement of an object when pushed or pulled; movement of a car are examples of fact.

Concepts: This means names of classes of items or ideas that can be exemplified. This includes classes of real objects or situations (Primary) or other classes of concepts (Secondary). A number of facts having common characteristics are usually categorised as concepts. For example, Motion, Force, Resultant Force, Velocity, Acceleration are examples of concepts.

Principles: Rules or principles are used to link certain concepts or facts in specific ways, enabling one to explain or predict phenomenon. For example, Law of parallelogram of forces, equations of motion may be the examples of principles relating to different concepts.

Procedure: This refers to knowing how to proceed with specific situations. This may be subdivided as chain (simple step by step procedures), discriminations (distinguishing similar information) or algorithm. For example, determination of resultant forces by numerical or graphical method may be an example of procedure.

The information on a particular topic is seldom of one type but is usually a combination of several types of factual and conceptual information.

CURRICULUM

Development of curriculum on scientific basis is relatively not much old in the history of education. India is one of the few countries in which curriculum development activity at school and other specific levels are carried out para-systematically. There is a need to relook at curriculum development processes in the context of socio-economic developments in a particular country, which accordingly changes from time to time. Thus, curriculum development process needs a scientific approach for taking into account present and future socio-economic and technological interventions in developmental scenario.

It has been experienced that the term *'curriculum'* is not understood properly by majority of teachers and administrators. It is unfortunate that even a large cross section of the teacher educators at various Institutions of Education as also institutions offering teacher education and liberal education programmes don't conceptualise the concept in proper way. Mostly, the term curriculum and syllabus are used interchangeably. Hence, it is important to define both the terms, for facilitating clear understanding between the two.

Definitions

Many authors have defined curriculum in varying contexts. A review of literature produced by various writers reveals marked differences in the way each perceives and defines the term curriculum.

Taba Hilda (1962) stated that a curriculum usually contains a statement of aims and objectives; it indicates some selection and organisation of content. It either implies or manifests certain pattern of learning and teaching, because the objectives demand them or because the content organisation requires them. Finally, it includes a programme of evaluation of the outcomes.

Saylor (1966) stated that curriculum encompasses all learning opportunities provided by the school i.e., institution that offers the learning opportunities.

Johnson (1967) described the term curriculum as 'structured series of intended learning outcomes'.

Burns and *Brooks* (1970) stated that a curriculum is a plan for arrangement of information and experiences which educator consider necessary for students to cope successfully in life. It is further stated that curriculum is defined as everything that is planned to happen to a learner with a view to enhancing, investigating or modifying predetermined behaviour.

Jenkins David et. al., (1976) expressed that a curriculum is the formation and implementation of an educational proposal, to be taught and learned within a school or other institutions, accepts responsibility at three levels, its rationale, its actual implementation and its effects.

Rubin (1977) stated that curriculum is to encompass the total impact of the school environment on the learner.

Lawton Danis et. al., (1978) defined curriculum as all the learning experience which are planned and guided by the school (or institution), whether it is carried out in groups or individually, inside or outside the school. He divides the curriculum into four aspects: curriculum objectives; knowledge; learning experiences; and curriculum evaluation.

Doll (1978) expressed that curriculum emphasises guided, pre-selected experiences to which children and youth should be exposed; plans for learning; ends and outcomes of being educated and system for achieving educational production.

Harris et. al., (1978) stated that the term curriculum is used in a broad sense to include the totality of what is to be taught in school, the relationship between subjects, teaching materials, teaching methods, technological and other aids and organisation of teaching learning.

Tanner Daniel (1980) stated that curriculum is a planned action for instruction.

Burshoff (1981) stated that curriculum is an education project for defining goals, aims and objectives of an educational action; ways, means, activities employed to achieve these goals; and methods and instruments required to evaluate the success of the action.

According to *UNESCO* documents published from time to time, curriculum is stated as an organised programme of both theoretical and practical studies, the successful completion of which is considered necessary to achieve specified educational goals corresponding to different levels of knowledge and qualification(s).

A publication of *CPSC* (1982) stated that curriculum of a course has been defined as an educational programme designed and implemented to achieve specified educational objectives.

Joyce (1987) stated that the curriculum is that set of courses and instructional experiences afforded to students.

Taking the above definitions into consideration, curriculum is viewed as a plan of intents about the learning outcomes, the processes (instructional and managerial) and resources in terms of physical, human, financial, informational etc., are designed and implemented to attain the specified goals of an educational programme for specified group of learners.

In other words it may be said that curriculum is a written document of an educational programme which states educational objectives, along with detailing of integrated sequence of curriculum areas (subjects) and detailed contents, recommended learning experiences to be given to students and methodology of student's evaluation for achieving the objectives in a stipulated period for a specific group of learners, according to pre-active, interactive and post-active phases of teaching.

In contrary, the term 'syllabus' is only a part of curriculum which means what is to be taught i.e., detailed contents comprising of concepts, principles, procedures and practices to be taught to students, whereas curriculum is a broad term which not only contains syllabus but the complete plan of action of teaching learning, including student's evaluation strategies and interpretation of assessment results, directed to achieve defined objectives in a stipulated time-frame.

From above detailing, it is clear that curriculum of a programme is an important document, based on which entire teaching learning process is planned to prepare suitable human resources. Curriculum is important for the learner to understand the scope of study; for the teacher to know what and how to teach and select appropriate learning experiences to be given to student for developing desired competencies in them, work field to understand the type of manpower and competencies possessed by the passouts from a programme and to facilitate Universities/State Governments/Directorate of specialised Education for planning physical, human, informational and financial resources for effective implementation of the curriculum. It also facilitates the Universities/State Board of Education to conduct examinations as per laid table of specifications for achieving desired levels of competencies.

Characteristics of Curriculum for Education Programmes

The curriculum for educational programmes has some special characteristics. These are briefly described below:

a) Data Based: It should be based on long and short range manpower requirements. Decisions about whether or not to offer a curriculum should be based upon related data. Curriculum contents cannot be worked out until the characteristics of students and the nature of occupation for which they are trained is clearly known.

Hence, following type of information will be quite useful for taking appropriate curriculum decisions:

- Employment opportunities
- Presentation of future developmental trends in terms of manpower requirements
- Activity and competency profile of specific target group.
- Existing facilities of educational system
- Availability of appropriate environment for effective implementation of curriculum.
- Availability of appropriate human resources and instructional resources.

b) Fully Articulated: It is essential that there should be integrated sequence of organised learning experiences to be given in a logical and chronological order of learning so as to achieve desired objective in stipulated time for a specific target group of learner.

Curriculum articulation may involve the resolution of content-conflicts across different areas or development of a logical instructional flow from one semester to other. Articulation may extend to determine the ways and means of the co–curricular activities which lend support to the rest of curriculum.

c) Student Oriented: The aim of a curriculum in professional subject is to develop specific competencies for gainful employment and hence students are required to learn by doing practical work in laboratories, workshops and in the industry. It is therefore, essential that curriculum should emphasise on student centered learning approaches.

d) Realistic: The curriculum cannot operate in vacuum. If the students are to be prepared for employment, the curriculum should focus on development of job related competencies. Contents should clearly specify knowledge and skill profile of human resource requirement of the future, so as to enable the teachers to provide appropriate learning experiences to students. Hands-on-experiences in studio, laboratory, and workshop or in industry provide the student with a relevant means of transferring knowledge, skill-sets and attitudes to the world of work. Curriculum should be realistic so that it is possible to implement in a given situation.

e) Dynamic: The curriculum has to keep pace with communication technology oriented development at work places. Hence, curriculum for any given programme should be dynamic, making provisions for bringing modifications from time to time.

f) Future Oriented: Educators, particularly, are very much concerned about the future. What technological changes might affect the students? What type of first-hand experiences would be needed twenty years from now? What sort of continuing education will be needed for the students undergoing education now? These are other questions which are often raised by teachers who think in futuristic terms.

Persons responsible for contemporary curricula need to ensure that ongoing curricula are considered in relation to what will or may occur in the future. As decisions are being made about curriculum content and structure, thought should be given to the future results that might come from those decisions. Any curriculum that hopes to be relevant tomorrow must be relevant to tomorrow's as well as today's needs. The extent to which a curriculum is successful in the times to come will be largely dependent upon the future oriented perspective associated with it.

g) Explicit Outcome: Not only the curriculum for a given programme is relevant to the world of work, it must be able to communicate the desired outcome to both the teachers and students. Broadly stated goals are also an important part of curriculum. Although, it is recognised that it is difficult to state all curricular outcomes in specific measurable terms, many of these outcomes may be written down in such a manner that broad curricular goals are made more quantifiable. This is perhaps the most commanding reason for ensuring that the curriculum outcomes are clear and precise.

Curriculum Development Stages

After understanding the characteristics of curriculum, it is important to know the stages of Curriculum-Development Process. Curriculum-Development comprises of the following four stages—(a) Need Analysis stage; (b) Curriculum Design stage; (c) Curriculum Implementation stage; (d) Curriculum Evaluation stage.

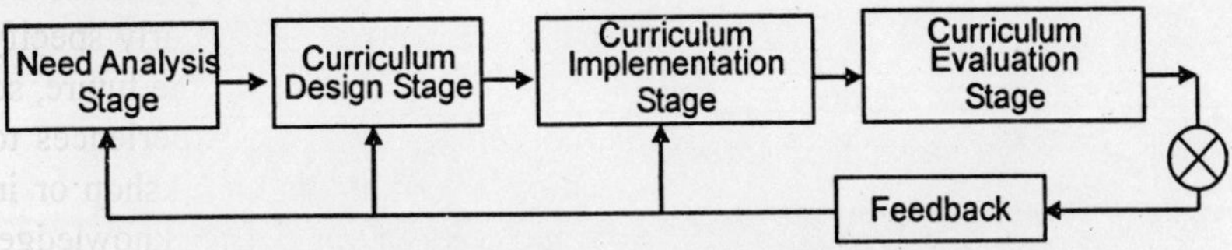

A Schematic Diagram of Stages of Curriculum Development

A brief description of the scope of each of above stages is given below:

a) Need Analysis: This stage deals with diagnosis of needs, which involves conducting market surveys for determining employment opportunities for specific target group, ICT application and allied technological development at work places and competency-profile of skilled manpower, keeping in view the present and future employment trends. Tnis also includes determination of the strengths and weaknesses of the system of respective education system.

b) Curriculum Design: The curriculum-Design stage involves devising or planning the intents of the curriculum. At this stage, decisions regarding curricular objectives for specified target group(s) are spelled out. From these objectives, curricula areas (subjects) are identified. Detailed contents are worked out to match the competency-profile of specific target group(s). After working out the time requirement for imparting desired knowledge, skills, values, ethos and attitudes, study and evaluation scheme is worked out, selection of appropriate methodologies and media for various curricula-areas is also detailed out. At this stage resources required (i.e., physical, human and information) for effective implementation of curriculum are also spellet out.

c) *Curriculum Implementation:* Once the curriculum document is ready, it will call for development of appropriate resources for the successful implementation of curriculum. This stage deals with harnessing of resources and their utilisation for providing appropriate learning experiences to students for developing desired competencies in them.

Networking with industry and other organisations for sharing resources is one of the important considerations for effective implementation of curriculum.

d) Curriculum Evaluation: Evaluation is considered in two stages.

The first stage is monitoring during implementation stage. During this stage, corrective measures are taken to improve teaching–learning process. Once the system has undergone corrective process for some time and got improved, a summative evaluation is undertaken for making changes at different stages for increasing the effectiveness and bringing improvement in the curriculum and the processes at different stages.

SECTION B

Instruction

4

Instructional Objectives

An instructional objective is a guideline for the performance of both teacher and learner in a learning situation. It is the intended learning outcome in order to achieve what the teacher plans his/her instruction systematically. Thus the instructional objective describes precisely as to what the learner can do or achieve after completing the process.

Mager first used the term 'behavioural objective' to emphasise that it is a statement what specifies what the student will be able to do. Later the term 'behavioural' was substituted by 'performance' and 'instructional' or 'specific'.

Meaning

An instructional objective is an intended learning outcome stated in such a way that its attainment can be observed and measured. It is a description of what learners will be able to do on completing a unit of instruction. They are called instructional objectives as they represent the goals of instruction. Such objectives are sometimes also labeled as measurable or behavioural since they specify outcomes in observable form.

Instructional objectives serve as guides for both teaching and learning, communicating the intent of the instruction to others, and providing guidelines for evaluating pupil learning. Objectives help a teacher to determine what s/he wants the students to learn and, what is to be measured.

Also they suggest how to measure what one wants to measure, whether the learners have achieved what is intended, areas in which one's instruction has been successful and unsuccessful.

The basic function of properly stated instructional objectives is describing the intended learning outcomes in performance terms. While viewing instructional objectives in terms of learning outcomes, it is essential to keep in mind that we are concerned with the products of learning rather than the process of learning. Well stated outcomes make clear the types of learner performance which we are willing one can accept as an evidence that the instruction has been successful.

Taxonomy of Instructional Objectives

Most of the specific learning outcomes can be classified under a relatively small number of headings. Though such a classification is necessarily arbitrary, yet it serves several useful purposes. It indicates types of learning outcomes that should be considered, provides a framework for classifying those outcomes and directs attention toward changes in pupil performance in a variety of areas.

This hierarchical pattern of classification is characteristic of the three domains.

For a broader classification, the objectives can be divided into three major areas as follows:

(i) ***Cognitive Domain***—Knowledge outcomes and intellectual abilities
(ii) ***Affective Domain***—Attitudes, interests, appreciation, and modes of adjustment or conglomerating a combination there of, which leads to feelings.
(iii) ***Psychomotor Domain***—Perceptual and motor skills.

Each of the three domains is subdivided into categories and subcategories. The major categories in the cognitive domain are knowledge, comprehension, application, analysis, synthesis and evaluation. These categories begin with the relatively simple knowledge outcomes and proceed through increasingly complex levels of intellectual ability as shown below:

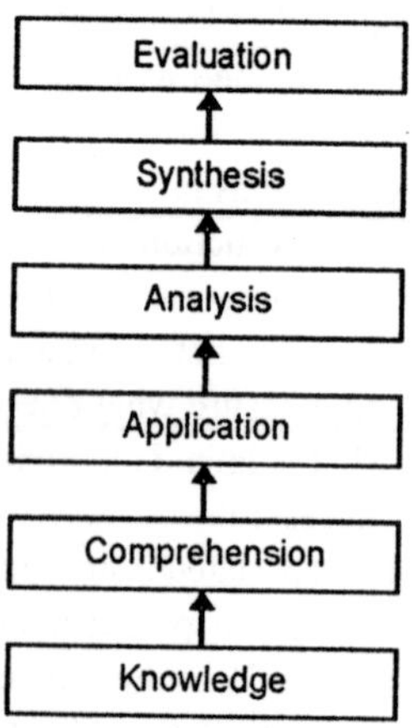

Hierarchy of Cognitive Domain (B.S. Bloom, 1956)

The Bloom's taxonomy has been revised in 2001, but has not been in much practice till now. The modified taxonomy accords the hierarchy of actions as follow:

Creating
↑
Evaluating
↑
Analysing
↑
Applying
↑
Understanding
↑
Remembering

Interestingly a matching of old and revised taxonomy of cognitive domain is perusing a little change which is presented as follows:

Evaluation	–	Evaluating
Synthesis	–	Creating
Analysis	–	Analysing
Application	–	Applying
Comprehension	–	Understanding
Knowledge	–	Remembering

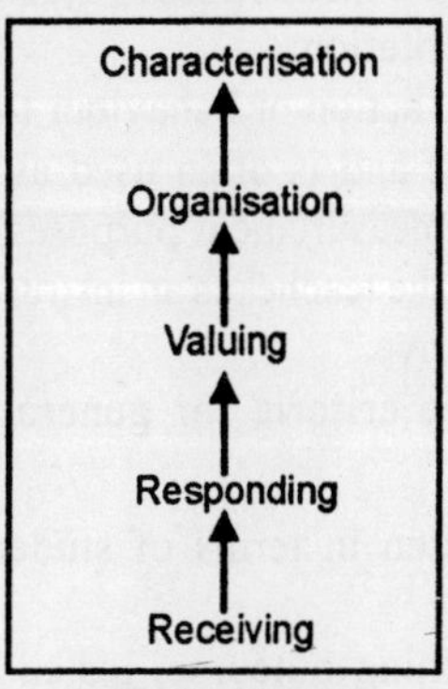

Affective Domain
(D. Krathwohl)

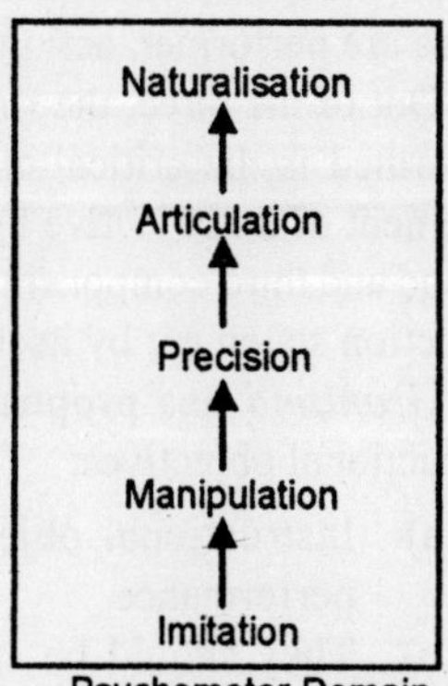

Psychomotor Domain
(R. H. Dave)

The taxonomy is mainly useful in identifying the types of learning outcomes that should be considered when developing a comprehensive list of objectives for classroom instruction. In this way important types of learning are not overlooked.

Robert Gagne (1985) has proposed five major categories of human performance or capabilities of the learner, which are:

- Intellectual skills
- Verbal information
- Cognitive strategies
- Motor skills and
- Attitude

This classification also contains the three primary taxonomies namely cognitive, affective and psychomotor. However in Gagne's taxonomy the cognitive category is stressed more than the other two.

How to Write Instructional Objectives?

When an objective is written, it has three parts:

(i) The action or behaviour that the learner is to perform.
(ii) The conditions under which the action or behaviour is to be performed for observation.
(iii) The criteria by which the action or behaviour is to be judged.

The three parts described above are given as the three basic criteria for writing instructional objectives by *Robert F. Mager*. They are performance (P), conditions (C) and criteria (C). In a different perspective the five components, instead of three, may be accorded in an instructional objective. These are performer, action, task, condition and criterion.

Out of the three, the first component, i.e., the action or behaviour to be performed is the critical element of the objective and is often used as the statement of an objective by itself. However, for measurement purposes the second and third components must be implied. For the teacher as an instructor, the action statement by itself suffices as the objective.

Gronlund has proposed the following five criteria for generating instructional objectives:

a) Instructional objectives are to be written in terms of student's performance.
b) They should be stated in terms of learning outcome, instead of learning process.
c) Mere description of subject matter should be avoided.
d) Only one learning outcome should be included in each learning objective.

e) To be specific, verbs having the proper level of generality should be used.

f) The action verb should be categorically 'measurable'; can be added to the list.

A teacher as a measurer essentially requires both the conditions, that is, when will the behaviour occur, and the criteria, that is how will the acceptability of the behaviour be judged for his/her objectives. A learner ought to know what s/he needs to perform during an instruction, thus an objective also helps in determining the goal of the learner during instruction.

Here, we will mainly emphasize upon the first component. Here, the emphasis is on the word 'action or behaviour' since this tells us what the student will be doing or what to test for. The action or behaviour is a descriptive statement of intended student performance. Because measurement requires an active response by the learner, the statement should include an action verb to depict the appropriate behaviour. For example, we can observe and measure whether a student can identify, describe or demonstrate something. As such, any verb that expresses action will suffice for writing an objective. Given below are some action verbs in each subcategory of cognitive and affective domains.

i) Cognitive Domain

1. For Knowledge: Define, describe, identify, list, name etc.
2. For Comprehension: Distinguish, explain, predict, generalise, summarise, etc.
3. For Application: Change, compute, predict, produce, relate, solve, use etc.
4. For Analysis: Differentiate, identify, select, separate, break down, illustrate etc.
5. For Synthesis: Combine, compose, create, design, rewrite, summarise, etc.
6. For Evaluation: Appraise, compare, conclude, describe, justify, interpret, summarize, etc.

It is interesting to note that the action verbs like 'describe', 'explain', 'discuss'—are lacking in terms of 'objectivity of the task assigned. Usually an instructional objective, if converted into an interrogative sentence, takes the form of a good 'question', or 'item'. Hence, it is advised not to use the above spelt action verbs in instructional objectives since the same lead to 'subjective' questions.

ii) Affective Domain

The term 'affective' denotes believing, emoting or feeling. Like the taxonomy of the cognitive domain, the taxonomy of the affective domain identifies a sequence of levels that may be used for structuring instructional objectives.

Some of the action verbs used for stating objectives in affective and psychomotor domains is given as follows:

- Choose,
- locate,
- practice,
- report,
- initiate,
- alter,
- Operate,
- draw,
- calculate,
- handle,
- fix,
- arrange,
- integrate etc.

The Need for Stating Instructional Objectives

Clearly stated instructional objectives serve the following purposes:

- Help a teacher to plan his/her instructional strategy so that the learners achieve the stated goal.
- Serve as a standard reference to which the learner can compare his/her achievement at various stages during a course and improving knowledge and skills wherever necessary.
- Helpful for preparing instructional materials.
- Provide guidance in evaluating the performance of learners.

Relationship between Instructional Objectives and Evaluation

Instructional objectives are quite useful for evaluating learning. Effective evaluation depends on a clear description of what is to be evaluated and determination of how to evaluate. Hence the instructional objectives should be stated properly.

Well-stated objectives facilitate the preparation of test items. If one's instructional goal is knowledge acquisition, measuring for comprehension or synthesis would be inappropriate. Objectives, therefore,

- Help a teacher to evaluate the appropriateness of his/her tests and items.

- Further, they help the teacher to know what to test for.
- They form the basis for the development of tests and test items.
- They help in constructing tests specially the teacher-devised achievement test items.
- Objectives represent a definite point of reference in the classroom system both for instruction and testing.
- Evaluation measures a broad range of objectives by a variety of techniques. The evaluation plan must integrate the results in to an understanding of the situation that will permit changes, which will result in better learning.

Objectives and evaluation are linked together as in the given flow chart with the four aspects inter related to each other.

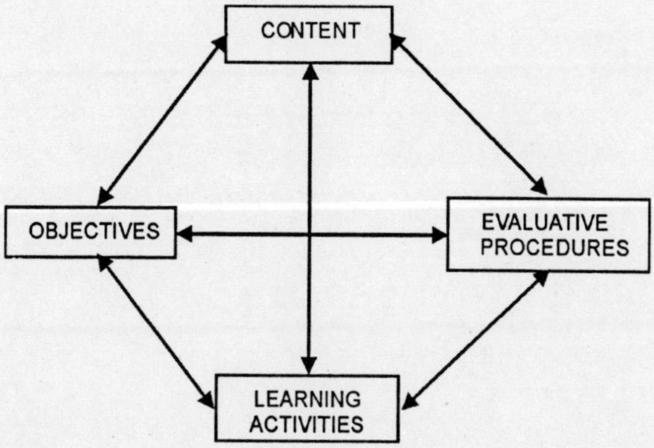

Conclusion

In fact, Instructional objectives identify the specific behaviour or performance, capability that the learner is supposed to achieve at the end of instruction. These are specific, observable and measurable. As a teacher therefore, one should be very careful in stating them precisely without any ambiguity.

5

Instructional Strategies and Instructional Methods

OVERALL INSTRUCTIONAL STRATEGIES

Overall instruction strategies are the translation of a philosophical or theoretical position regarding instruction into a statement of way in which instruction should be carried out in specific circumstances. The primary objective of instruction is to enable the students to learn. As such the strategy should be based on the learning activity of a learner. Learning takes place through processing of information received during instruction. Learning activities are described as *deductive* or *inductive,* depending upon the type of reasoning in which the learners are involved. It may also form the combination of the two, heading to inducto-deductive reasoning.

Deductive Reasoning

It is a thinking process, which moves from the general to specific. A common form of deductive reasoning is the syllogism, which can be defined as an argument containing two statements of propositions, called premises and a conclusion. The famous example of this argument is:

Major Premise- (*Generalisation*)	All men are mortal.
Minor Premise- (*Observation*)	Socrates is a man.
Conclusion- (*Predictive Inference*)	Therefore, Socrates is mortal.

The major premise in a deductive sequence, which is either a concept, definition or a generalisation. The minor premise is a fact or observation. The conclusion is either explanatory or predictive.

Inductive Reasoning

The concepts and generalisations used in deductive reasoning are often acquired through direct experiences with environment. Inductive thinking is a reverse process of deductive thinking and thinking proceeds from the specific to general. In inductive thinking, the individual does not have prior knowledge of the abstraction but only arrives at it after observing and analysing the observations. The data used in inductive reasoning can take various forms, like observations, pictures, words or graphs.

Types of Strategy

Two strategies are identified related to the process of learning and instruction.

- **Expositive** strategy *(for Reception learning)* based on deductive reasoning model and
- **Experiential** strategy *(for Discovery learning)* based on inductive reasoning model.

The two strategies have the following main steps—

Expositive Strategy

1. Present information. This may be achieved through explanation or through practical demonstration.
2. Test for reception, recall, and understanding. Repeat or rephrase the message if it proves to be necessary.
3. Present opportunities for learners to practice applying the general principles to a range of examples. Test for correct application. Modify the quantity and difficulty of examples when necessary to correct performance.
4. Present opportunities for the application of the newly learned content based on information to real situations and problems.

Experiential Strategy

1. Present opportunities to act and observe the consequences of one's actions.
2. Test for understanding of the cause and effect relationship. This may be done by questioning or simply by observing the reactions of learners. Present further opportunities to act, if necessary.
3. Test for the formation of the general principles underlying the cases presented either by questioning or by observing further activity. Present further cases as required until the general principle has been learned.
4. Present opportunities for the application of the newly learned information to real life situations and problems.

There are many variations on these two basic strategies. It is possible to construct a continuum of discovery or expositive strategies, ranging from totally free discovery to totally controlled expositive learning.

Applicability of Strategy

It is expected that both expositive and experiential strategies will be needed for instruction on topics depending on the type of content. The question is which strategy should be used when. There are no hard and fast rules, but it is possible to establish some guidelines, which makes the instructon logical.

Fact: It is possible to discover facts. Fact, by definition, does not have examples- –they exist independently.

Concepts: Primary or concrete concepts are usually learned by experiencing a number of examples and hence discovery learning approach will be an ideal approach. A secondary or defined concept is, in a sense, a rule for the classification of simpler concepts. In such case, the use of clearly worded definitions and thus expository strategy would be useful.

Principles: Principles can be learned through exposition. However, there is overwhelming evidence that principles learned through discovery are remembered more efficiently and applied in transfer of learning situations with more success than those learned through reception learning. Finally, the learning of principles by discovery, which employs the solution of problems as an instructional method, exercises the learner's problem solving skill. For all these reasons, it would seem reasonable to use experiential strategy for teaching of principles, whenever this practically feasible and economically justifiable.

Procedures: These are a category of fact-systems that answer the question '*How do I do it?*' in a unique and unambiguous way. It would seem therefore, that, like facts, procedures should be taught by expositive strategy. However, the procedures based on concept and principles can also be taught by a guided discovery approach. This would require a process of reflection and construction to take place during initial learning. This would help in recollecting the procedures at later stage.

Instructional Tactics

The selection of appropriate tactics for specific lesson is a process of creative design or adaptation of explanations and definitions; illustrations, examples, analogies; learning activities, drill sand games; feedback questions, tests, exercises.

All these should be appropriate to the content, the proposed objectives and the learner characteristics.

Some tactics are suggested below for different category of information.

Fact

Presentation and repetition of information in a form, sequence and frequency conducive to memorisation.

Concept

- Provide set of appropriate examples clearly illustrating the concept and non-examples.
- Develop cues/questions to draw attention of students to the critical attributes, similarities and differences in examples and non-examples.
- State clear definition of concepts.
- Develop analogy, compare/contrast, and diagrammatic representation to place the concept in context with other related previously known concepts.

Principles (Cause-Effect Relationships)

Expositive Strategy- RUL-EG
The definition and rules related to the principles are explained first. This is followed by illustrations with examples by applying the rule to specific cases. The tactics is more applicable for pedagogic setup.

Experiential Strategy- EG-RUL
The examples are illustrated first usually through simulation. The students observe and study a phenomenon and attempt to formulate the principle or rules from observations. The tactics is more relevant for androgogic setup.

Procedures
Divide learning task into stages and teaching in 'parts' and 'progressive parts' for chain procedure.

For discriminating procedure comparison/contrasting between alternative courses of action should be shown.

As algorithms are combinations of chains and discrimination, teacher may use the same tactics as above.

In sum, a teacher has to identify the categories of information before deciding on the strategies to be adopted. It has been established that adoption of experiential strategy encourages growth of learning *with thinking capability* among the learners.

However, a teacher should make a judicious mix of instructional strategies, taking into consideration the category of information to be presented, learners' characteristics and available resources for imparting an effective instruction.

INSTRUCTIONAL METHODS

It is a generic term used to mean *'ways of doing something'*. The method is to be selected on the basis of type of knowledge on which instruction is to be imparted.

The instruction may be provided through different methods and the common methods employed in classrooms of educational institutions are as below:

1. Lecture Method
2. Laboratory Method
3. Tutorial Method
4. Project Method
5. Discussion Method
6. Seminar Method.

There are 4 stages involved in each of the instruction methods. These are

(1) Planning
(2) Preparation
(3) Implementation
(4) Evaluation.

All the four stages must be followed diligently to make any instruction method effective.

Lecture Method

This is the easiest, most accepted, 'safest' and basic method used in the higher education system. A lecture may be defined as a teaching period occupied wholly or mainly with continuous exposition by a lecturer. Research studies has established 'lecture method' to be very much effective for conveying information.

If delivered properly, usually the students like this method for the following reasons

(a) It does not require anything except paying attention, better to say, concentration in following.
(b) It is a traditionally accepted method,
(c) It can provide new information to students in new areas,
(d) It provides a summary of topic(s) suitable for memorisation,

(e) It provides opportunity to take notes, and
(f) It is interesting to listen to a lecturer having good presentation skills.

It is popular among the teachers for the following advantages:

(a) It is very helpful for
   (i) Conveying information,
   (ii) Providing framework for detailed study of a topic to be undertaken by students,
   (iii) Managing large sized class,
   (iv) Quick coverage of the course,
   (v) Greater content coverage,
   (vi) Stimulating interest of the students, and
   (vii) Generating understanding of students.
(b) It normally does not require any other material for the classroom.
(c) It has gained stature through tradition as being the method used by the teachers of a teacher.
(d) It provides the opportunity to the teachers to exhibit their skills of (i) memorisation, (ii) sequential presentation of facts, (iii) oratory.
(e) It is economical, however you may question of cost of a 'teacher'.
(f) It is the only method available to teachers of the institutions, which cannot provide facilities for use of other effective methods.
(g) It allows an unprepared teacher to hide his/her weaknesses by giving uninterrupted lecture.

The lecture method though popularly used has been found to have the following limitations

(1) It does not ensure effective participation of students in teaching-learning process.
(2) It often does not lead to effective learning by students.
(3) It is generally a one-way communication encouraging the students to be passive and dependent.
(4) It does not cater to individual difference among students.
(5) It generally does not encourage stimulation of thought process.
(6) It is often boring for students.
(7) It is not useful in case of training of skills.

The following guidelines will help a teacher to deliver a lecture more effectively:

- Fit the material to be presented to the time at your disposal.

- Seek unrelentingly for precise examples and illustrations and for ways of breaking up a single presentational mode.
- Begin by stimulating the interest of the students and continue to sustain the interest during the lecture.
- Provide the students with frequent breathing spaces and opportunities for questioning.
- Provide an ending for every lecture but maintain continuity with what has been presented and what will be presented.
- Deliver and use a range of voices and gestures and physical movements appropriate to the material being presented.
- Be guided by the students before whom presentation is being made.

In spite its various limitations, the lecture method will continue to be the major method to be used by the teachers in Indian higher education system due to paucity of resources. However, if proper thought is given during planning and preparation stages for applying the appropriate instructional strategies, the lecture method may be developed to lead to effective learning by students.

Laboratory Method

This is considered to be a quite important method for imparting skill-training to the students in programmes of any discipline. It involves experiments and demonstrations for development of manual skills and process of scientific inquiry among the students.

In laboratory methods various types of experiments are designed to be performed by the students with the following aims:

- Understand concepts
- Understand principles
- Discover rules and relationships
- Solve problems
- Develop ability to observe and measure
- Identify sources of errors and methods for minimising equipment/ instrument/material
- Develop manipulating skills such as setting, adjusting and handling of equipment
- Follow standard procedure of testing and assessing
- Write formal and informal reports
- Work in groups (team work) successfully

- Develop habit of inquiry
- Observe safety precautions
- Interpret the results/data
- Locate fault in equipment/instrument/circuits
- Judge magnitude without actual measurement.

In spite of its importance in development of a professional, little thought is given to the application of instructional strategies in design of laboratory experiments. The conventional type of experiments provides little freedom to students, little scope for student initiative and limits the conclusions to be drawn. The stress should be given on Discovery type, Investigative type and Problem-solving type experiments in the laboratory. Problem solving type experiments can be used very effectively for developing a scientific process of inquiry among the students.

Tutorial Method

This is a student-centered approach offering step by step guidance in student learning. It gives stress on individual development, which is normally neglected in classroom lecture. The tutorial takes care of individual differences among students, especially slow learners getting compensatory treatment and gifted learners getting enrichment treatment.

This method is quite useful in development of skill in manipulation of data and numerical computations. It may consist of assignments to be done in tutorial class itself. The assignments are evaluated at the spot and outcomes are discussed with individual student. This provides opportunities for individual student to clear his/her doubts, if any.

Ideally, the teacher-pupil ratio in tutorial method should be 1:1. Generally in Indian condition, a tutorial class group consists of 5 to 10 students which is actually a deviation from its objectives. In adopting the tutorial method, a number of techniques such as exposition, demonstration, coaching, questioning, guided practice or a combination of those is chosen as constituents. The teacher has to be real resource with multiple requirements on subject matter, reference materials, techniques and approaches of inter-personal relationship in order to make a tutorial a successful method of instruction.

Heavily loaded theoretical part in curriculum, knowledge based examination pattern and rigid time schedule are not conducive to the adoption of tutorial method. In practice, in most of the higher educational institutions, adequate time is not available to the faculty members for arranging adoption of effective tutorial method.

Project Method

This is a student-oriented effective method of instruction and is widely used to enrich the classroom teaching. It may be defined as a significant practical unit of activity of a problematic nature, planned and carried out to completion by the students. A project, in the sense used in education system is an open-ended assignment, the outcome of which is not known at inception and whose progress depends mostly on the intelligence, skills, creativity and energy of the students.

Its purpose is to expose the students to real-life problems and introduce them to procedures used to reach the acceptable solutions so that they gain confidence in taking decisions and tackling problems on their own. It is possible to integrate and reinforce through this method the skills acquired by the students in separate courses of study.

This method of instruction develops among the students

- Attitude of inquiry
- Confidence and ability to tackle new problems
- Ability to interpret events and results
- Ability to work as leader and member of a team
- Ability to observe and measure physical phenomenon
- Ability to develop communication skill
- Ability to plan, prepare, select materials and tools to reach perfection through experimentation
- Creative thinking
- Ability to analyse and synthesise problem and thereby to think critically.

A project has a problem or task as a theme. It aims at solving the problem or acquiring mastery of the task. In project method, a scheme is formulated for the purpose. The scheme is continuously evaluated and changed as and when necessary on the basis of feedback from evaluation. This continues till the conclusion of the project. The projects may be of various types and can be taken up through observation, library study, practical work etc. The success of this method is dependent on the ability of the teacher to facilitate and guide the students to exhibit the skills necessary for undertaking the project.

Discussion as a Method

It is a small group instructional method and is defined as a group work using different instructional techniques to attain a predetermined objective. It is primarily based on 'question and answer' technique punctuated by short narration. Discussion method has been found to be helpful in development of skills of speaking, listening and group leadership; critical thinking and inquiry skill among the students. The teacher has a twin role to play in this method-guiding and directing. Based on the content and procedure the discussion may be categorised in 3 types: Direct discussion, developmental discussion and Problem-solving discussion.

Direct Discussion

Its purpose is to acquire better understanding of and to apply known fact, principles and processes. For making the discussion effective, the topic of discussion should be announced in advance and teacher has to provide a lot of guidance for the students' to prepare themselves and to effectively participate in the discussion.

Developmental Discussion

Its' purpose is to pool all knowledge for developing principles, rules, hypothesis through discussion in which all members are equal partners. It is not possible to set any specific objective for such developmental activities. The teacher may elicit contributions from the participating students after presenting the issue for discussion and may balance their participation during the course of discussion.

Problem-solving Discussion

This is a higher-level discussion organised to discover a solution to a common problem. The teacher defines the problem and encourages maximum participation by the students. The discussion passes through all the stages of problem solving i.e. identification of problems, analysis of data, formulation of alternate solutions, evaluation of the solutions and selection of viable solution(s).

The success of the discussion method depends on the teacher who should take efforts to guide the project as a student-centered approach and play only the role of the facilitator. Equal participation of all members, avoidance of dominance of any member(s), democratic handlings of situations are important considerations for leading an effective discussion.

However, inhibition of majority of students in Indian condition is a barrier in conducting effective discussion and brainstorming approach may be effectively used to overcome this barrier.

Interestingly the author came across the discussion method adopted by the teachers, at post graduate levels where the teacher is not familiar with the medium of instruction leading to a 'chaos' in adopting the method.

Seminar Method

Seminar is also a group-work with extensive participation with focus on exclusive study of a topic or interrelated topics. Generally a topic of common interest is specified for the seminar and students prepare on different aspects of the topic and make presentation before a small group. All the members of the group need not be presenters but all should prepare adequately to ask relevant questions or add new and unique view points to the presentation made. Participation in a seminar helps in development of critical thinking, formulation of hypothesis, analysis and evaluation skills.

The teacher should play the role of a catalyst as the moderator. S/he is to introduce the topic at the beginning, supposed to explain the themes linked to the topic and set the rules for presentation and discussion. S/he also has to summarise at the end the views expressed and relate it to learning. This can be used as an effective technique in higher levels of academic programmes.

In sum, a teacher has to make a judicious mix of instructional strategies and methods, depending on the learning objectives, and available resources for imparting an effective instruction.

6
Designing Classroom Instructional Plan

Human being always thinks in advance about the things they want to do and make preparations that enable them to do the things. We being rational creatures, tend to deliberate about what to do. The deliberation always takes time and we rarely have time, at the time of action, to deliberate at length about exactly how we want to act. Hence, we deliberate in advance, deciding how we intend to act at some future point, and this deliberation is called *planning*. We engage in planning on a regular basis.

Why Instructional Planning?

It has already been justified in the volume that the instructional system is a complex phenomenon. The primary activity of a teacher is to deliver instruction to the students, particularly in classroom situation, so that students can achieve learning to a specified level. It is an accepted fact that even a simple activity like daily marketing needs prior planning. Hence, in the complex instructional system, the activities to be performed by the teacher during the process of instruction obviously need to be planned for effective learning by the students.

Everybody is Doing it—in a Variety of Ways

While all teachers plan about teaching, they all do not plan in exactly the same way. Some may jot down a few notes in lesson-plan book, others may write outlines detailing lessons or units they intend to deliver. Studies have shown that few experienced teachers plan according to the recommended procedure. It has been observed that teachers in higher educational Institutions normally focus on the content of the topic and its explanation. Since students' achievement is related to their attention and on-task behaviour, the importance of involvement of students have to be kept in mind during instruction.

The systematic instructional planning helps in motivating the students, sustaining their level of interest during instruction and also helps the teacher to obtain feedback about the level of learning achieved. It is recommended that novice teachers should always prepare plan, put it in writing on paper or in MS Word before delivery. However, with experience, every teacher develops his/her own style of planning keeping into consideration the basic principles of planning.

What is a Lesson?

For convenience of instruction and learning, the topics/sub-topics of a subject is divided into a number of units called lessons. It is

- ✓ An arbitrarily chosen unit of teaching/learning and not a time-table period
- ✓ a two way activity between teacher and students, designed to facilitate student learning
- ✓ A combination of presentation and activity methods supported by the appropriate media to be decided on the judgment of the teacher.

What is a Classroom Instructional Plan or Lesson Plan?

- ✓ A series of learning experiences, which occur in a single block of time in a particular day
- ✓ An organised, sequential statement of general and specific means by which the goals are to be attained by the students during the lesson
- ✓ Preparation by the teacher to outline his/her behaviour during the lesson to enable the students to achieve the specific goal.

Advantages of Lesson Plan

The lesson plan helps the teachers to organise the contents of their lessons or units in such a way to bring about the best conditions for learning. This serves as an organisational tool, assisting them to organise time, activities and materials for a lesson. It can be used as a guide for interaction with the students. A written plan can ensure that directions are structured in exactly the right way when an activity has begun. There are other advantages of carefully planned lessons. They provide the teachers with a sense of security thus giving the teachers, particularly the new teachers, more confidence while teaching in the classroom. It also provides a framework for later evaluation of a lesson assisting the teacher in identifying productive learning activities and for self-appraisal.

Learning Phases

It must be emphasised at this point that there is no one fixed and formalised plan that will suite all lessons and a set plan cannot be recommended for any type of lesson or unit. The teacher must adopt a flexible approach arising out of particular objective one has in mind in relation to the classroom situation. Such flexibility will depend on the teacher's understanding of the psychopedagogical processes underlying an act of learning and how these relate to the behaviour of the teacher and learner.

It is possible to distinguish the components of comprising the complexities of a complete learning sequence. Gagne has identified eight such phases, which are:

1. Motivation phase
2. Apprehension phase
3. Acquisition phase
4. Retention phase
5. Recall phase
6. Generalisation phase
7. Performance phase
8. Feedback phase

These phases refer to the internal processes that take place during an act of learning, which may be influenced by external factors. The forthcoming Table indicates how the internal learning phases, together with their attendant processes, relate to the possible instructional events deemed appropriate by the teacher.

Learning Phase/Instructional Events Model

Learning Phase	Process	Instructional Events
1. Motivation	Expectancy	Arousing interest; Stating learning objectives, Creating rewarding learning situations
2. Apprehending	Attention, Perception, Understanding	Exposition; Introducing the subject; Directing attention to significant features; Explaining
3. Acquisition	Coding, Storage entry	Suggesting means of coding
4. Retention	Storage	Not known, however attention, interest, drive often contributes.
5. Recall	Retrieval	Stimulating recall; Suggesting schemes and cues for recall; Providing learning guidance
6. Generalisation	Transfer	Promoting transfer by providing a variety of contexts for retrieval; Cuing
7. Performance	Responding	Instances of performance
8. Feedback	Reinforcement	Information feedback providing verification or comparison with a standard.

Elements of Planning

While planning a lesson, the internal consistency among three components of instruction should be maintained. These components are:

1. Lesson Objectives.
2. The teaching methods, materials, media, aids, learning experiences and/or exercises and their organisation.
3. Evaluative procedures.

These are referred as the 'Anchor Points' in the design of instruction, constant reference to which keep the lesson 'on target'. Mager has expressed the same elements in terms of fundamental interrogatives as:

1. ***Where am I going?***—Objectives.
2. ***How will I get there?*** —Steps by means of which objectives are achieved.
3. **How will I know, *When I have arrived?***—The use of appropriate evaluation procedures.

Linkage between Lesson Plan and Learning Phases

The different stages of a class lesson, derived from the learning phase/ instructional event model is shown in Table below:

Table

Learning Phase	Class Lesson Plan stage
MOTIVATION	INTRODUCTION
APPREHENSION ACQUISITION	PRESENTATION
RETENTION RECALL	CONSOLIDATION
GENERALISATION	CONCLUSION
PERFORMANCE FEEDBACK	EVALUATION

Stages of Lesson Plan and their Functions

This corresponds to the motivation phase of learning model and will be the point in the lesson where the instructional events designed to arouse interest among students are planned. A desire is created in the students to take part in lesson and an atmosphere conducive to learning is created. Thus the functions of lesson introduction are to:

- Establish contact
- Create mental setup
- Arouse interest
- Draw attention
- Initiate motivation
- Explain need for lesson
- Outline lesson objectives.

This may be done in several ways

(a) Stating a historical, topical or current problem related to the lecture content.
(b) Explaining the relationship of the lecture content to laboratory exercise, professional career interest etc.
(c) Relating lecture content to previous information learned.
(d) Demonstrating some experiment, the outcome of which will lead to a question that can be answered in terms of the new information to be learned.
(e) Raising a question to be answered at the end of lecture.
(f) Creating motivation by mediating between what is previously known and what is to be learnt.

Presentation

The presentation stage embraces the apprehending, acquisition and retention phases in the model. This will be the point where new information or content that to be learnt or studied is introduced. Depending on the nature and extent of the content, the presentation stage may be broken down in further sub stages.

The functions of presentation are:

(a) Ensuring sufficient clarity of matter through introduction of appropriate methods/media.
(b) Explanation with illustration and examples/non-examples.

This stage pertains to the sequential development of the content structure, which is to be done according to the abilities of the students. This can be achieved through the following steps (not suggested in hierarchical order)

(a) Organising content in some logical way such as to divide and sequence new information into small units, each having logical and psychological meaning.

(b) Determining the key points which can be effectively developed during a lesson, striking a balance between length and depth of coverage.
(c) Preparing relevant examples to illustrate the key ideas to help in understanding and learning
(d) Planning small units, containing some key ideas (of 3 to 5 minutes duration) and providing transition between key points or ideas.
(e) Preparing some significant questions for posing to the students or to the teacher himself/herself to establish a dialogue.
(f) Planning for involvement of students during the lesson.

Consolidation

Although recall phase, together with the generalisation and performance phase are included in the consolidation stage, it must be remembered that it will also play a part in the preceding presentation stage. It will be the point in the lesson where the students will have the opportunity to demonstrate what they have learned and it will therefore be incumbent on the teacher to provide opportunities for testing the newly acquired knowledge and/or skills and for using them in novel situations.

The functions of the consolidation stage are to:

- Reinforce new material presented
- Ensure application
- Carryon formative evaluation
- Cater for individual difference
- Initiate closed student-teacher interaction

Following suggestions may be adopted for consolidation.

(a) Asking a few students to restate (non-verbatim) the key points, ideas and concepts presented and developed in the lesson.
(b) Allocating time to summarise key points, ideas and concepts.
(c) Keeping allowance for some flexibility in the presentation in order to respond to students' questions and comments.
(d) Evaluating formatively.

Conclusions or Summary: While introduction is the initiating activity in a lesson, conclusion is the culminating activity. It refers to those actions or statements by a teacher that are designed to bring a lesson presentation to appropriate closure. This is the time to revise and/or highlight the main points of the lesson. Any of the following activity may be used for this purpose

(a) Answering the question(s) raised at the beginning of the lesson.
(b) Providing closure for the lesson by
    (i) briefly summarising lesson content and previewing what lies ahead, or

(ii) relating lesson content to past or future presentation, or

(iii) re-stating what is expected of the students by gaining the new information.

Evaluation

A teacher often needs to know the extent of learning/understanding achieved by the learners, particularly at the end of discussion of a topic or at the end of a class discussing solution of numerical problems or the like. Further students need to practice for acquiring the skill of solving numerical problems. This objective is achieved through Home Assignments given by the teachers. Assessment of these home assignments is credited to Internal Assessment of students, and form an integral part of Evaluation scheme.

Time Factor

The instructional events should not only lead to the achievement of objectives but they must also fit into the time available. The timing of the lesson usually becomes instinctive with experience and practice. However, for beginners, one way is to begin by allocating time to each stage of lesson as a notional guide (e.g. 45 minutes lesson could have a 5 minutes introduction, 25 minutes presentation, 10 minutes consolidation and 5 minutes conclusion).

It is important to distinguish between the allotted and the actual duration of lesson, particularly when the students have to move from one classroom to another between subsequent lessons.

Structure of a Classroom Instructional Plan (also known as Lesson Plan)

The structure of an instructional plan for classroom situation has been suggested in the Sample Lesson Plan-I. However it should be kept in mind that the suggested format is not sacrosanct and it may be modified by the teacher according to the requirement, keeping into consideration the objectives and basic stages of the plan.

The *heading* of the plan should include information about the nature of class, students, subject, topic/sub-topic, unit lessons and name of the teacher.

The *objectives* should contain the following elements:

1) An indication of who is to perform the desired behaviour (e.g. individual student or group of students or class etc.)
2) A precise statement of the expected specific terminal behaviour or learning outcome using clear, observable action verbs.

SAMPLE LESSON PLAN - I

A. Class Profile
   1. Name of Institution
   2. Year/Semester
   3. Branch- Mechanical Engineering
   4. No. of students - 30
   5. Total time for lesson - 1 Hr.
   6. Name of Teacher—XYZ

B. Lesson Profile
   1. Subject : Manufacturing Processes
   2. Topic : Electro Discharge Machining (EDM)
   3. Lesson Title : Introduction to EDM

C. Instructional Overview
   1. Instructional Objectives-After attending the class the students will be able to
      a) Define electro-discharge machining
      b) List the main components of EDM system
      c) Explain the principle of EDM process
      d) List the functions of dielectric fluid
      e) List the desirable characteristics of EDM tool materials
      f) Describe the advantages of EDM process
   2. List of Media/Teaching Aids:
      a) Chalk Board and Coloured Chalks/Marker Pen and White Board
      b) O.H.P/LCD Projector
      c) Transparencies for presentation/ppt. slides
   3. List of Pre-requisite Knowledge:
      a) Common machining processes
      b) Idea of sparking
      c) Dielectric medium

TEACHING POINT	TEACHING METHODS		STUDENT ACTIVITIES
	TEACHER ACTIVITIES	MEDIA/ TEACHING AIDS	
(1)	(2)	(3)	(4)
	Lesson stage 1. INTRODUCTION		Time Allotted- 10 minutes

(*Contd.*)

(1)	(2)	(3)	(4)
SET INDUCTION 1. Draw Attention to motivate students	Ask questions, encourage and help students to respond with desired answer Q1. How do you make a small circular hole in an aluminum block? Q2. What will be the cutting tool? Q3. What should be the tool material? Q4. What will be the tool material if the work material is mild steel?		Respond by giving answers
2. Checking Previous Knowledge	Ask Questions and Give feedback on students' responses		
	Q1. Have you seen sparking in electric circuits? Q2. What happens there? Q3. What is the effect?		Respond by giving answers
3 Declaration of topic	Explain the difficulty of machining many modern materials by conventional methods. EDM is a special method to machine electrically conducting hard materials.		
4. Objectives	Announce the topic and write on top of board. Explain the lesson objectives as stated, invite questions.		Ask questions to clarify doubts
	Lesson stage 2. (a). PRESENTATION		
Knowledge Category- CONCEPT Definition of EDM	State definition and write on board. Explain salient features of definition.	chalkboard	Write in note book Ask questions
	Lesson stage 3. (a). CONSOLIDATION		
Reinforce understanding of concept	Ask question Q1. What is EDM? Correct the students' responses, if necessary. Repeat definition. Respond to students' question to clarify doubts.		Respond Ask questions for clarification

(Contd.)

(1)	(2)	(3)	(4)
	Lesson stage 2. (b). PRESENTATION		
Knowledge Category-FACT Names of basic elements of EDM	State and Draw/Display labeled sketch of EDM System	Chalkboard/Transparency 1) Tool 2) Work piece 3) A.C. Power supply Fig. 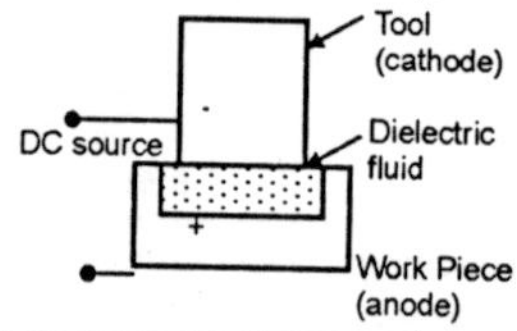	Listen and Note down
	Lesson stage 3. (b). CONSOLIDATION		
Assess retention of information	Ask questions about names.		Students Respond
	Lesson stage 2. (c). PRESENTATION		
Knowledge Category-PRINCIPLES Basic principles of EDM	Explain the basic principle of EDM process in steps.	Display Transparency	Respond
	Lesson stage 3. (c).		
Assess understanding	Ask questions. Clarify doubts of students.		Respond Ask questions to clarify doubts
	Lesson stage 2. (d). PRESENTATION		
Knowledge Category-PROCEDURE Functions of dielectric fluid	Display the functions of Dielectric fluid on board/transparency and Explain.	Chalkboard/Transparency 1. Acts as insulator until potential is high 2. Flushing medium 3. Cooling medium	
	Lesson stage 3. (d). CONSOLIDATION		Time Allotted-
Assess learning	Ask questions. Clarify doubts of students.		Respond Ask questions

(*Contd.*)

(1)	(2)	(3)	(4)
Lesson stage 2(e). PRESENTATION			
Knowledge Category-CONCEPT Desirable characteristics of tool material	Display to Describe and Explain desirable characteristics of tool material, on board / transparency.	Chalkboard/ Transparency 1) High electrical conductivity 2) High thermal conductivity 3) High melting temperature 4) Cheap in price 9) Easy to manufacture	
Lesson stage 3(e). CONSOLIDATION			
Assess learning	Ask students question and give feedback Q1. What are the characteristics of tool material?		Respond
Lesson stage 2(f). PRESENTATION			
Knowledge Category-FACT Advantages of EDM process	Describe the advantages of EDM process. Display list on board/ transparency.	Chalkboard/ Transparency "Advantages of EDM"	
Lesson stage 3(f). CONSOLIDATION			
Assess learning	Ask students question on applicability and give feedback		Respond
Lesson stage 3 (e). CONSOLIDATION			
Assess learning	Ask students question and give feedback Q1. What are the characteristics of tool material?		Respond
Lesson stage 2 (f). PRESENTATION			
Knowledge Category-FACT Advantages of EDM process	Describe the advantages of EDM process. Display list on board/transparency.	Chalkboard/Transparency "Advantages of EDM"	
Lesson stage 3 (f). CONSOLIDATION			
Assess learning	Ask students question on applicability and give feedback		Respond

Power point presentation slides on Advantages of EDM Process

1. The process is applicable for machining any electrically conductive material irrespective of properties like strength, brittleness.
2. It is simple and straightforward method of form producing dies for drop forging, drawing and extruding.
3. It is simple method for making complex cavities in moulds and dies for plastics, glass and ceramic manufacturing.
4. The high rate of heating and cooling at the treated surface renders some extra hardness to the surface.
5. Simple geometrical shape configurations can easily be produced by piercing or die sinking in hard ended die-plates with required accuracy and surface finish eliminating much complicated grinding and lapping

Teaching point	Teaching methods		Student Activities
	Teacher Activities	Media/Teaching Aids	
	Lesson stage 4. CONCLUSION		Time Allotted- 5 minutes
Summary of Information presented Formative evaluation	Summarise the main points of the lesson. Ask objective type questions to assess achievement of objectives. Clarify Doubts.		Respond
	Lesson stage 5. EVALUATION		Time Allotted-3 minutes
Assess level of understanding and learning of lesson	Give Home Assignment.	Chalk board	Respond

The stages of lesson plan is recommended to be prepared in a tabular format and body of the plan be divided in vertical columns—the Teaching Point on the left hand side of page, Method in the middle and Students' Activities on the right hand side. The Method column is subdivided in two vertical columns—the Teacher's Activity on the left hand side column and Media/Teaching Aids on right hand side column.

The teacher may state clearly and concisely the key points of what s/he is going to do in content column. The lesson content is divided into suitable small units (key points) and categorised into different types of information, in sequential order and will be included under teaching point column. The teacher activity column should indicate the strategy and/or tactics to be used i.e. how s/he intends to teach the expressed content of the lesson.

The method corresponding to each small unit (e.g. lecture, question/answer, demonstration, group discussion, problem exercise etc.) will be indicated in this column. The corresponding media and teaching aids to be used will be indicated in teaching aid column (e.g., chalk and board, charts/maps/posters/slides/film strips/power points or the like. and audio, visual, audio-visual media etc.)

The student activity column will include the expected student responses appropriate to the instructional activities performed by the teacher (e.g. listens, reads, writes, draws, responds, computes etc.).

The *introduction* should indicate

(a) List of requisite previous knowledge for effective learning of lesson to be discussed.
(b) The probing questions to assess whether requisite previous knowledge has been acquired by the students along with correct responses.
(c) The ideas/examples to be discussed for motivating the students by arousing the interest of students about the lesson and transition from previous to new knowledge. (***Set Induction***)
(d) The objectives of the lesson.

The teacher should be announcing the title of the lesson (recommended to be written on the top of the board) during introduction. This may be done at the beginning of introduction or after set induction, according to the preference of the teacher.

The *presentation and consolidation* be developed for each teaching point separately appropriate to each objective.

The *conclusion* should include the summary of chalkboard layout, highlights of key-points, points for discussion and the like.

The *evaluation* should include the home assignments comprising questions/problems/worksheets and the like.

Suggested Steps for Classroom Instructional Planning (Lesson Planning)

1) Select the Topic/sub-topic to be taken-up for instruction.
2) Organise the content of the topic/subtopic by dividing and sequencing into small meaningful unit lessons, taking into consideration the allocated time.
3) Identify the key points (which can be covered in short duration) to be developed during the lesson.
4) Categorise the information contained in each key point via, Fact, Concept, Principle and Procedure.

5) Identify the instructional objectives related to the category of information.
6) Select appropriate overall instructional strategy to be adopted during the lesson matching with the lesson content and learners' characteristics.
7) (a) Identify the previous knowledge required to be possessed by the learner for learning new information to be presented during the lesson.
   (b) Frame appropriate questions and responses for testing the previous knowledge.
   (c) Select appropriate instructional activities by the teacher for introducing the lesson to achieve 'set induction'.
   (d) Identify the anticipated student activities matching with the instructional activities by the teacher.
8) (a) Identify appropriate instructional tactics matching with the objective and category of information to be provided at Presentation and Consolidation stages.
   (b) Select appropriate instructional activities by the teacher according to the tactics identified.
   (c) It is preferable to develop the presentation and consolidation for each objective in sub-stages.
   (d) Identify the anticipated student activities matching with the instructional activities by the teacher.
9) (a) Summarise the presentation listing the key points.
   (b) Frame appropriate questions/responses for use during conclusion
10) Frame appropriate questions/problems/worksheets for evaluation of students' achievement, usually provided as Home Assignment.
11) Allocate adequate time corresponding to each stage/sub-stage within the total allocated time.

Evaluation of Instructional Plan

The lesson planner should evaluate the plan to assess the suitability of existing material for use in the lesson. We shall discuss the technique of *Pedagogical Evaluation* leaving the *validation* part.

This will concentrate on the designer's task of evaluating the soundness of the materials from a pedagogical viewpoint. This will include the verification of the quality of materials as instructional resource; whether they are likely to achieve the specific objectives for which they are being selected/prepared; whether they are well structured, easy to use, clear, and use the special effects of specific media to full pedagogical advantage, etc. Given hereunder a checklist, suggested by Professor Romiszowski, that may be used for the pre-evaluation of existing materials in terms of both suitability in a given lesson and general pedagogical quality.

CHECK-LIST FOR EVALUATION OF INSTRUCTIONAL PLAN

ASPECTS	Your rating			
	Yes	Partly	No	Cannot say
1.0 General				
1.1 Do all the materials specified in the lesson plan actually exist, and are they available for inspection?				
1.2 Have the materials passed the technical validation stage, and are they considered suitable in content?				
1.3 Is the type of material appropriate relating to the strategies and tactics specified in the plan?				
1.4 Does the material appear to be adequate to achieve the objectives set for it in the lesson plan?				
1.5 Are the materials really necessary? Do they contribute to the lesson in a manner that justifies the time/cost?				
1.6 Are the media employed appropriate for the objectives to be achieved and the content?				
2.0 Written Text				
2.1 Are the style and language used appropriate for the target students?				
2.2 Does the material really say what it sets out to say? Are the sentences logically structured, well organised, etc.?				
2.3 Are sufficiently well chosen examples included to define all new concepts clearly and adequately?				
2.4 Are there sufficient well-chosen examples included to define all new concepts clearly and adequately?				

ASPECTS	Your rating			
	Yes	Partly	No	Cannot say
2.5 Are sufficiently well designed illustrations and graphics to support or summarise the text adequately?				
2.6 Is good use made of spacing, blocks, underlining, colour, typography and other aids to communication?				
2.7 Are worked examples, self-test, practice exercises, introductions, summaries, glossaries, references and indexes used adequately and to good effect?				
3.0 Visuals				
3.1 Are the notations, conventions and graphic symbols used in the visuals known to learners?				
3.2 is the intended message well conveyed by the visual? Does it use the visual medium to good effect?				
3.3 Are the size and style of lettering used appropriate to the size of classroom?				
3.4 Is the layout of the visual clear and uncluttered, illustrating the key points of the message?				
3.5 Are the quality of artwork and the use of colour and shading adequate for communication?				

Instruction: Tick the appropriate column against each question and answer only the question that applies to a given case.

CLASSROOM INSTRUCTIONAL PLAN STRUCTURE (LESSON PLAN)

A. Class Profile

1. Name of Institution-
2. Year/Semester-
3. Branch-
4. No. of students-
5. Total time for lesson-
6. Name of Teacher—

B. Lesson Profile

1. Subject:
2. Topic:
3. Lesson Title:

C. Instructional Overview

1. Instructional Objectives-After attending the class the students will be able to-
   a)
   b)
2. List of Media/Teaching Aids:
   a)
   b)
3. List of Pre-requisite Knowledge:
   a)
   b)

D. Lesson stage

1. INTRODUCTION (Time Allotted- mins.)

TEACHING POINT	METHODS		STUDENT
	TEACHER ACTIVITIES	MEDIA/	ACTIVITIES TEACHING AIDS
Set Induction a) Checking previous Knowledge b) Drawing attention c) Lesson objectives d) Announcement of lesson title	Strategies and tactics to be adopted		

* Announcement of topic may be done at the beginning of introduction or after the set induction.

2. (a)PRESENTATION (Time Allotted- mins)

TEACHING POINT	METHODS		STUDENT ACTIVITIES TEACHING AIDS
	TEACHER ACTIVITIES	MEDIA/	
Statements of key points of information. Knowledge category.	Strategies and tactics to be adopted		

3.(a) CONSOLIDATION (Time Allotted- mins)

TEACHING POINT	METHODS		STUDENT ACTIVITIES TEACHING AIDS
	TEACHER ACTIVITIES	MEDIA/	
Reinforcement	Strategies and tactics to be adopted		

2.(b) PRESENTATION (Time Allotted- mins)

TEACHING POINT	METHODS		STUDENT ACTIVITIES TEACHING AIDS
	TEACHER ACTIVITIES	MEDIA/	
Statements of key points of information. Knowledge category.	Strategies and tactics to be adopted		

3. (b) CONSOLIDATION (Time Allotted- mins)

TEACHING POINT	METHODS		STUDENT ACTIVITIES TEACHING AIDS
	TEACHER ACTIVITIES	MEDIA/	
Reinforcement	Strategies and tactics to be adopted		

4. CONCLUSION (Time Allotted- mins)

TEACHING POINT	METHODS		STUDENT ACTIVITIES TEACHING AIDS
	TEACHER ACTIVITIES	MEDIA/	
List of Key Points. Questions related to formative evaluation. Linkage to next lesson	Strategies and tactics to be adopted		

5. EVALUATION (Time Allotted- mins)

Home Assignment problems/worksheets.

Conclusion

The principles of designing a classroom instructional plan (lesson-plan) on the basis of learning phases/instructional events have been discussed. The instructional strategies and tactics appropriate for different categories of information have also been suggested. It is reiterated that either the pattern developed or the labels used are not fixed and rigid, but are determined by the lesson objectives and the sequence of events leading to the achievement of the same. The later will be controlled by the particular phases of learning that the teacher wishes to use. The teacher him/herself is the best person to decide on the need for committing the plan on paper in written format. However, it is recommended that the teachers who have joined the profession recently should prepare written lesson plans before delivering the lesson in the class.

Mind it, You are the teacher of the students and not of the subject.

SECTION C

Learning Styles, Motivation and Communication

7
Learning Styles

In order to understand how our students learn, it is essential to be familiar with the several styles of learning. The students or learners have their own characteristic ways to receive and process information. Owing to their individual learning style, students focus on different types of information, tend to operate on perceived information in different ways, and achieve understanding at different rates. Teachers use a variety of teaching methods in their course delivery. In order to have an effective teaching-learning system, the *Learning Styles* of students need to be compatible with the teaching methodology of the teacher.

Need for Knowing the Learning Style of Students

Information about the learning style of students help the teachers in designing learning experiences that match the style of learning. Studies have shown that identifying a student's style and then providing instruction consistent with that style contribute to more effective learning. Even for counselling of of the students, this information may suggest appropriate counselling approaches for particular student. In orientation, it can help students understand their own preferences and strengths in learning and be a stimulus for developing new ways of learning.

A student's learning style may be defined in part by the following considerations:

- The type of information that the student preferentially perceives:
  Sensory—sights, sounds, etc.
  Intuitive—memories, ideas, insights, etc.
- The mode through which sensory information is most effectively perceived:
  Visual—diagrams, graphs, demonstrations, etc.
  Verbal—Sounds, written and spoken words and formulae.
- The type of organisation of information to which the student is most comfortable:
  Inductive—facts are given and underlying principles/laws/rules are inferred.

Deductive—Principles/laws are given and applications are deducted from them.

- The way in which the student prefers to process information:
  Actively—through engagement in physical activity or discussion.
  Reflectively—through introspection.
- The way in which the student progresses towards understanding:
  Sequentially—in a logical progression of small incremental steps.
  Globally—in large jumps, holistically.

These are some of the dimensions of learning style.

However, the pattern of learning, the references on a given scale may be strong, moderate or almost nonexistent. It may change with time, and may vary from one subject or learning environment to another.

Learning Style Models

Before we initiate exploration about the teaching strategy that suits all styles, let us look into some learning style models.

The Myres-Briggss Type Indicator (MBTI)

Students are classified into following four types according to MBTI:

(a) ***Extroverts*** (try things out, focus on the outer world of people) or introverts (think things through, focus on the inner world of ideas).

(b) ***Sensors*** (Practical, detail-oriented, focus on facts and procedures) or intuitions (imaginative, concept-oriented, focus on meanings and possibilities).

(c) ***Thinkers*** (skeptical, tend to make decisions based on logic and rules) or feelers (appreciative, tend to make decisions based on personal and humanistic considerations).

(d) ***Judgers*** (set and follow agendas, seek closure even with incomplete data) or perceivers (adapt to changing circumstances, resist closure to obtain more data).

The above mentioned preferences can be combined to form sixteen different learning style types.

Kolb's Learning Style Model

This model classifies the learners as having a preference for

(a) concrete experience or abstract conceptualisation (how they take information in), and

(b) active experimentation or reflective observation (how they internalise information). The learners can be classified into four types as tabulated below.

Types	*Characteristic question of the type*	*Characteristics of learners*	*Role of the teacher*
Type-1 Concrete, reflective	Why?	Respond well to explanations of how course material/content relates to their experience, interests and future careers.	Motivator
Type-2 Abstract, reflective	What?	Respond to information presented in an organised, logical fashion and benefit if they have time for reflection.	Expert
Type-3 Abstract, active	How?	Respond to having opportunities to work actively on well-defined tasks and to learn by trial-and-error in an environment that allows them to fail safely.	Coach
Type-4 Concrete, active	What if?	They like applying the content learnt in new situations to solve problems.	Has to provide more opportunities for the learners to discover things for themselves.

Felder-Silverman Learning Style Model

As per Felder-Silverman Learning Style Model, students are classified as described below:

(a) ***Sensing learners*** (concrete, practical, oriented toward facts and procedures) or intuitive learners (conceptual, innovative, oriented towards theories and meanings).

(b) ***Visual learners*** (prefer visual representations of presented material—pictures, diagrams, flow charts) or verbal learners (prefer written and spoken explanations).

(c) ***Inductive learners*** (prefer presentations that proceed from the specific to the general) or deductive learners (prefer presentations that go from the general to the specific).

(d) ***Active learners*** (learn by trying things out, working with others) or reflective learners (learn by thinking things through, working alone).

(e) ***Sequential learners*** (linear, orderly, learn in small incremental steps) or ***global learners*** (holistic, systems thinkers, learn in large leaps).

According to the classification given by *Alan Mumford* and *Peter Honey*, learners may be classified into four types as *active, reflectives, theorists* and *pragmatists.*

(a) ***Active***—They always have a keen to go and are open-minded and flexible.
(b) ***Reflective***—They are cautious, careful and methodical. Sometimes they bring judicious insights about the work they have been doing and criticise themselves constructively.
(c) ***Theorists***—They tend to be rational and logical. They take what they do, turn it into ideas, and work with these ideas in an abstract way.
(d) ***Pragmatists***—They are planners and practical. They enjoy trying things out and making them work. They seek early opportunities to experiment with applications.

Teaching Strategies Suiting the Learning Styles

It has been found that teachers usually present lectures rather than emphasising active class involvement and cooperative learning. This method may suit only a few learners. To reach all types of learners a teacher should firstly explain the relevance of each new topic, present the basic information and methods associated with the topic, provide opportunities for practices in the methods and encourage exploration of applications. Some suggestions for teachers in this regard those appeals to a range of ***Learning Styles*** are listed below:

(a) Teachers may establish curricular experiences that focus on helping students learn how to learn.
(b) Theoretical material may be taught by first presenting phenomena and problems that relate to the theory.
(c) Conceptual information may be balanced with concrete information, such as descriptions of physical phenomena, demonstrations etc.
(d) In addition to lectures and written explanations, teachers should make extensive use of sketches, plots, vector diagrams, computer graphics, physical demonstrations, etc.
(e) To illustrate an abstract concept or problem-solving algorithm, teachers should try to supplement that with a few numerical examples.
(f) To illustrate the magnitudes of calculated quantities, teachers can use physical analogies and demonstrations.
(g) To present a general principle, law etc. teachers may use inductive method.
(h) Sufficient time is to be provided to the learners to think about the material being presented and also for their active participation.
(i) Teachers can correlate subjects while teaching a particular topic and help students develop higher-level thinking ability. For example, while teaching a particular topic, they can point out connections between that and other relevant material in the same, in other topics in the same discipline or even in other disciplines as well as in everyday experiences.

In this way teachers can contribute effectively in improving teaching and learning practices in higher education.

In sum, while there are a variety of approaches of learning style, they typically share four core assumptions.

1. There are individual differences in learning.
2. An individual's style of learning is fairly stable across time.
3. An individual's style of learning is fairly stable across tasks/problems/ situations.
4. Learners have a dominant preference to learn in a certain way.

At school level, teachers should help the students in building their skill-sets in both their preferred and less preferred styles of learning so as to match the teaching strategies of most of the teachers. They should try to adjust well in all learning styles. Whether the teachers are designing a curriculum, preparing instructional material, promoting cooperative learning among students or helping them to develop interpersonal, leadership and communication skills, they should take care of the learning styles of the target group and try to cater to the needs of the majority of them.

8

Principles of Motivation and Motivating Students in Classroom

Motivation is the drive within individuals that leads them to action. Actually it is a goal-directed behaviour. It energises, directs and sustains a particular behaviour or performance.

Motivating students is a concern for all teachers as it is a prerequisite for learning and one of the important factors affecting performance of the learners. In planning an instruction it is important to think of the factors that will energise the students and arouse the class. These are the motivational factors. Motivation is important for any sort of activity. As such it makes the learners interested in what the teacher wants them to learn. It is rightly referred to as an energy change in an individual associated with behaviour directed towards the attainment of a goal. Motivation is an essential component of a classroom atmosphere which maximizes personal and social development.

The Process of Motivation

Motivation is the driving force within individuals, which impels them for action. Unfulfilled needs, wants and desires lead to tension. The individual must reduce this tension by engaging in an appropriate behaviour which can provide the desired goal. It should be noted that tension provides the necessary driving force and the appropriateness of behaviour is determined by learning and cognitive processes of the individual. Goal or need fulfillment finally leads to tension reduction.

Ability includes skills, knowledge and judgment to perform a task. It is a vital performance factor but only an enabling capacity. Teachers have to create a learning environment for the learners so that there is active involvement of one and all in the learning process. It has been found that degree of involvement varies from one learner to the other. This is because of difference among them in their desire to learn. To create and sustain this desire, motivation of learners has to be ensured.

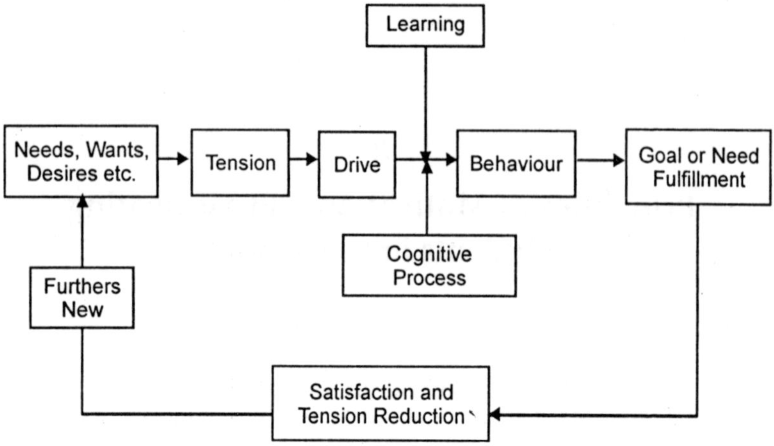

Fig. 8.1: A simple flowchart relating Motivation and other factors to performance as stated by *Cummings* and *Schwab* (1973) is given as follows:
Performance = f (Motivation + ability + environment)

Need for Classroom Motivation

During classroom instruction, students are expected to perform a set of activities to show the desired terminal behaviour (performance). In order to prepare the students for such activities motivation takes the lead role for several reasons as given below:

- ***Arousal function***: An aroused learner is active and will exhibit dynamism in his/her learning activity.
- ***Expectancy function***: In the process of learning, learners have to work towards achieving a goal and the expectancy of this achievement. The goals may be immediate or long-term goals.
- ***Incentive function***: Learning is affected by the incentives provided to the learners in the form of teachers' praise, encouragement, rewards, certificates, grades, recognition or the like by peer group.
- ***Disciplinary function***: The disciplinary function of motivation requires the teacher to control deviant behaviour using positive (rewards) and negative reinforcement.

A teacher has to integrate the four motivational functions in order to initiate, sustain and continue the learning behaviour of students.

Motivational factors initiate and direct behaviour. The intensity and persistence of behaviour is also often determined by motivation. However, it varies in nature and intensity from person to person depending on the particular mixture of influences at any given moment.

Motivation has the lead role in the social development and personality development of a learner. It is like fire -unless one keeps adding fuel to it, it dies; but if the source of motivation is belief in inner values, it becomes long-lasting. Motivation is very powerful as it can persuade, convince and propel an individual to action. It is the motive for action. This can be better viewed in following figure.

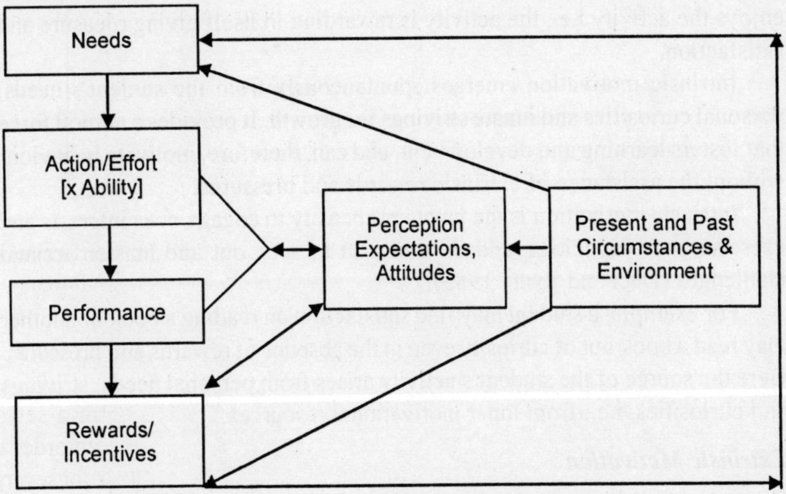

Fig. 8.2: adopted from *Roger Buckley* and *Jim Caple*, 1995

Types of Motivation

The two broad categories of motivation are **intrinsic** and **extrinsic** motivation. *Morgan* and *Taylor* (1984) classified motivation 'into two sub-types according to whether the students were directly interested in the content of the course or whether they were studying the course merely as a means to an end. These sub-types were labeled intrinsic and extrinsic respectively'.

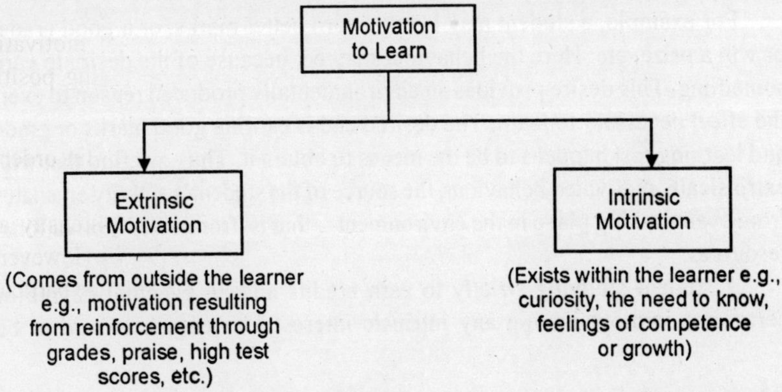

Intrinsic and Extrinsic motivation produce significant differences in students' classroom experiences and in the qualities of their academic work.

Intrinsic Motivation

When an individual finds an activity as self-rewarding, the motive arises from within the person. It is referred to as intrinsic motivation. Here, the person enjoys the activity i.e., the activity is rewarding in itself giving pleasure and satisfaction.

Intrinsic motivation emerges spontaneously from the student's needs, personal curiosities and innate strivings for growth. It provides a natural force that fosters learning and development, and can, therefore, motivate behaviour without the assistance of extrinsic rewards and pressures.

Intrinsic motivation is the innate propensity to engage ones interests and exercise ones capacities, and, in doing so to seek out and master optimal challenges (Deci and Ryan, 1985).

For example, a student may find satisfaction on reading a book or another may read a book out of curiosity even in the absence of rewards and pressures. Here the source of the student's activity arises from personal needs, strivings and curiosities, i.e., from inner motivational resources.

Extrinsic Motivation

Contrary to intrinsic motivation, if the individual takes up an activity to get an external reward, like teacher's praise, a better grades, good marks, scholarship etc. (motive is external), then the type of motivation is extrinsic motivation.

Extrinsic motivation arises from external contingencies. It is an environmentally created reason to carry out an action. Extrinsic motivation is a ***means-to-an-end*** type of motivation in which the means is the behaviour and the end is some attractive consequence (or the prevention of an unattractive consequence).

For example, a student may learn to earn better marks, or a good grade, or win a prize, etc. Here the behaviour may be, because of the desire to earn something. This desire provides an environmentally produced reason to exert the effort necessary to learn. The desired end is earning good marks or grade and learning just happens to be the means to obtain it. Thus, we find that with extrinsically motivated behaviour, the source of the student's activity emanates from events taking place in the environment—that is, from outer motivational resources.

A student studying strictly to earn credits and an eventual degree or certificate without having any intrinsic interest in a course is said to be extrinsically motivated. If one enjoys learning and also looks forward to a good grade, degree, a well-paid job, s/he has both intrinsic and extrinsic motivation.

Implications for Teachers for Motivating Students

Studies have shown that when extrinsic motivation is introduced, intrinsic motivation tends to decrease. Therefore, a teacher must always try to emphasise on intrinsic motivation. The ultimate goal of the teacher should be to inculcate within the students intrinsic motivation towards learning by gradually withdrawing all external motives. Verbal praise is quite effective in enhancing intrinsic motivation. Praise and social approval also intensify intrinsic motivation.

However, some individuals can continue with the task at hand without the help of any extrinsic reward as they enjoy doing the task and feel satisfied working on it. There may be still others who enjoy the task momentarily and therefore, require some extrinsic reward (motivator) to keep it up.

While using extrinsic motivators, teachers have to be very careful and can always bear the following three principles in mind:

- Positive attitude towards learners' response(s)
- Novelty in introducing and even during presenting the content
- Minimising failure in the class.

Motivational Techniques in Classroom

Motivation of students is crucial to their learning as learning inevitably starts with motivation. Students will easily learn, what they want to learn and will have great difficulty in learning material that does not interest them. Again some students seem enthusiastic about learning but many may need or expect their teacher to inspire and stimulate them. *Motivation is a necessary but not sufficient condition for learning.*

A student will feel motivated to learn when s/he feels that his/her needs will be satisfied through learning and thus will take interest towards learning. A teacher, in a classroom, has to create sufficient interest among the students to learn and also has to sustain the interest during the class. Effective learning by students in the classroom depends on the ability of the teacher to maintain the interest that brought the students to attend the class. The level of motivation, with which a student enters the class, will be transformed, for better or worse, by what happens in the classroom.

A teacher, thus, has to adopt different techniques for motivating the students to achieve an effective classroom instruction. Unfortunately, there is no single magical formula for motivating the students. The motivation of students to learn is dependent on different factors, some of which may be beyond the control of the teacher. Further, these factors also vary from student to student. However a conscious and planned effort by a teacher to motivate the students in the classroom helps students in achieving their learning goals.

Some general principles of motivation, strategies and some commonly applicable motivational techniques are presented below. It is expected that these will help the teachers to develop motivational techniques for application in their own classroom environment.

Principles

Some basic principles of motivation that are applicable to learning in any situation are:

(a) *The environment can be used to focus the attention of students on what are needed to be learned*: A warm and accepting yet business-like classroom atmosphere promotes persistent effort and favourable attitude towards learning. Interesting visual aids such as booklets, posters or practice equipment motivate learners by capturing their curiosity and attention across the level of study.

(b) *Incentives Motivate Learning:* Incentives include rewards, or praise from the teacher. Nature of incentive and its timing appropriate to the learner is to be determined by the teacher. Students must find satisfaction in learning based on the understanding that the goals are useful to them.

(c) *Internal (intrinsic) motivation is long lasting than external (extrinsic) motivation*: The internal motivation is more self-directive than external motivation and later has to be repeatedly reinforced by praise or concrete rewards. However, some individuals have less capacity for internal motivation and must be guided and reinforced constantly. Caution should be exercised in using external rewards only when they are absolutely necessary.

(d) *Learning is most effective when an individual is ready to learn*: An individual is ready to learn when one wants to know something. Teacher's role is to develop this readiness among the students and ensure that the desired behaviour occurs. If a student is not ready to learn, s/he may not be relied to follow instructions.

(e) *Motivation is enhanced by the manner of organisation of the instructional material*: The properly organised instructional material conveys the information as meaningful to the individual and thus enhances motivation. One method of organisation is to relate new tasks to those already known. Other ways to relay meaning are to determine whether the persons being taught understand the desired final outcome.

General Strategies for Motivating Students

(i) *Focus on the Students' Existing Needs*: Students learn best in a classroom when their need for enrolling in the course is satisfied. The needs brought by the students in the classroom will vary from person to person, such as, need to learn something in order to complete a task; need to seek new experiences; need to perfect skills; need to become competent; need to feel involved. Satisfaction of such needs is rewarding in itself and such rewards sustain learning more effectively. Assignment questions, in-class activities and discussion questions should be designed by the teacher to address these kinds of needs.

(ii) *Active Participation of Students in Learning*: Students learn better by doing, making, writing, designing, creating, solving etc. Passivity dampens motivation and curiosity of students. Involving students in discussion through posing questions or encouraging them to suggest approaches to a problem can lead students to actively participate in learning.

(iii) *Analysis by Students about Causes of 'Motivating' Classes*: A recent research study carried out by the author among a sizable group of students across India in specific gamut of education, in which students were asked to list the various aspects of, one highly motivating and one substantially low-motivating class, recently attended by them. The following characteristics were found to be common in all 20 studies made:

1. Teacher's enthusiasm
2. Relevance of the material
3. Organisation of the course
4. Appropriate difficulty level of the material
5. Active involvement of students
6. Variety
7. Rapport between teachers and students
8. Use of appropriate, concrete and understandable examples.

Motivational Techniques

Motivating Instructional Behaviours: Holding high but realistic expectations from students—The teachers' expectations have a powerful effect on the performance of students. If the teacher acts as though s/he expects the students to be motivated, hardworking and interested in the course, they are more likely to be so. Realistic expectations should be set for students when making assignments, conducting discussions, give presentations etc. 'Realistic' means that standards are high enough to motivate the students to do their best work but not so high that they are not achievable by students. To develop the drive to achieve, students need to believe that achievement is possible.

***Helping students set achievable goals for themselves*:** Students feel disappointed and frustrated when they fail to attain 'unrealistic' goals. Students should be encouraged to focus on their continuous improvement and not on the marks or grade in any one test or assignment. Students may be encouraged to criticise their own work, analyse their own strength and work on their weaknesses and thus help them to evaluate their progress.

***Telling students what they need to do to succeed in the course*:** Students ought not to struggle to figure out what is expected of them. Students may be reassured that they can do well in their course, and be told exactly what they must do to succeed.

Strengthening students' self-Motivation: Messages reinforcing the power as a teacher or that emphasising extrinsic rewards be avoided. Instead of saying, 'I require', 'you must', or 'you should, stress 'I think you will find.' or 'I will be interested in your reaction'.

Avoiding creating intense competition among students: Competition produces anxiety, which can interfere with learning. Students' tendencies to compare themselves to one another be reduced. It has been found that students are more attentive, display better comprehension, produce more work, and are more favourable to the teaching methodology when they work cooperatively in groups rather than compete as individuals. Criticisms of students' performance in public and comments or activities that pit students against each other must be avoided by the teachers.

Be enthusiastic about your subject: A teacher's enthusiasm is a crucial factor in student motivation. If you become bored or apathetic, students will too. Typically, a teacher's enthusiasm comes from confidence, excitement about the content and genuine pleasure in teaching. If you find yourself uninterested in the material, think back to what attracted you to the field and bring those aspects of the subject matter to life for your students. Or challenge yourself to devise the most exciting way to present the material, however dull the material itself may seem to you.

Structuring the Course to Motivate Students

Work from students' strengths and interests: Find out why students are enrolled in your course, how they feel about the subject matter, and what their expectations are. Then try to devise examples, case studies, or assignments that relate the course-content to students' interests and experiences. For instance, a Physics professor might devote some lecture time to examining the contributions of chemistry to resolving environmental problems. Explain how the content and objectives of your course will help students achieve their educational, professional, or personal goals.

When possible, let students have some say in choosing what will be studied: Give students options on term papers or other assignments (but not on tests). Let students decide between two locations for the field trip, or have them select which topics to explore in greater depth. If possible, include optional or alternative units in the course.

Increase the difficulty of the material as the semester progresses: Give students opportunities to succeed at the beginning of the semester. Once students feel they can succeed, you can gradually increase the difficulty level. If assignments and examinations include easier and harder questions, every student will have a chance to experience success as well as challenges.

Vary your teaching methods: Variety reawakens students' involvement in the course and their motivation. Break the routine by incorporating a variety of teaching activities and methods in your course such as: *role playing, debates, brainstorming, discussion, demonstrations, case studies, audiovisual presentations, guest speakers,* or *small group work.* These will enhance the level of motivation among students.

De-emphasising Grades/Marks: Emphasise on mastery and learning rather than grades. Researchers recommend de-emphasising grading by eliminating complex systems of credit points; they also advise against trying to use grades to control nonacademic behaviour (for example, lowering grades for missed classes) Instead, assign un-graded written work, stress the personal satisfaction of doing assignments, and help students measure their progress.

Design tests that encourage the kind of learning you want students to achieve: Many students will learn whatever is necessary to get the grades they desire. If you base your tests on memorising details, students will focus on memorising facts. If your tests stress over on the synthesis and evaluation of information, students will be motivated to practice those skill-sets when they study.

Avoid using grades as threats: The threat of low grades may prompt some students to work hard, but other students may resort to academic dishonesty, excuses for late work, and other counterproductive behaviour.

Motivating Students by Responding to Their Work: Give students feedback as quickly as possible. Return tests and papers promptly, and reward success publicly and immediately. Give students some indication of how well they have done and how to improve. Rewards can be as simple as saying a student's response was good, with an indication of why it was good, or mentioning the names of contributors.

Reward Success: Both positive and negative comments influence motivation, but research consistently indicates that students are more affected by positive feedback and success. Praise builds students' self-confidence, competence, and self-esteem. Recognise sincere efforts even if the product is less than stellar. If a student's performance is weak, let the student know that you believe s/he can improve and succeed over time.

Introduce Students to the Good Work Done by their Peers: Share the ideas, knowledge, and accomplishments of individual students with the class as a whole:

- Pass out a list of research topics chosen by students so they will know whether others are writing papers of interest to them.
- Make available copies of the best papers and essay examinations.
- Provide class time for students to read papers or assignments submitted by classmates.
- Have students write a brief critique of a classmate's paper.
- Schedule a brief talk by a student who has experience or who is doing a research paper on a topic relevant to your lecture.

Be Specific when Giving Negative Feedback: Negative feedback is very powerful and can lead to a negative class atmosphere. Whenever you identify a student's weakness, make it clear that your comments relate to a particular task or performance, not to the student as a person. Try to cushion negative comments with a compliment about aspects of the task in which the student succeeded.

(a) Avoid Demeaning Comments: Many students in your class may be anxious about their performance and abilities. Be sensitive to how you phrase your comments and avoid offhand remarks that might prick their feelings of inadequacy.

(b) Avoid Giving 'The Answer" to Homework Problems: When you simply give struggling students the solution, you rob them of the chance to think for them. Use a more productive approach:

- Ask the students for one possible approach to the problem.
- Gently brush aside students' anxiety about not getting the answer by refocusing their attention on the problem at hand.
- Ask the students to build on what they do know about the problem.
- Resist answering the question "is this right?" Suggest to the students a way to check the answer for themselves.
- Praise the students for small, independent steps.

If you follow these steps, your students will learn that it is all right not to have an instant answer. They will also learn to develop greater patience and to work at their own pace. And by working through the problem, students will experience a sense of achievement and confidence that will increase their motivation to learn.

Motivating Students to Read

(a) Assign the Reading at least Two Sessions Before it will be Discussed: Give students ample time to prepare and try to enhance their curiosity about the reading: 'This article is one of my favourites, and I'll be interested to see what you think about it'.

(b) Assign Study Questions: Handout study questions that alert students to the key points of the reading assignment. To provide extra incentive for students, tell them you will base examination questions on the study questions.

(c) Ask Non-threatening Questions about the Reading: Initially pose general questions that do not create tension or feelings of resistance within students. Such as:

'Can you give me one or two items from the chapter that seems important?'
'What section of the reading do you think we should review?'
'What item in the reading surprised you?'
'What topics in the chapter can you apply to your own experience?'

Use Class-time as a Reading Period: If you are trying to lead a discussion and find that few students have completed the reading assignment, consider asking students to read the material for the remainder of class time. Have them read silently or call on students to read aloud and discuss the key points. Make it clear to students that you are reluctantly taking this unusual step because they have not completed the assignment.

Prepare an Examination Question on Un-discussed Readings: One faculty member asks her class whether they have done the reading. If the answer is no, she says, 'You'll have to read the material on your own. Expect a question on the next examination covering the reading'. The next time she assigns reading, she reminds the class of what happened the last time, and the students come to class prepared.

Give a Written Assignment to those Students who have not done the Reading: Some faculty-member asks at the beginning of the class who has completed the reading. Students who have not read the material are given a written assignment and dismissed. Those who have read the material stay and participate in class discussion. The written assignment is not graded but merely acknowledged. This technique should not be used more than once a term.

In sum, researchers have begun to identify those aspects of the teaching situation that enhance students' self-motivation. To encourage students to become self-motivated independent learners, teachers can do the following:

- Give frequent, early, positive feedback that supports students' beliefs that they can do well.

- Ensure opportunities for students' success by assigning tasks that are neither too easy nor too difficult.
- Help students find personal meaning and value in the material.
- Create an atmosphere that is open and positive.
- Help students feel that they are valued members of a learning community.

Research has also shown that good everyday teaching practices can do more to counter student apathy than special efforts to attack motivation directly. Most students respond positively to a well-organised course taught by an enthusiastic teacher who has a genuine interest in students and what they learn. Thus activities undertaken by a teacher to promote learning will also enhance students' motivation.

9

Principles of Communication and its' Application in Classroom

A professional teacher influences his students' behaviours by using three basic competencies, which are listed as follow:

(a) ***Diagnosing:*** being able to understand the situation the teacher is attempting to influence,

(b) ***Adapting:*** being able to adapt his own behaviour and the other things that the teacher has control over to the contingencies of the situation, and

(c) ***Communicating:*** being able to put the message in a way that the students can easily understand and accept.

Communication is usually taken to mean the transfer of information and understanding from one person to another. It is the transfer of meaning or information between the sender and the receiver.

When communicating with other people, the message or information passes through perceptual 'filters' of both the sender and the receiver. And because of these filters, there is the potential for a communication breakdown at any point in the communication process. Information is meaningfully understood depending on the nature of perception of the information. Perception is a process through which we organise and interpret information brought to us by our senses. Attention is a process of perceptual grouping or structuring.

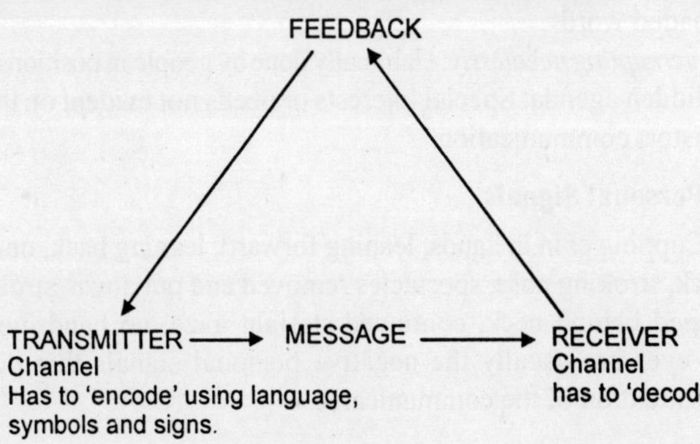

The transmitter in the communication process transmits the message. The teacher has to express it in such a way that it is easily understood (i.e., in the right language the right level of knowledge, the right approach and attitude and so on).

The receiver gets the message. The student must de-code this in the way intended by the transmitter, the teacher.

It is the feedback which tells the transmitter whether the decoding is correct, or not.

There is always some loss of information or message depending on the nature of the channel. The channel (usually a media-mix) must be properly chosen to minimise channel-loss.

Five Types of Communication

1. Cognitive communication to transmit content or information.
2. Expressive communication to express our attitude and feeling.
3. Persuasive communication attempting to influence others.
4. Social communication getting to know people or acknowledging their presence (maintenance of human relations).
5. Non-verbal communication-communication through facial features, eyes and mouths and also through postures and gestures (body languages).

Communication Barriers to Effective Communication

Following are the barriers in the process of communication which often hinder the process:

1. *Passing judgment*: Judgmental responses like ordering, warning, advising, moralising etc.
2. *Stereotypes*: Wide spread generalisations that have little or no basis in fact e.g., physically attractive and well groomed people are likely to be accepted.
3. *Anxiety and self-centeredness*: When we are anxious, aroused or wrapped up in ourselves, we do not communicate well.
4. *Over reacting to emotional words*: Emotionally aroused and prejudiced people often distort communication by using emotionally loaded words.
5. *Interrupting needlessly*: Habitually done by people in positions of power.
6. Hidden agenda: Special interests or needs not evident on the surface distort communication.

Negative Personal Signals

Yawning, Cupping chin in hands, leaning forward, leaning back, one hand on back of neck, stroking nose, spectacles removed and put down, stroking chin, hands clasped behind neck, continued straight gaze, no hand movements, narrowing eyes are usually the negative personal signals that denotes or diminishes attention of the communicatee.

Positive Personal Signals

Smiling, asking open questions, introducing and summarising, the seating, avoiding interruptions, asking for opinions, expansion of ideas, nodding, not being judgmental, showing you are concentrating, highlighting the positive, leaning forward are the expression of positive personal symptoms of enhanced level of communication.

Communication Grid

In business, general communication must move to specifics and opinions must be supported by facts if understanding is to become action. However, opinions and judgments must also be brought to bear. The same is a fact in academia too.

In communication, people generally exhibit broadening and specifics tendencies. The concepts of the two are as follows:

To broaden: use open questions, ask for other ideas or options, restate, give cues to explore issues and encourage participation and contributions before coming to conclusions.

To focus on specifics: Remind yourself and others of the purpose of the discussion and control the time spent on general discussions. Ask specific questions and get to the point more quickly, identifying a clear line of action and responsibilities.

Communication Skills

Communication skills can be divided into several groups, the important ones are—

- Expressive,
- Receptive,
- Non-expressive,
- Social,
- Influencing,
- Presentations,
- Giving feedback,
- Meetings and
- Interviews.

Transactional Analysis (TA)

Transactional Analysis (TA) is a means of diagnosing interpersonal communication problems. TA is based on the concept of Ego-States of an individuals. There are three ego-states of an individual. The three ego-states are *Parent (P), Adult (A)* and *Child (C)* ego-states.

When we communicate we use our ego-states and try to hook the ego-states of other individual. Parallel transactions help the process of communication while crossed transactions may pose serious communication problems. The important functions of the three ego-states can be utilised in controlling and improving our communications in the classroom.

Parent: Sets limit, gives advice, disciplines, guides, protects, makes rules, teaches, nurtures, judges and criticises.

Adult: Senses problems. Gathers information, diagnoses situations. Generates alternatives, evaluates alternatives' and makes choices.

Child: Belongs capacities for being natural, loving, spontaneous, creative, carefree, fun-loving, exciting, adventurous, curious, trusting or joyful.

Rules for Communication

Following are the basic rules of communications:

1. Fitness for purposes: will it achieve its objectives; what, why, when, where, how select the most effective way of achieving the objective.
2. ABC: Accuracy, Brevity, Clarity.
3. K I S S - Keep It Short and Simple.
4. The Three Stages —
   i) Tell them what you are going to tell them.
   ii) Tell them.
   iii) Tell them what you have told them.

Improving Your Communication

A. Communicator

1. Adopt an accepting attitude (trust and positive regard towards others)
2. Be physically attentive (appropriate eye-contact, certain postures and gestures)
3. Listen for the total meaning (not only just factual information and feelings)
4. Share responsibility for the communication (Be an active participant)
5. Observe non-verbal communication (Body language)
6. Express yourself clearly and effectively (choose words carefully and speak in a way that makes people want to listen to you).
7. Be assertive
8. Use 'I' messages
   Four components
   i) An objective, non-judgmental description
   ii) The concrete effects on me
   iii) How I feel about this, and
   iv) What I would prefer the person do instead
9. Be a good listener

10. Appear well prepared and confident
11. Use the three–stage approach i.e.;
    - tell them what you are going to tell;
    - tell them and
    - tell them, what you have told them.
12. Include visuals.

B. Receiver

When you are a receiver,

1. Listen actively
2. Ask questions
3. If confused, say so
4. Request more information
5. Give non–verbal signals
6. Restate complex parts.

COMMUNICATION IN CLASSROOM

Human beings cannot do without communication as all human activity is based on communication. It is one of the basic activities of the human race and a skill through which human make magnificent successes and startling failures. Our ability to communicate on a higher level separates us—the human beings from other animals. Communication is an essential function of civilisation. Teaching is only one of the many occupations that depend upon it and depend upon it absolutely. A teacher influences the students in the most serious ways by his or her communication. A teacher who is a mediocre scholar can be an excellent teacher if s/he is good in communication. A teacher can create a climate of learning through his/her manner of communication with the students.

Meaning

The term '*communication*' has been derived from the Latin '*communicare*' meaning to share and from the French '*communis*', meaning common. Communication can be defined as a process in which commonness is established between the persons communicating, firstly the sender of the message and secondly the receiver of the message. When persons communicate, they try to establish a certain degree of commonness with the communicator by sharing some information, an idea or an attitude.

Communication refers to the act of communing, transmitting, imparting and exchanging thoughts, ideas, opinions, sentiments and information. In the words of Martin P. Anderson (1959), '*Communication is the process by which we understand others and in turn Endeavour to be understood by them'*. Professor S. S. Stevens (1950) defines communication as *'the discriminatory response of an organism to a stimulus'*.

Communication Process

While talking of communication, we talk of the transmission of information in its broadest sense. Information and communication are two interlinked terms for communication since it is impossible without information and vice versa.

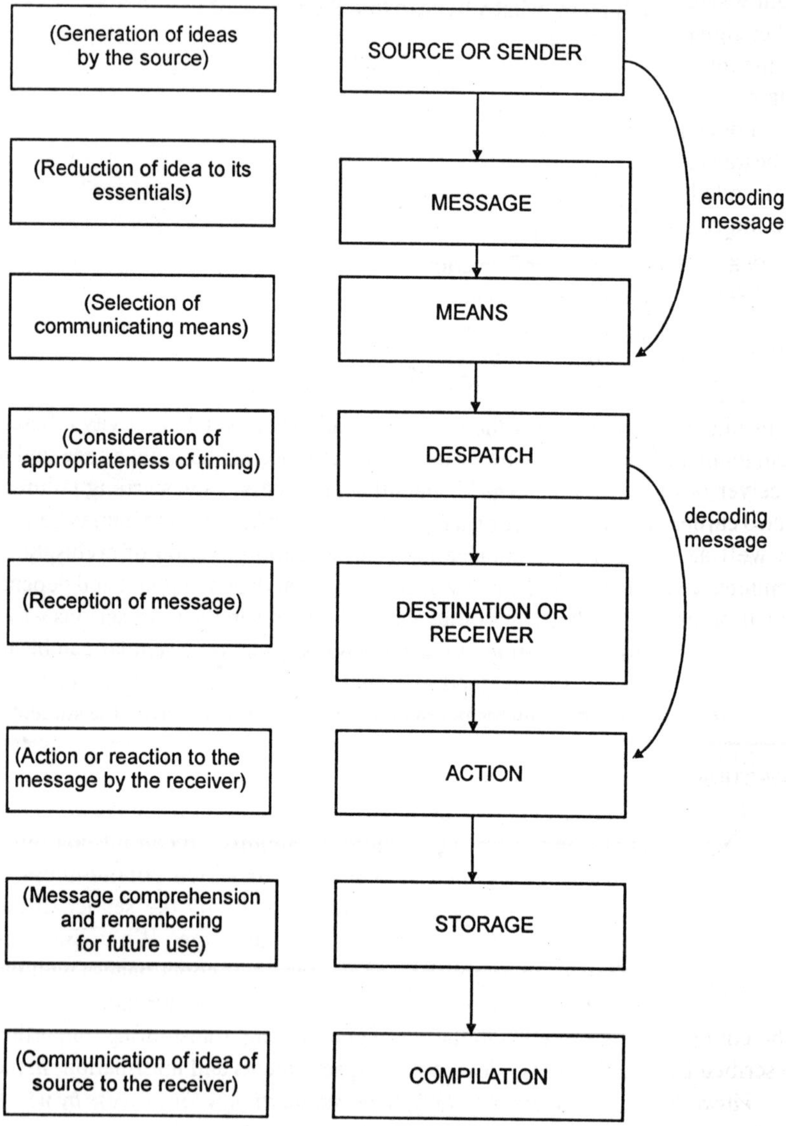

Fig. 9.1: The Communication Process

Communication is a continuous process and requires at least three basic elements—the source, the message, and the destination. Source, also referred to as sender or initiator of information, is the point at which the messages originate. Message may be in the form of written or printed text, sound or light waves in the air, impulses in the electric current, or in the form of any other signal which is capable of being interpreted meaningfully. Destination or the intended target of the message is the final level in the communication chain.

For communication process to take place, the source encodes the message to be transmitted into a form suitable for transmission. This transmitted message is decoded by the receiver or destination end. Thus encoding and decoding are the two steps in the communication process. It may be assured that the message once received has been considered and understood, this is too vital for a classroom situation.

Communication Cycle

The communication process depicts a linear model in which the source transmits the message and the destination receives it. In actual practice, the communication process does not end up with the receiving of message by the receiver or destination. In fact, communication is a continuous process, as stated earlier, in which each individual or institution functions as the transmitter as well as the receiver of messages. In this way we can describe the communication process to be working in a cycle in which each individual functions as the encoder, interpreter and the decoder of information.

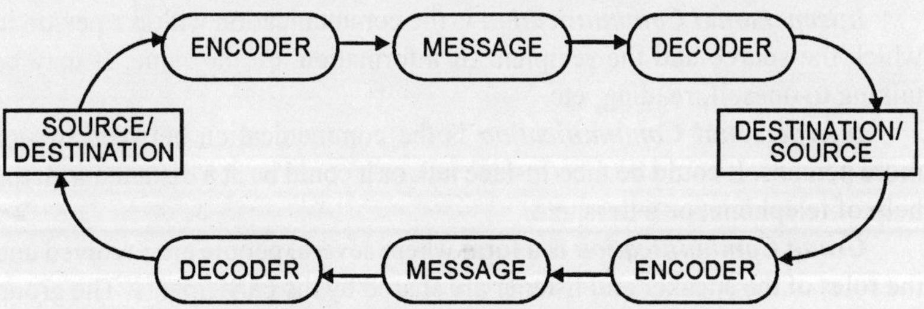

Fig. 9.2: The Communication Cycle

Types of Communication

The communication systems may be categorised into various categories as described below.

Vocal Communication refers to any form of communication that uses the human vocal chords. It can range from shouting to spoken languages.

Non-Vocal Communication refers to the use of signs, signals and symbols, gestures etc., in the communication process.

Verbal Communication refers to the use of words. The era of verbal communication began with the development of language.

Non-Verbal Communication includes actions such as gestures, vocalisations, facial expressions, tone of voice, touch, etc. Non-verbal communication is usually used to communicate feelings, likings and preferences.

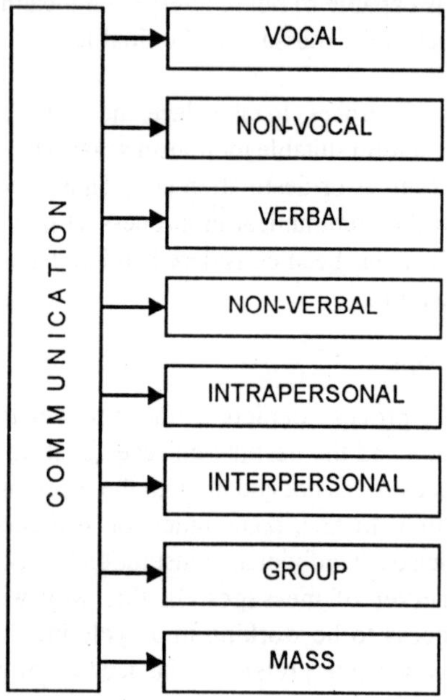

Intrapersonal Communication is the communication within a person in which the source and the recipient of information are the same. It may be talking to oneself, reading, etc.

Interpersonal Communication is the communication between two or more persons. It could be face-to-face talk or it could be at a distance with the help of telephone, or letters, etc.

Group Communication is a form where several people are involved and the roles of the speaker and listener are shared by the participants. The group may be small consisting of two or more persons, usually not more than 25, or a large group where there is communication by one or several persons to an audience of 25 or more persons.

Mass Communication also referred to as public communication, is the communication from one person or a group of persons to large audience via some special media.

Whereas interpersonal communication is one-to-one exchange, mass communication is one to many exchanges in which a few sources transmit to a vast number of destinations.

Communication in the Classroom

Once the teacher has planned the instruction, s/he has to communicate the knowledge (according conceptual, factual or both) of it to the learners. A teacher has to be a good listener too.

For an effective communication in a classroom, message delivered by the teacher must lead to a true learning, i.e., the learner should be able to use that information appropriately in subsequent occasions. Teaching as an art of communication should succeed in making a permanent and meaningful addition to the student's own communication skills. Classroom communication requires inter-communication between students and teachers, mutual sharing of experiences and a continuous feedback process.

In a classroom situation, we may have different patterns of communication. The two common patterns are depicted in following figures:

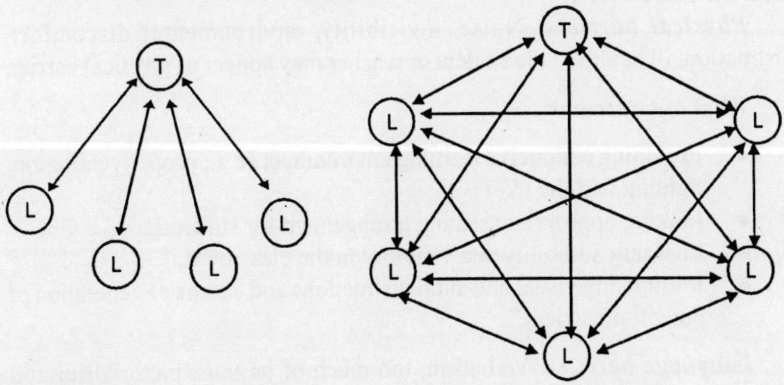

(i) (ii)

T – Teacher
L - Learner

(i) Teacher—Controlled Pedagogic Model

(ii) Group—Controlled Andragogic Model

Fig. 9.3: Communication Patterns

Situation (i) depicts a limited pattern of communication as compared to situation (ii).

In the former case, the pattern involves a succession of transfers of information between the teacher and the individual learners.

Situation (ii) refers to a multi-way communication pattern in which the learners can interact freely among themselves. In fact, in such a learning environment the teacher only acts as a facilitator once the communication has been set-off in the right direction. In order to create a suitable environment for effective communication, a teacher may take care of some considerations, a few of which are listed below:

- Psychological state of the learners
- Social Environment
- Linguistic competence of the learners.
- Academic maturity level of the learner.

Barriers to Communication

Any difficulty—Physiological, Sociological or Psychological or maturity relate, caused to effective communication as a barrier. For an effective communication, clarity, loudness and pace of delivery are important. Factors like simplicity, clarity and intelligibility of the message affect its reception and understanding. A message which is too slow or too loud, too simple or too complex may be regarded as a noise or barrier to communication. Some of the commonly observed barriers and suggestible methods of overcoming them are listed below:

Physical barriers: Noise, invisibility, environmental discomfort, distraction, ill health of the student or teacher may appear as physical barrier.

Ways to Overcome

- Providing conducive learning environment (e.g., proper ventilation, lighting and the like)
- Making appropriate seating arrangement for students.
- Ensuring audibility and visibility in the classroom.
- Minimising visual and aural distractions and causes of generation of potential barriers.

Language barriers: Verbalism, too much of jargons, pictorialism, too much.

Ways to Overcome

- using clear and simple language
- employing appropriate methods of communication
- explaining and using graphic symbols
- preparing necessary handouts
- using audio-visual aids effectively
- taking continuous feedback.

Psychological Barriers

Inattention, lack of interest and motivation, prejudice, anxiety, unfulfilled curiosity, on part of students may appear as psychological barriers.

Ways to Overcome

- Motivating the learner

- Showing sympathy and extending support services
- Providing required assistance
- Satisfying curiosity in real time.

Background Barriers

Previous learning, cultural disparities, and the like.

Ways to Overcome

- Getting knowledge of the learner's background.
- Employing different strategies and tactics.

Role of a Teacher

The different principles and theories of learning are useful for successful communication in the teaching-learning process. Thus a teacher needs to be well acquainted with all such aspects. Good teaching demands something more from the communication process. It needs interaction in the classroom or inter-communication between the teacher and the learners. With the help of suitable audio-visual aids, a teacher can provide the learners with real-life experience bringing the outside world with the learning environment.

A teacher should be well versed with the different aids and be able to apply them judiciously. S/he should try to bridge the communication gap in the classroom as the students come with different socio-cultural, linguistic and economic background from various environments. The teacher must motivate the students and facilitate multi-directional communication in the classroom.

A teacher can take the help of educational technology to break through the communication barriers in the classroom. Since classroom communication depends on the external and internal conditions of the learner, a teacher must select the external conditions wisely and utilise the internal conditions properly for effective communication.

In sum, Classroom communication involves more than the unilateral presentation of information by the teacher in the form of mere lecturing, or dictating class-notes or reading out the texts or yellow notes. The communication should be kept wide open and made lively by free interaction of the teacher and the learners. Teachers should try to make their communication interesting and meaningful by the adequate and justified utilisation of modern methods and media.

SECTION D

Skill-sets for Teaching and Instructional Media

10

Overview of Instructional Media

Media are the carriers of messages from some transmitting source (which may be a human being or an inanimate object) to the receivers of the message (the learners). These carriers of information provide stimuli to the learners which interact with the learner through his/her senses. The learner may use any of his/her senses to receive the information.

Quite often, messages are received by a combination of senses in order to render the desired communication complete. Media facilitate learning because learning cannot occur unless there is some event or fact or symbol or the form of stimulation. Learning starts with stimulation. Stimuli vary in both quantity and quality. The sequential relation between stimuli and learning is shown in figure below.

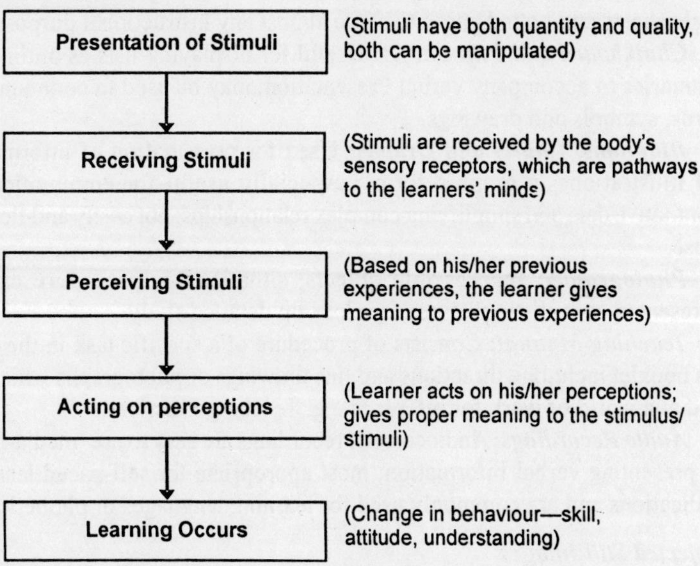

Classification of Media

Real Things

***Guest Speakers*:** Qualified and experienced guest speakers can motivate as well as inform a group of learners. The guest speakers may be from academic institutions with high academic or research experiences and activities. As they have vast experience they can describe the content or information to the learner, which may enlighten them. The experienced experts are generally invited in the institutions to describe different aspects as practiced in field. The managers from corporate houses are also invited for the same purpose. These resource persons may deliver their lectures vocally or they may use different teaching media for better communication or better understanding.

***Objects and Devices*:** Seeing and manipulating real things in actions are directly beneficial for learning.

***Models and Mock-ups*:** Tangible simulations can substitute for real items which are too big or too complex to be made available in the classrooms or learning laboratory. Models are frequently smaller than the original as essential elements can be omitted. Mock-ups are often larger and simplified. Each permits learning of operation through careful study of its functional methods.

Non-projected (Two-dimensional) Materials

***Printed Handouts*:** Most common resources for use by learners; includes single sheets and bound pages to serve almost any instructional purpose.

***Chalkboard and Flip Charts*:** Useful for displaying lists as outlines or summaries to accompany verbal Presentation; may be used to communicate words, symbols and drawings.

***Diagrams, Charts and Graphs*:** Used for presentation of information and illustrations in graphic forms; especially useful for communicating quantitative data and simplifying complex relationships; not costly and flexible to use.

***Photographs*:** Inaccessible objects, situations or procedure can be represented as realistic pictures for close-up detailed study.

***Teaching Manual*:** Consists of procedure of a specific task in the form of a booklet including directions and line drawings or photographs which are used at a world of work for reference e.g. Teaching Practices.

***Audio Recordings*:** Audiocassette recordings are easy to use 'media-form' for presenting verbal Information; most appropriate for self-paced learning applications and are commonly used for learning languages or phonetics.

Projected Still Images

***Slides*:** There are colourful realistic reproductions of original subjects and may contain verbal graphic and photographic forms of information. Useful for presentations to support a lecture or for individual study. There are relatively inexpensive to prepare and use and can be rearranged and updated easily.

Filmstrips: Similar to slides, but images are always in same order for use. They cannot be rearranged or revised and are inexpensive when a number of copies are required.

Overhead Transparencies: Though now a day's used quite rarely, however Overhead Transparencies are easy to use for presenting verbal and graphic information to groups. Simple methods are available for making black and white and colour transparencies. Various techniques can be used for systematically disclosing information on a transparency to hold audience interest. This is possible by juxtaposing transparencies one over another to present a sequential content. However now-days these are rarely used since the place is occupied by LCD projectors and powerpoint presentations.

Computer Programme: These display information and instructions on video screen, are interactive and self-pacing with assured learning through careful application of learning principles. Skill is programmed preparations are made and numerous programmes are available for drill. These are useful for an acquisition of information, concept development, simulation and gaming exercises. Most common forms of the same may be film strips and powerpoint presentations, abbreviated as ppt.

Projected Moving Images

Films: There are widely used commercial medium when motion (regular speed. slowed down or speeded up) relationships and dramatisations are to be shown; being replaced by video recording in many instructional programmes.

Video Recording: Preferred medium for producing motion pictures with visual and audio elements recorded in synchronisation; permits results to be viewed immediately; can permit incorporation of other media forms (for example, slides, transparencies, films etc.)

Interactive Videos: Interactive videos are very popular medium. The video programme is controlled by computer programming. It needs authoring language software along with video recording. It is self-learning device and self-paced system and easy to copy but difficult to produce because lot of expertise are necessary.

Multimedia

Latest form of learning media is multimedia system. It is a combination of computer hardware, software, video and audio system. It may be an open learning system or a programmed learning system. It's sky-high limitation and wide range of application makes the system acceptable all over the world. The learner may avail the facility of programmed instruction or s/he may collect information from different information centers through local area network or through satellite communication system. S/he is also free to enter into the video programmes through interactive computer network. The learner is also free to collect the hard copy of the information through network system.

Senses are the avenues of communication between the teacher and learner and they are the gateways to knowledge. Teachers should strive to constantly improve their means of communication. They use a variety of media to bring the outside world in the classroom.

Based on the different human senses, the media can be broadly classified as audio, visual, audio-visual.

In all these types we have number of media that can be listed as follows:

(a) *Audio*—Tape recorder, Radio
(b) *Visual*—Charts, posters, models, maps, slides, flip charts, flash cards, transparency, chalkboards.
(c) *Audio Visual*—Video films, Computer based instruction, TV., powerpoint presentation with audio effects.

Effect of Media

Burton says that audio-visual media are 'those sensory objects or images which initiate or stimulate and reinforce learning'.

The most popular saying is '*I hear I forget, I see I remember and I do I understand*' is quite true in this paralance. *Edgar Dale* arranged all the audio-visual aids in the form of a 'cone of experience'. The cone itself is a visual aid. Further the teacher is also an audio-visual aid, as learners can see and hear from the teacher. Teacher can use one or more of the media to make their classes more effective. Teaching should not be only chalk and talk.

The effects of using visual media are listed below:

1. *Makes easy recalling*: Visual media of any form assist learners to recall important information at later date. They are embedded in our memories with the result that any associated information is more easily recalled.
2. *Develop attitude to learn:* Experiences reveals that most of the classes suffer from boredom with a prolonged vocal instruction or dictating notes even at University level. A visual media breaks the monotony, through colour which attracts people, and excites the students with its dynamism resulting in development of attitude to learn.
3. *Invent new ways*: No learning process is complete unless it is verified by the application of the knowledge. The visual media shows the ways and means of applying knowledge, as well as it helps to innovate new ideas to perform the teaching in a better way.
4. *Perform practical skill*: Practical skill is chiefly concerned with the

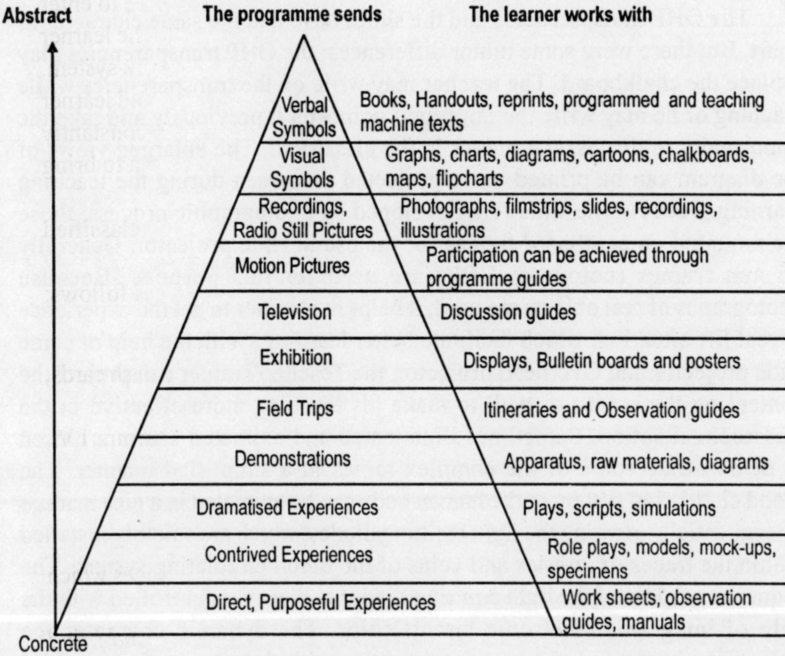

Fig. 10.2: Dales Cone of Experience

ability to physically manipulate objects around a learner. For example preparing a ppt. is a practical skill, because it requires the learner to perform good many competencies. A series of diagrams showing the different views of different step by step tasks can give clear instruction of the process which helps to develop skill.

5. *Simplify potentially complex topics by providing a visual analogy:* Visual media assist in understanding whenever learning proceeds from simple to the complex. For learning mathematics it would be unusual for someone to be able to understand the idea of subtraction without first knowledge of how to add up. The visual aids can facilitate this simple to complex transition by providing simple analogies, which can pave the way for more sophisticated explanations

Features of Projected Visual Media

The projected media are those, which are used in the classroom by projecting image on the wall and screen. The graphics, diagrams and charts carrying some information or message can be projected in the classroom to complement the verbal lecture.

The OHP transparencies and the slides have had the same character as chart. But there were some minor differences; the OHP transparencies may replace the chalkboard. The teacher may write on the transparencies while teaching or he may write the important points on it previously and take the opportunity to discuss the matter in the classroom. The enlarged views of the diagram can be printed on it, projected on screen during the teaching learning process. The slides are developed by photographic process; those are mounted on cardboard frames for the use in slide projector. Generally 35 mm frames (colour or B/W) are used for this purpose. Because photographs of real objects are used, it helps the learner to get the experience of real life situation, which facilitate better learning. With the help of some slide projector and Overhead projector, the Teacher/Trainer can project the content on the screen or wall to make his teaching more effective in the classroom situation. Sometimes illuminated and animated charts are used to demonstrate some of the complex topics in a simplified manner. The blood circulation system of the human body can be animated in a nice manner by sequentially glowing the light emitting diodes, which are suitably installed within the traces of arteries and veins of the blood circulating system. The sequence of glow of the light emitting diodes is however controlled with the help of integrated electronic circuit chips. The dynamic character the animated charts make it very attractive and help to transfer required information to the students.

The filmstrips or films can be used in the classroom situation. Generally 16 mm/8 mm films or filmstrips are used for educational purpose. The documentary films can be used for this purpose also. There are some companies who produce this type of films or movies based on scientific and educational topics. Because these programmes are used to substantiate the classroom lecture, the duration of these programmes does rarely exceed 20 minutes. For projecting this type of programme it requires film projector, power supply units and screen. It requires some skill to operate and so it has become unpopular by a section of teachers. Now-a-days educational video programmes have replaced these.

Slide tape combination, several slides are selected in such a manner that they are logically related to each other. A well-structured audio content is previously recorded in an audio tape recorder. There is a coherent relation between the audio material and visual slides logically, meaningfully and sequentially. Normally in this situation the teacher has the role of operator only. Because it is a programmed instruction, it does not require any further instruction to be communicated to the student.

Video Programme has the same character as movie. It is also a programmed instruction. Instead of projecting it on a big screen it is projected on a 51 cm CRT screen. Sometimes the CRT screen of size more than 51 cm is available. Further enlarged projection of Video System is available for larger gathering.

In computer aided instruction, special software are developed to present the teaching material to the student through computer. Computer is being used as a learning media. A teacher or a group of teachers along with computer experts develop this computer programmes. The programme is developed in such a manner that it contains relevant text material, diagrams, animated diagrams and questionnaire. Questionnaires are supplied after each chapter for the formative evaluation of the students' performance.

Questionnaire for final evaluation are also supplied at the end of the programme for the overall assessment. Generally the four option type multiple choice questionnaires are used. Feedback messages are also supplied along with each item for guiding the students to reach at the correct answer. This method eliminates the presence of a teacher as required in the class room situation. The student has freedom to select topic, or sub-topic. He may quit the programme or continue it. The main disadvantage of this programme is that it cannot involve the student to experience the real life situation as available in film show or video programmes. In video programme and movie, the student has no option or control while learning process is continuing.

The main drawback of Computer Aided Instruction (CAI) can be overcom by using interactive video. The movie part of the programmes is stored in a series of video frames along with the sound and music. Instead of using video tape, video disc player or CD-ROM drivers are used. With suitable hardware arrangement in the CPU of the computer the video system is operated as and when required by the Computer Aided Instruction programme. The main advantage of the Interactive Video system is that it provides all the facilities available in Computer Aided Instruction system which are providing the facility of video-programme. This system also eliminates the presence of a teacher as required in the classroom situation. Because it is a programmed instruction; the scope of obtaining further information is limited here. Here the teaching learning process is not open-ended. However this can be compensated by further study in the library. A nicely organised programme can facilitate efficient learning among the learners.

The following table gives a summary of characteristics of different types of instructional media.

Table 10.1: Summary of Characteristics of Instructional Media

Material	*Advantages*	*Limitation*
Printed Media	1. Include common types of materials 2. Have wide variety of applications 3. Simple types quick to prepare	1. Sophisticated types are costly to prepare 2. Requires suitable reading ability
Display Media	1. Useful in any kind or room without special adaptations 2. Allows user to be flexible for making changes as presentation proceeds 3. Easy to prepare and use materials	1. Limited to use with small groups 2. Requires some showmanship on part of speaker 3. May not be accepted as important media forms when compared with projected types
Overhead Transparencies	1. Can present information in systematic, developmental sequences 2. Use simple-to-operate projector with presentation rate controlled by instructor 3. Require only limited planning 4. Can be prepared by variety of simple, inexpensive methods 5. Particularly useful with large groups	1. Require special equipment, facilities, and skills for more advanced preparation methods 2. Are large compared with other projectors
Audiotape Recordings	1. Easy to prepare with regular tape recorders 2. Can provide applications in most subject areas 3. Equipment for use is compact, portable, easy to operate 4. Flexible and adaptable as either individual elements of instruction or in correlation with programmed materials 5. Duplication easy and economical	1. Have a tendency for overuse, as lecture or oral textbook reading 2. fixed rate of information flow 3. Low fidelity of small portable recorders

(Contd.)

Material	*Advantages*	*Limitation*
Slide Series	1. Require only filming, with processing and mounting by film laboratory 2. Result in colourful, realistic reproductions of original subjects 3. Prepared with any 35mm camera for most uses 4. Easily revised and updated 5. Easily handled, stored, and rearranged for various uses	1. Require some skill in photography 2. Require special equipment for close up photography and copying 3. Can get out of sequence and be projected incorrectly if slides are handled individually
	6. Increased usefulness with tray storage and remote control by presenter 7. Can be combined with taped narration for greater effectiveness May be adapted to group or to individual use	
Filmstrips	1. Are compact, easily handled, and always in proper sequence 2. Can be supplemented with recordings 3. Are inexpensive when quantity reproduction is required 4. Are useful for group or individual study at projection rate controlled by instructor or user 5. Are projected with simple lightweight equipment	1. Are relatively difficult to prepare locally 2. Require film laboratory service to convert slides to filmstrip form unless special camera available 3. Are in permanent sequence and cannot be rearranged or revised
Multi-Image Presentations	1. Can demand attention and create strong emotional impact on viewers 2. Can compress large amounts of information in short presentation time 3. Provide for more effective communications in certain situations than when only a single medium is used	1. Require additional equipment, complex setup, and careful coordination during planning, preparation, and use 2. Equipment and production costs high for complex programmes

Material	*Advantages*	*Limitation*
Video and Film	1. Particularly useful in describing motion, showing relationships, and giving impact to topic 2. Allow instant replay of video recording 3. Videotape reusable 4. Easy to record lip sync on videotape 5. May include special filming techniques (animation, time-lapse) 6. Combine still and motion on videodisc 7. Standardized film projector available everywhere	1. High cost for studio production equipment 2. Resolution limited with video for fine detail close-ups 3. Incompatibility of video format types 4. Value of investment in motion picture equipment reduced as video replaces film
Computer-Based Instruction (CBI)	1. Presents text information and graphic images 2. Interacts with learners on individual basis through asking questions and judging responses 3. Maintains record of responses 4. Adapts instruction to needs of learner 5. Controls other media hardware 6. Can interface computer and video for learner-controlled programmes	1. Requires computer and programming knowledge 2. Requires essential hardware and software for development and use 3. Resolution of graphic images limited on microcomputer systems 4. Effective when used by only one or few individuals at a time 5. Incompatibility of hardware and software among various systems

Selection of Media

Media selection is one of the important skills that should be acquired by every teacher. The teacher must base the selection of media on various priorities like availability of resources, the objectives, the topic and its content.

The traditional approach to selecting media was based on a search for application for a new item of equipment recently appeared in the market. Now we speak of a different approach termed the development approach. We first think of the type of problem we face in the teaching learning situation and then think of the media that would help us in this regard. Although both the approaches have their value but for the practicing teacher the developmental approach is more appropriate.

The major factors to be considered in the selection of media for use in teaching—learning process is shown in Figure 10.3:

The two basic rules that we may follow in choosing our media are:

(i) *Selection by rejection*: This means we should eliminate first those media which we consider to be unsuitable for our purpose.

(ii) *Selection from the remaining ones* on the basis of the economic and practical constraints and teacher and learner preferences and skills.

The important considerations that should be kept in mind while we take decisions on the selection of media are –

(a) Effective Communication: Some of the important points to be considered at this stage of media selection are:

(i) Which media would appeal most to the learner?

(ii) Do we need to transmit just some information or we need to get some feedback too?

(iii) Whether our teaching objectives are rigid or flexible?

(iv) Which medium would help us in achieving our Objectives?

(b) Cost Effectiveness: The number of students who would be benefited as well as the proportion of capital and receiving costs are two important determining factors here. We should also consider whether we can use any existing media and what their worth is compared to any new media to be purchased.

(c) Practicability: The practicability of use of different media is to be determined with reference to the time available for presentation and the human and material resources available.

(d) Preferred Learning and Teaching Styles: The learners' preferences for particular media should be taken into account. As the learners differ in the manner of their learning so do teachers in the way they teach. Different teaching strategies and plans call for the use of different sensory channels of instruction.

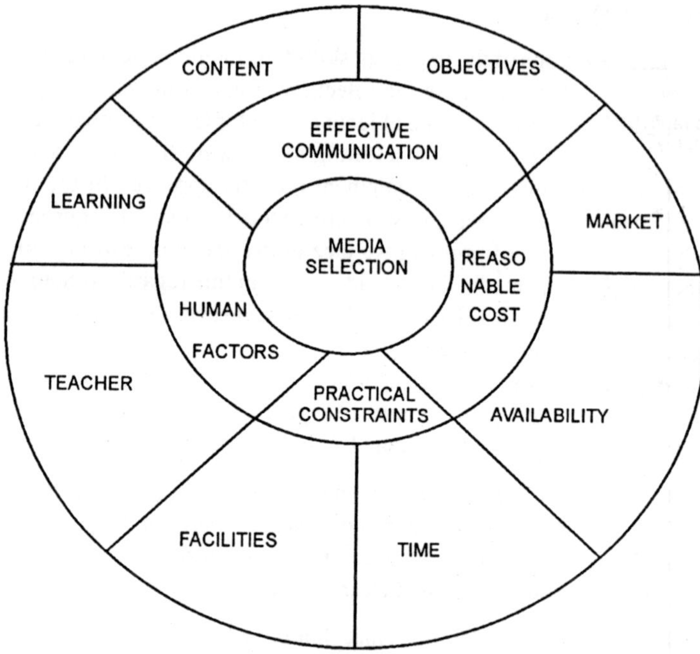

Fig. 10.3

One should take into account the different aspects of the learning environment and choose media keeping in view our overall strategy, methods and techniques of instruction, the learning behaviour to be affected and the instructional events to be arranged for.

After selecting the most appropriate media for our instruction, we should think of putting them to effective use. Consideration at the phase accords the following issues:

- When should they be used? Whether at the beginning of teaching, during the course or towards its end?
- Whether the same medium is to be used always?

Change of media is always desirable wherever possible. Figure 10.4 shows diagrammatically the attributes to be considered for selection of media on the basis of learning objectives and subject content for presentation to regular size classes.

Role of Media

Media serves to bring the outside world into the classroom. It is possible to provide a variety of learning experiences with their help. The importance of

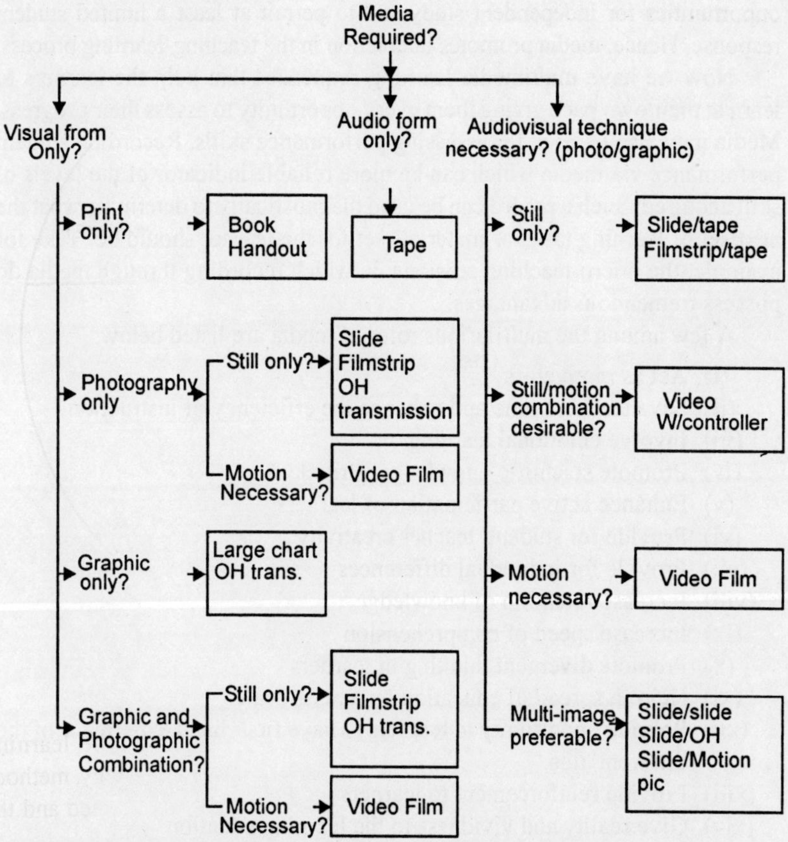

Fig. 10.4: Media Selection Diagram for Presentation to Regular Class Size

the use of different media in instruction is now increasingly being realised. Resource centers are being established at different levels making it possible for teachers to borrow and use the media they require, however mostly by the private agencies, especially in eastern India. Revolutionary changes are taking place in the field of education by the contribution of various media, which are contributing for increasing effectiveness of teaching learning.

Media are instruments of communication and a vital part of teaching-learning process. Media enables us to record information in a variety of forms thus there can be repetition of the content taught. This leads to more independent and individualised patterns of learning. Media offer a much wider range of learning experiences, presenting simulations of reality or even the reality, in audio and visual modes, in motion, colour, magnification, reduction and animation. The media takes into consideration the need to reach more students, to reach them with an improved range of learning materials, to offer greater opportunities for independent study and to permit at least a limited student response. Hence, media promotes interaction in the teaching-learning process.

Now we have multimedia learning sequences that help the learners to learn at their own pace giving them every opportunity to assess their progress. Media may also be used for assessing performance skills. Recording student performance via media which can be more reliable indicator of the levels of skill acquired. Such a record can be used diagnostically to determine what the next set of learning tasks or materials set for the learner should be. Take for example, the micro-teaching sessions, in which recording through media do possess tremendous advantages.

A few among the multifarious roles of media are listed below:

(i) Act as motivators
(ii) Save teachers time and enhance the efficiency of instruction
(iii) Involve emotional learning
(iv) Promote scientific knowledge, attitude.
(v) Enhance active participation of learners
(vi) Provide for student, teacher creativity
(vii) Provide for individual differences
(viii) Increase retention of knowledge
(ix) Increase speed of comprehension
(x) Promote divergent thinking in learners
(xi) Help in spread of education on a mass scale.
(xii) Provide opportunity to learners to have first- hand experience of the different aids.
(xiii) Provide reinforcement to learners
(xiv) Give reality and vividness to the learning situation
(xv) Supply a concrete basis for conceptual thinking.

Thus the media give the way to the two-way communication of instruction.

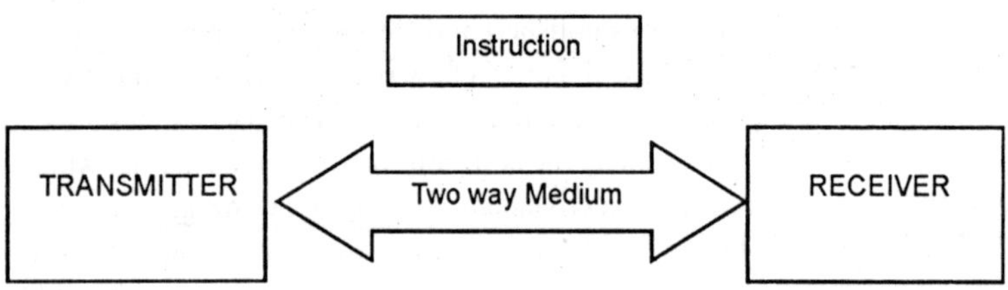

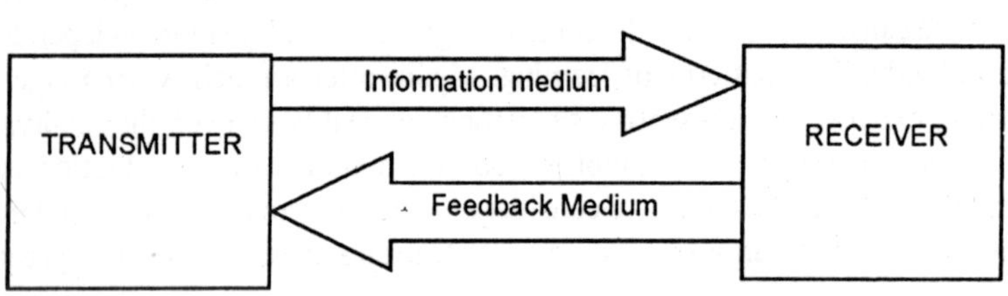

Conclusion

In sum, if the use of audio-visual resources needs to be planned, only then it can improve quality of teaching-learning in a cost-effective way, in a country like India.

The media serve an important role in completing an instruction. However, its effectiveness depends on the competence of the teacher as to how s/he selects and uses them in order to create a meaningful learning environment. A learning resource centre can be set up in the institution and to begin with teachers can contribute their own learning resources like different charts, working and non-working models, slides and the like. Students can also be assigned some project work to complement this.

11
Principles of Visual Media Design

It has been established that visual media plays an important role in the retention process of a learner. The projected 'still images' may be pictures, charts, diagrams, drawings or written material which can be displayed through projection on a screen. Overhead transparency is a cheap and simple media which can be prepared and used by the teachers themselves. The discussion herein will focus on design of such media.

Principles Governing the Selection of Still Images

The major consideration which underpins these principles concerns the sense of sight. Visual aid of any description utilises the learners' ability to see as a means of helping him/her learn.

Principle 1: The image to be used must have relevance, as something that is relevant to the content of presentation or needs of learners is more lively to arouse interest. It is known that interest is very important for learning as it draws the attention and encourages effort which is the key to achievement motivation.

Principle 2: An image must achieve a balance between what is understandable and what sets a problem. The image should be thought provoking.

Principle 3: An image should Challenge some sort of response on the part of the learner since learning stems from activity rather than passive absorption. Images can play a big part in encouraging learner activities.

General Principles of Design of Still Image

The most important principle to be kept in mind while designing still images is the CLARITY of both the image and the message transmitted. A beautifully developed visual will lose much of its impact if either the students at the back of the classroom has to *squint* to see it or if they find the message too obscure.

Principle 4: Learners will tend to see an image better if Maximum Contrast is established between content and background. In other words, the important information must stand out from less important. COLOUR is an important aspect for contributing to the attractiveness of an image. Colour should be used judiciously keeping into consideration the psychological impact as some colours are automatically associated with a particular object. Colours selected, should be harmonious together because dissonant colours (of equal intensity and complementary on the colour wheel like Orange-Blue, and Red-Green) create annoyance in the audience and consequently interfere with a clear perception of the image.

Other emotional aspects of specific colours have been identified. Some common ones are

- **Red**-danger or action, arouses feeling
- **Orange**-warmth or energy
- **Blue**-aloofness or clarity, cooling
- **Green**-freshness or restfulness
- **Violet**-depression
- **Yellow**-cheerfulness
- **Black**-darkness, gloom
- **Violet Blue**-stern, unyielding.

When selecting colours for visual materials, attention should be given to three specific aspects:

(a) ***Hue***: the choice of a specific colour (red, blue and so on)
(b) ***Value***: the value of the colour, meaning how light or dark the colour should appear in visual with relation to other visual elements.
(c) ***Intensity***: the intensity or strength of the colour for its impact or coordinated effect.

Most commonly, colour is used diagrammatically to differentiate areas when a subject is complicated.

Principle 5: Visual clarity of an image will improve if the Letering is easily recognisable. The legibility of the words, numerals and other data that the learners are expected to read is frequently neglected during planning and preparation of visual images. It is much important that proper attention be given to the shape, size and style of lettering, which also control the amount of information to be presented in one visual.

The suitability of lettering also depends on shape and size of the classroom, type of screen surface and the amount of ambient or outside light which cannot be controlled. Since these factors are often variable, It is advisable that as a general guide or '*minimum standards*' be adopted for lettering for convenience of reading by the students.

As a general rule, *lower case* letters be used as far as possible. The minimum standard size of letters is fixed on the basis of the maximum anticipated viewing distance.

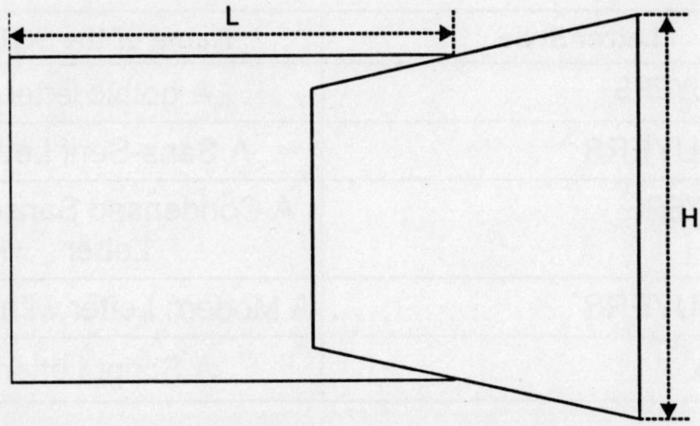

The standard maximum viewing distance (L) is considered on the basis of the vertical dimension of the picture on screen (H), depending on the type of projected image. Maximum viewing distance for transparency is 8H, while for vide it ranges from 16H to 24H.

Table 11.1: Minimum letter size for different projected media

Medium	*Maximum viewing distance*	*Maximum ratio of letter height to image height*	*Minimum letter height (lower case letter) for image area 15x22 cm*
Slide **Filmstrips** **Transparencies**	8H	1 to 30	6 mm (18 pints/1.5 pica)
Video	16H—24H	1 to 25	6 mm to 9 mm (18 to 27 points/1.5 to 2.23 pica)

As a rough guide in helping to determine the size of projected *lowercase lettering* the following table may be referred.

Viewing Distance (m)	36m	18m	9m	4.5m
Minimum Lettering height	100mm	50mm	25mm	12mm

The following guidelines are recommended for obtaining good legibility.

To assist with good legibility, the following guidelines are recommended:

I. Select a readable letter style, like a sans-serif or gothic type, which is composed of evenly drawn, medium-width strokes.
II. Avoid script letter styles because the letters are difficult to distinguish, one from another.

Letter Style	Name of the Style
MANY BUYERS	A gothic letter
MANY BUYERS	A Sans-Serif Letter
MANY BUYERS	A Condensed Sans-Serif Letter
MANY BUYERS	A Modern Letter with Serifs
Many Buyers	A Script Letter

- For a visual, or series of related visuals consisting of verbal information, use no more than three different typefaces (two are preferred). The typefaces should harmonise with each other. They can be of various sizes.
- Use capital letters for short titles and labels, but for longer captions and phrases (six words or more use lowercase letters with appropriate capitals since the lowercase letters are more easily read.

A HISTORY OF OUR TEMPLE	Vs.	The Fourty Most Common Deciduous Trees and Shrubs In Vernon County

- As stated previously, include no more than 15 to 20 words in a single projected visual. Also, leave extra blank space around the edge of the visual so it appears non-crowded. This tends to increase readability
- Separate lines within a caption so that adequate white space is left for ease of reading—about 1 ½ times the height of the lowercase letter *m*, measured from an *m* on one line to an *m* (or comparable letter) on the next line.

  Extensive research has been made by educationists in both professional and liberal aspects.

Extensive research has been made by educationists in both professional and liberal aspects.	Too Close
Extensive research has been made by educationists in both professional and liberal aspects.	Too Far
Extensive research has been made by educationists in both professional and liberal aspects.	Good

- Space letters *optically*. Equal measured distances between all letters do not look equal. *Make spaces look equal*, regardless of measurement.
- Thickness of line is important to legibility. A thin line is difficult to see. A moderate, bold line is preferred because it increases the area of a letter that is visible to the viewer. Extremely bold lines reduce legibility because parts of letters that should be open appear somewhat filled in.

EDUCATION	Too thin
EDUCATION	Too thick
EDUCATION	Good

- Space letters so they do *not* appear to either blend together or lose their continuity for forming letters.

TRAINING	Too close
T R A I N I N G	Too far
TRAINING	Good

- Allow 1½ letter widths for the space between words and 3 widths between sentences. Too much or too little space again makes reading difficult.

Holdlidfirmly. Raisearm.	Too close
Hold lid firmly. Raise arm.	Too far
Hold lid firmly. Raise arm.	Good

- Contrast the lettering in colour or tone with the background so that separation contributes to good legibility.
- Light letters against a dark background have greater visibility than do dark letters against a light background.
- For satisfactory legibility, dark letters on a light-coloured background require a wider width stroke than do light letters on a dark background.

Principle 6: The visual image content should be easy on eyes and contain uncluttered information. Simplicity should be the basic characteristics of clarity of message transmitted through image. The most effective images are usually simple and/or brief and kept to one or two points. Charts, graphs and diagrams suitable for handouts may not be acceptable for images as they usually contain large amount of information.

Generally speaking, the fewer elements into which a given space is divided, the more pleasing it is to the eye. The complex or lengthy information should be subdivided into a number of easy-to-read and easy-to-understand related materials. The verbal content for projected visuals should be limited to 15 or 20 words.

Hardware for Transparency Projection

The basic hardware comprise-

i) Equipment by which image is projected, for example, *Over Head Projector* (OHP),
ii) Medium on which presentation image is prepared, for example *Transparency* and
iii) Surface on which image is projected, for example *Screen.*

Over Head Projector (OHP): It is the device as already stated, projects a still image onto the screen. The common variety has a box with a glass plate or *Optical Stage* on the top. A Fresnel lens is kept just below the *stage*, which can concentrate light into a particular direction. The box contains a lamp, a reflector and a fan used to cool the projector during running.

Above the box, a Head attachment, supported by column, contains (i) an objective lens which can be moved up and down for adjusting the focal length or focusing for sharpness and clarity of projected image and (ii) an adjustable mirror, (up to 45° angle) for adjusting the vertical position of the projected image.

OHP Transparencies: An OHP transparency is a piece of plastic or acelate on which the still image is prepared. When it is placed on the optical stage of a running OHP, a silhouette of the image will be projected on the screen. The OHP will also project colour when translucent coloured materials and inks are used to create images. Transparencies usually come in two sizes—250mm x 250mm and 200mm (width) x 280mm (height) (A4 size). The former has same area as the area of the standard optical stage.

OHP Pen: OHP Pens contain a fast drying ink which will not bubble on the films and which is translucent. Ordinary pens and felt-tips do not have these qualities. Pens are available in a range of colours and several line widths—fine, medium, broad.

There are two major varieties of pen—Non-Permanent and Permanent. Non-permanent pens usually contain water-soluble ink which can be erased using a damp cloth. Permanent pens contain spirit-based ink and can be erased using a special solvent.

The impression of permanent pens has long *shelf* life but is difficult to erase when modifications or corrections are required.

Non-permanent pens facilitate imprompt presentation and material can be easily erased. However, the impression is easily smudged if dampened.

Screen: Screen is not essential for Over Head Projection and any smooth white surface such as a classroom wall or white board can be used for the purpose. Whiteboards reflect back the light and a screen with a matt white finish is preferred. The screen may be fixed on the wall, which can be pulled down or it may be a tripod-mounted, portable screen.

Advantages of Using OHP

i) ***Large image***: A very large projected image can be obtained in a minimum projection distance. The projected image size depends on (a) focal length of the projector's object lens and (b) the distance between projector and the screen. The closer the OHP is to the screen, the smaller the image will be. The image size usually ranges between 0.50 and 0.80 sq. m.

ii) ***Facing the audience***: It allows the teacher to face the class, maintaining eye-to-eye contact with the students.

iii) ***Identity with the user***: The audience sees the visualisation from the same point of view as the presenter. Thus a feeling of oneness between the teacher and students is established.

iv) ***Lighted room***: The projected image, unlike power-point projection, is bright enough to be seen clearly in a normally lit classroom. Only when strong daylight is directly falls on the screen, some shading of the screen would be necessary. The existence of natural light promotes the continued personal link between the teacher and the students and the presence of natural light also help students to make notes during presentation.

v) ***Controlled Pace***: OHP allows for controlling the rate at which information is presented. This flexibility helps the students to clarify their understanding of complex topics. This can be achieved either by showing several transparencies in a sequence or by projecting one transparency which incorporates different components which are gradually displayed. The three main techniques are known as Revealation, Masking and Overlay.

vi) ***Aid-Memoire***: The prepared material being projected on to the screen is also available for viewing by teachers. Thus a teacher has on view an excellent *aide memoire* which assists him/her to maintain a smooth flow of presentation without having to peer down at written notes as prompts.

vii) ***Portability***: OHP being light weight makes it portable.

viii) ***Flexibility***: It enables a teacher flexibility to integrate the visualisation into the total presentation. The teacher may move from verbal to visual exposition and vice-versa, by switching on or off the OHP, without any break in communication. This enhances the fluency of the delivery/presentation.

Limitations of OHP

i) The lamp gives a bright dazzling light.
ii) The machine generates a great deal of heat and to reduce the heat, most of the models have automatic fans. These fans often make loud distracting noise during presentation.
iii) The lamps of OHP are very delicate. Excessive movement of OHP, especially when lamp is hot, may cause the lamp to be extinguished.

OHP Presentation Technique

Setting the Machine: After plugging in the machine, the lead should be arranged such that no one, particularly the presenter can trip over it. The worrying of fan and lamp should be checked.

Focusing the OHP: Focusing can be done by lowering or raising the object less and/or increasing/decreasing the distance between OHP and screen. A specially prepared transparency containing extremely fine details such as lettering is preferably used to check the visibility during focusing.

Positioning the Screen: The screen should be positioned as high as possible and as low as possible. It should be ensured that the *Head attachment* does not obscure the students' view and is obtained when the screen is placed across a corner position, on the window side, with bottom of the screen 1.5 to 2 meters above the floor. Presenter's problem relative to the screen is also important. Teacher should ensure that s/he does not position between projector and screen to avoid blocking the view.

Prior Rehearsing: The transparencies to be used should be arranged sequentially prior to presentation for smooth presentation. When handling a series of transparencies in one session, it is a good idea to number them and have them ready in presentation order alongside the projector. A handy space should be kept available for replacing the transparencies after use.

Positioning of Presenter: As a general rule it is advised to the teacher to remain facing students during presentation. A pointer or even a pen can be used for pointing at the transparency on the projector.

Scheduling of Session: Prior planning should be made in respect of time to be devoted for presentation of each transparency, flexibility to take into account possible digression arising due to unplanned interaction with students.

Presentation of successive transparency should be timed such that the visual material and accompanying verbal explanations are synchronised.

Timing for exposure of transparency-information should also take into consideration the purpose of the visual—whether being used as cueing device to encourage thinking or as advance organiser. Sufficient exposure time should be ensured to enable the students to consider the material and assimilate the information.

Revelation: This enables the teacher to simply but effectively focus the students' attention only on what the teacher wants them to see and when s/he wants them to see. It is achieved by moving a piece of card or paper towards the presenter revealing one section of the information at a time. This will encourage students to concentrate on current points without looking ahead to points not yet relevant. This technique is most appropriate to the disclosure of verbal points, although in some instances graphic information lends itself to this type of display.

The major problem for the presenter in this technique is that since part of the transparency remains covered, the information to be revealed is not accessible to the presenter. A presenter may be in difficulty if s/he is relying on OHP as an aide-memoire. The difficulty may be overcome by using semi-transparent material such as tissue or tracing paper as covering device.

This will prevent light projection but allows the presenter to view, in advance, the information to be received. However, care should be taken to put some weight on covering material, as these being very light are prone to be blown away by draught from fan which would lead to loss of full effect of revelation.

Revelation technique leads to build up of complex topics, as it is known that assimilation of new information often depends on its linkage with familiar information.

Masking: This technique in many ways is similar to revelation as it also reveals information one bit at a time. In this case exposure is achieved by raising flaps which are taped to the frame or by opening windows within a cover card Blocks of information can be displayed separately in this technique.

Unlike revelation, semi-translucent papers cannot be used as such paper does not make efficient flaps or windows. It is advisable to note on each *window* or *flap* indicating information underneath. It is worth rehearsing the opening up sequence to avoid getting into confusion and revealing information before it is due.

Masking can be used to build up relatively complex topics and act as a step-by-step accomplishment to verbal presentation. The major facility offered by masking and not by revelation is its capacity to allow flexibility in sequence of presentation of information. The order of presentation can be changed depending upon the impact desired to be achieved. This also has the advantage of covering back the information displayed earlier to enable the students to focus attention only on the information currently being presented.

Overlay: In overlay transparency, further information is layered on to a base transparency by means of additional transparency placed at appropriate points. Any problem, process or other forms of information can be divided into logical elements, prepared separately as transparency sheets and then shown progressively for effective presentation.

For preparing transparency in overlay form, first a sketch of the total content is made. Next decision has to be taken regarding elements to be *base* (projected first) and the elements of original sketch to comprise each *overlay*. Separate *masters* are made for the base and each overlay. Then transparencies are made from each master. Guide masks should be indicated at same position on each of two corners of each master, base and overlay transparencies to ensure proper alignment of all layers. Overlays can have great impact on a viewing audience, but care should be taken in following aspects in order to maximise the impact:

- Respective *overlay* transparencies should be accurately aligned to preceding ones.
- Sequence of exposure should be rehearsed before the presentation.

Usually it is possible to overlay between 4-6 transparencies at most on OHPs. Overlay is also used, like revelation and masking to build up complex topics by visually reinforcing, stressing clarifying the explanations. Overlay, however, has some advantages which are only possessed by previous two techniques. It allows for *breakdown* of a topic as well as *builds up* of a topic—starting with the whole and gradually dismantling, it can be equally illuminating as build up to the whole.

- It can be used to present graphic information much more effectively than revelation or masking.
- The major strength of this technique lies in its ability to show relationships within objects, processes, procedures and operations since each aspect of a component can be first of all viewed separately and then linked to other aspects of components through the addition of additional transparencies.

Animation: OHP is usually associated with still images, this can be used to represent simple animation and can make a substantial contribution to the development of insight into relationships which learners otherwise may find difficult to grasp. The specialized OHP display technique can be divided into following categories.

(a) ***Moving diagram***—It is a logical extension of overlay including a fixed base and one or more movable transparencies e.g., to show movement.

(b) ***Moving Shapes***—This involves cutting the shape of objects from coloured fill and a card of a silhouette is required and moving them by hand or pushing them into position with a pointer. e.g., Perspex blocks containing key points may be moved around the optical stage.

(c) ***Working Model***—These would consist of those diagrams which are built from card, wood ~ Perspex and which attempt to reproduce, in a 2-dimensional form, a key mechanism e.g., movement of eye to measure eye-voice-span.

(d) ***Projected experiment***—It is possible to display experiments as they are performed using OHP. This improves visual access during carrying out a scientific demonstration e.g., wave phenomenon, formation of magnetic field using magnet and iron fillings, formation of drops, surface tension effect etc.

Preparing OHP Transparencies

The OHP transparency can be prepared by hand or reprographic methods. Other methods require special facilities from skilled person which are normally not available in educational institutions.

A rough plan should be drawn on a plain paper while preparing transparency by hand. Use of squared paper for planning would ensure that information on the transparency has a balanced or symmetric finish. A margin of about 12mm (1/2″) space should be left all around as the projection at the edges can become distorted. It is convenient to work within a rectangular area having height to width ratio of about 4:5. Projection in horizontal position is preferred as the eyes have a greater field of vision horizontally.

Diagrams/graphics from printed material can be directly photo-copied on transparency sheet. However, the sheets should be of thicker, special variety to avoid melting under high temperature in the photocopier, i.e. xerox machine.

While preparing transparency by photocopying from printed material, due attention should be given to following points.

- The formats to be copied are often vertical rather than horizontal, as recommended above.
- The quantity of information in printed material may be more than what can be presented in a single transparency.
- Printed material may be too dense and thus not suitable for projection which permits viewing for only limited time.
- Unnecessary details should be eliminated
- Visual elements may be modified and lettering may be replaced with lettering suitable font and size.
- Complex diagrams may be simplified by dividing its segments for separate transparencies.

Conclusion

Overhead projection technique is a very simple, cheap, flexible and effective means for using projected visual instructional media.

Development of the skill of designing and using this technique among the teachers would lead to an effective teaching-learning process. A summary of guidelines for using this technique effectively is provided below.

DO's and DON'Ts when Using OHP

- Position the transparency on stage before turning on the light.
- Keep the projected information towards the top of screen.
- Use the revelation technique when several lines or points are projected.
- Keep the material on transparency simple.
- Use a maximum of 6 or 7 words per line in a visual.
- Don't stand between the projector and the screen.
- Don't leave the projector light on when nothing is projected.
- Don't move the projector when the lamp is switched on.
- Don't switch off power supply or move the projector until the lamp is cooled, which is indicated by automatic stoppage of thermostatically controlled fan.

12
Teaching Skills

Concept of Teaching Skills

Teaching may be said to be the process whereby the environment of an individual is deliberately manipulated to enable the individual to learn.

Learning is a relatively permanent and desirable change in behaviour as a function of reinforced practice or experience.

Skill may be defined as a physical, mental or social ability that is learned through practice, repetition and reflection in which it is probably always possible for the individual to improve.

It is recognised that teaching is a very complex task, affected by a large number of variables, all of which may influence the behaviour of the participants and many of which are extremely difficult to cater for. The personality, sex, age, social background and previous experiences of both teacher and students would affect the classroom behaviour of a teacher. In addition, the attitudes of both teacher and students to one another will affect any interaction between the two parties. Other variables in operation include the subject matter and its level of difficulty, the academic interest and orientation of teachers and students, institutional environment and economic and social factors.

Since teaching is a complicated task involving many related tasks, it would be convenient if teaching could be broken into specific skills or competencies. Such skills or competencies then would become the basis not only of training programmes but also of attempts to evaluate teaching effectiveness.

Technical skills of teaching are specific aspects of teaching behaviour that are considered to be particularly effective in facilitating desired learning. These technical skills are not linked with subject matter and were derived from an analysis of teaching process into specific techniques. The technical skill approach was initially developed at Stanford University in early '60s. Each skill has an observable and easily countable teacher response linked to specified and easily countable student behaviour. The first technical skill used at Stanford University was 'how to begin a lesson'. Subsequently other skills were added and a list was developed which included the following 14 components of skills of teaching important for instructional stage:

---

* The simantic determination of the term 'skills' is not beyond debate however it has been accepted in Education.

1. ***Set Induction***—Preparing students for a lesson by clarifying its goals, relating it to students' prior knowledge and skills, through using analogies, demonstrations and posing stimulating problems.
2. ***Stimulus Variation***—Using stimulating material and variations in movement, gestures, interaction techniques and sensory channels in order to minimise boredom and inattentiveness.
3. ***Reinforcement of Student Participation***—Encouraging students to respond through the use of praise and acceptance as well as non-verbal cues such as nodding and smiling.
4. ***Silence and Non-Verbal Cue***—Reducing reliance on 'teacher talk' by encouraging teachers in the proper use of pauses and in effective use of facial expressions, body movement, head movement and gestures.
5. ***Fluency in Asking Questions***—Eliminating unnecessary hesitations and repetitions of questions.
6. ***Probing Questions***—Skill in framing questions, which lead students to elaborate on or raise their level of response.
7. ***Higher Order Questions***—Questions, which elicit responses requiring higher intellectual levels from students instead of responses, that involve only stating of facts or description.
8. ***Divergent Questions***—Questions that elicit student responses that are unconventional, imaginative and cannot be judged simply as correct or incorrect.
9. ***Recognising 'Attending Behaviour'***—Recognising non-verbal signals from students indicating their interest/disinterest in the presentation made by the teacher.
10. ***Illustrating and Use of Example***—Use of examples and seeking examples from students in such a way so as to help the students to comprehend new concepts by modifying and extending their previous acquired concepts.
11. ***Lecturing***—Treated as the basic teaching skill.
12. ***Planned Repetition***—This is essential for reinforcement of learning.
13. ***Completeness of Communication***—Avoiding *'Joti Babu'* syndrome, when a sentence is never uttered completely.
14. ***Closure***—Assisting students to establish links between new and past knowledge by reviewing and applying material to familiar and new examples, cases and situations.

Detailed discussion about these has been covered in the next section.

Australian Advisory Committee on Research and Development in Education had identified 140 teaching skills.

Teaching Skills Development Project at University of Sydney (TSDP) considered the following skills for formulating teacher development programmes—

1) Set Induction
2) Explanation
3) Variability
4) Questioning
5) Reinforcement
6) Discipline and Classroom management
7) Small group and individualised teaching skills
8) Skills relating to development of discovery learning and creativity in student

An Australian team of authors developed a system for classifying teaching skills under which, seven categories emerged. These were:

a) ***Motivational skills*** including reinforcing student behaviour, varying the stimulus, set induction, encouraging the student involvement, accepting and supporting student feelings, displaying warmth and enthusiasm and recognising and meeting students' needs.
b) ***Presentation and communication skills*** including explaining, dramatising, reading, using AV aids, closure, silence, encouraging student feedbacks, clarity, pacing and planned repetitions.
c) ***Questioning skills*** including refocusing and redirecting, probing, higher level questions, convergent and divergent questions, stimulating student initiatives.
d) ***Skills of small group and individual instruction*** such as small group work, developing independent learning counseling, encouraging cooperative activities and student to student interaction.
e) ***Developing student thinking*** such as fostering inquiry learning, guiding discovery, developing concepts, using simulations, role playing and gaming to stimulate thought, developing students' problem solving skills, encouraging students to evaluate and make judgments and developing critical thinking.
f) ***Evaluative skills*** including recognising and assessing student progress, diagnosing learning difficulties, providing remedial techniques, encouraging self-evaluation, handling evaluative discussion.
g) ***Skills from Classroom management and discipline*** including recognising attending and non-attending behaviour, supervising class group work, encouraging task-oriented behaviour, giving directions and coping with multiple issues.

Specifically identified components of skills as important for teaching in higher education are as follows:

1. Set induction
2. Explanation
3. Closure
4. Questioning skill
5. Stimulus variation
6. Reinforcement skill
7. Recognising attending student behaviour
8. Silence and non-verbal cue

The subsequent section discusses in details these components of skills.

The technical skill approach to teaching has often been criticised, as it is believed that this leads to mechanisation of the teaching-learning process and the teachers develop the tendency to follow over-simplified prescriptions or recipe ignoring the variations in context and individual differences in both teachers and students. Further, this approach emphasises the behavioural aspects of teaching to the detriment of intellectual and creative aspects. However, this approach has been used universally in teacher training programmes for development/improvement of teaching skills.

Components of Teaching Skill

Set Induction

During sprinting competition in athletics, the sprinters commence running at the starter's instructions: "On Your Marks." "Get Set." "Go." These simple instructions contain the basis of Set Induction. In teaching, as in athletics, a teacher has to gain the general attention of the learners, direct them specifically and see that they proceed in right direction for effective learning.

'Set Induction' may be defined as any device or process which induces a learner to attend and learn and refers to those actions and statements by the teacher that are designed to relate the experience of students to the objectives of the lesson. It directs the learners' attention to a specific task or learning sequence and it has been demonstrated that differences in set induction affects learning outcomes. It is analogous to the introduction provided at the start of a chapter in books. Effective teachers use set induction to put learners in a receptive frame of mind that will facilitate learning. Inducing a set also excludes the perception and learning of other activities.

Purposes

The first purpose of set induction is *to focus learners' attention on the lesson.* The first motivational function of the teacher is "to engage the student in learning".

As its second purpose, set induction attempts *to create an organising framework for the ideas, principles or information that is to follow.* It is suggested that teachers can best shape the behaviour of the students when students have been told in advance what is expected from them. This is said to be the 'expectancy function' of a teacher. Some experts have suggested use of 'advance organisers', i.e. telling students in advance how a lecture is organised during lecture introductions, which is likely to improve their learning.

The third purpose of set induction is *to extend the understanding and application of abstract ideas through the use of example or analogy*. It is difficult for many students to comprehend an idea or principle that is abstractly stated and even those students who can understand may have difficulty in applying their knowledge to new situations. The clever use of examples or analogies helps in overcoming such limitations.

The fourth and last purpose of set induction is *to stimulate student interest and involvement in the lesson.* The active involvement at the beginning of a lesson increases the curiosity and stimulates the students' interest in the lesson.

Usage

Set induction has to be used in following instances:

- Commencement of a new topic
- Introduction of new concept/principles
- Initiating a discussion
- Presentation of guest speaker
- Initiating Question and Answer session
- Beginning a laboratory exercise
- Preparing for a field visit.

Techniques of Set Induction

Set Induction may be used by adopting the following techniques:

- By employing an activity, event, object or person that relates to student interest or previous experience to focus the students' attention on the presentation, the teacher is about to make.
- Providing a structure or framework that enables the students to visualise the contents or activities of presentation.
- Clarifying the goals of the lesson presentation.
- Providing a smooth transition from known or already covered material to new or unknown material by capitalising on the use of examples, analogies and student activities.
- Evaluating previously learned material before moving on to new material or skill building activities, by employing student-centered activities.

Steps in Using Set Induction

1) Preliminary attention gaining: It should be ensured by the teacher that the students are attentive at the commencement of the class. This can be achieved by pausing, looking around the class and waiting till the class is ready. Taking attendance may also be used for this purpose.
2) Orientation: An event, object, process or device, preferably from day-to-day experience of students, be selected which will interest the students and match the objectives of the lesson. The choice should be appropriate, provide a structure or focus for the students and make the objectives of the lesson clear to the students.

An effectively designed set induction will provide answer to the question 'why a student will be interested to learn about the topic to be discussed in the class?' The duration of set induction may vary from a few minutes to even one class hour depending on the situation e.g., set induction to a subject at the commencement of the session may last even for one class hour. This skill is the most important among all the skills, as effective learning will not take place unless the interest of students is aroused about the topic. But it is observed that teachers usually do not give sufficient time to design appropriate set induction.

Examples of Set Induction

Some examples of the set induction used in teaching different technical topics are listed below:

- Analogy of preparation of pioneer from milk for introducing the topic of coagulation in treatment of water.
- Demonstration of gradual clearing of a glass of water containing suspended particles to introduce the topic of settling in treatment of water.
- Example of an electric fan and description of its components to introduce the topic on electric motor.
- Example of finding directions/locations in an unknown place from a map to introduce the subject relating GPS.

Explanation

Explanation may be defined as the activity to give understanding to some-one else. So the act of explaining involves 'an explainer', 'explainees' and 'something to be explained'. It refers to planned 'teacher talk' designed to clarify any idea, procedure, process not understood by a learner. Every teacher, as well as every student, knows the importance of being able to give clear explanations. Teachers rely heavily on this skill in lesson presentation and usually devote most of their time and energy in this activity during a class.

Students know only too well the difficulty of learning from the teacher who lacks this critical skill.

The use and importance of explaining behaviour extend far beyond the classroom. We encounter the use of explanations, both oral and written, in every aspect of our personal life. Unfortunately, the explanations heard in varied situations are not very satisfying. Though teachers are extensively involved in providing explanations, systematic approach to designing explanations would improve their professional competence and also optimise the time spent in classroom.

Purposes

An efficient way to begin acquiring the skill in explaining is to first understand the underlying purpose of an explanation. The purposes of an explanation may be divided into following categories.

- ***Interpretive:*** These give the answer to the question 'WHAT?' and specify the central meaning of term or statement or they clarify an issue. Examples are 'What is entropy?', 'What is water quality?', 'What is environmental pollution?' 'What is education?', 'What is Training'? etc.
- ***Descriptive:*** These explanations describe or illustrate processes, structures and procedures and provide answers to the question 'HOW?' Examples of such explanations are: 'How does a centrifugal pump work?', 'How Bacteriological analysis of water is done?', 'How steel is manufactured?' 'How education differs from training'? etc.
- ***Reason giving:*** These involve principles or generalisations, motives and causes and answer the question 'WHY?' The purposes of these may be further classified for convenience of designing as under:
  - To show a direct cause-and-effect relationship
    Examples are 'The effect of pollutants in air', The effect of heat on liquid', 'The effect of an unclear communication', the effect of training over the level of understanding etc.
  - To show that a particular action is governed by a general rule or principle or law
    Examples are 'Why painting is done on a steel structure?'
  - To show the intent of an action or process

Examples are 'Why annealing is done in metallurgical manufacturing?', 'Why steel is used in reinforced concrete?' How 'CBCS is a better choice than former system of education?'

These types of explanation are mainly used in teaching. However, a particular explanation may involve all the types and the teacher has to decide the sequence of the different types of explanation.

Steps in Designing Explanation

Explaining ideas to students can be a challenging task. Explaining behaviour is a teaching skill that depends a great deal on a teacher's knowledge and creativity. However explanation is a vague action verb in process of determining instructional objectives and also in the process of setting question papers. A systematic approach for designing explanation is suggested below.

Step 1. **Identification of purpose**: It is to be first decided precisely what are to be explained by identifying the purpose. It is not enough to decide that the topic 'Environmental pollution' is to be explained. It should be further decided whether explanation is to be provided for 'What is environmental pollution?' or 'Why environmental pollution occurs?' or 'How environmental pollution is caused?' or ' What are the effects of environmental pollution?' and the explanation is to be designed accordingly.

Step 2. **Finding the hidden variables:** The key words are to be underlined in the questions and relations between them are to be set out. If this cannot be done, the answers to the questions cannot be given. Often the relationship is not direct, but contains hidden variables. For e.g., the question why environmental pollution occurs will lead to further questions like what are environment and pollution, what are the materials that cause pollution, where from these materials come, what is the measure of the pollution and so on.

Step 3. **Stating the key points:** Once the hidden variables are identified, the key points should be selected and stated. It is preferable to write the key points in question form. Each major section of explanation should yield a key point and the summary at the end should contain all of them.

Step 4. **Designing the keys:**

(a) Statement of key points: The key points are stated in a simple statements using minimum of technical terms and avoiding unnecessary complex sentences. Some suggested useful openings to the first key may be 'Put simply….', 'Put very briefly…….,' 'The essential point is….'or like that,. Useful openings to the subsequent keys may be 'Now the next point is…', 'Let's look at the second feature……' etc.

(b) Choice of examples or illustrations: One or two appropriate examples or illustrations are chosen to clarify the keys. These should be brief and unambiguous and relevant to the key being discussed.

During presentation of explanation of the rules or principles the steps (a) and (b) may be interchanged according to the strategy adopted. In the 'expository' strategy the order noted is followed which is called 'rule-e.g.' method. In the 'exploratory strategy' the reverse order i.e., 'e.g.-rule' method is followed.

(c) Giving major qualifications of key points: The major qualifications or elaborations including the exceptions or limitations of the key points should be stated. It is suggested that non-examples should also be cited to encourage the students in discrimination learning.

(d) Restatement or extension of key principle: It is recommended, if possible, to restate or extend the key point in different words. This increases the probability of clearly understanding the explanation.

Step 5. **Summarising the main points:** The main points are brought together to reach a conclusion, which should provide answers to the question formulated in step 1, i.e., identification of purpose. Summaries are crucial for effective explanation.

Step 6 **Designing the set induction:** The objective is to design a lead in orientation to direct the attention of the explainees to what is to be explained. This is important since unless the attention of the explainees can be gained and held during explanation they may not listen to or understand the explanation.

Step 7. **Writing the design:** This is very useful for the new teachers in particular and also for experienced teachers for planning the sequence and allocation of time. Only the main points and the links are to be noted and it should be checked that the question intended to be explained is effectively explained.

Characteristics of Effective Explanation

The effectiveness of explanation is that the explainees understand it. They should be well-structured and they should generate interest among the listeners. Brevity in an explanation and is important so that the listeners can easily recall and understand it, but it should cover the essential features of the point being explained. Each key point should be dealt preferably for not more than 10 minutes beyond which the interest of the listeners may not be sustained. Often the listeners' non-verbal cues provide a clear signal of their interest or boredom and skill in interpreting these will be dealt with in *'recognising attending behaviour'* later on.

However, a well-designed explanation will not be effective if the explainer is unable to convey his/her interest, enthusiasms and confidence in the topic being explained during presentation . The skills of 'stimulus variation', 'silence and non-verbal cue', to be discussed later on, have to be integrated to make the presentation interesting. The capability of understanding maturity of the group of explainees, particularly with respect to the age and level should be taken into consideration while designing explanation. The explanation of the same topic, which is effective for the final semester students will not be so if presented to the first semester students.

Tips for an Effective Explanation

Actions to be taken	*Actions to be avoided*
1. Pause, look around the group and wait until they are ready	1. Starting when only one or two are listening
2. Make the opening remarks in a friendly way	
3. Look at members of the group and watch their reactions	2. Staring hard at the ceiling and floor
4. Use some gestures to emphasise points	3. Semaphore
If you want to, move about a little	4. Marathon walk
5. When you use visual aids like blackboard, slides or projected transparencies make sure they can be seen by the listeners	5. Showing your back to the explainees, even if it's your best feature
6. Use connecting links	6. Confusing asides and irrelevancies
7. Keep the keys and examples brief and interesting	7. Excessive qualifications, highly technical words and complex sentences
8. Pause before making an important point or asking a question and look at the listeners	8. Dropping your voice and looking at your toes while saying something important
9. Try to vary the pace of delivery	9. Uniformly slow or high speed delivery

Closure

Closure may be defined as directing attention to the completion of a specific task or learning sequence. It refers to those actions or statements by teachers designed to bring a lesson presentation to an appropriate conclusion. Teachers use closure to help students bring things together in their own minds, to make sense out of what has been going on in the class during the presentation made by the teacher.

Closure may be considered to be complementary to the set induction. While set induction is an initiating activity of the teacher, the closure is the culminating activity. Research in the 'psychology of learning' indicates that learning is more effective when teachers make a conscious effort to help students organise the information presented to them and to perceive relationships based on those information which may be explored in some part of the book.

There are two important types of closure: *cognitive and social.* Cognitive closure aims to consolidate what the students have learnt by focusing their attention on the major points covered in the lesson or lesson segment. Social closure is concerned with giving the students a sense of achievement such that they are encouraged to continue striving for learning. Usually social closure is used only at the end of a lesson or at the end of a particular difficult learning sequence. The techniques of social closure, which mainly consist of praising and encouraging students, will be discussed along with the skill of reinforcement later on. The focus of this section is on the cognitive closure.

Purposes

The basic purpose of closure is ***to draw attention to the end of a lesson or lesson segment.*** The unstructured forms of closure ignore the fact that effective learning depends on proper sequencing of lesson presentations and effective sequencing provides the opportunity for feedback and review. The teacher who uses closure effectively understands the importance of cuing students to the fact that they have reached an important point in the presentation and it is the time to wrap it up. This activity must be planned as carefully as set induction and the timing is critical. The teacher must be aware of the clock and should initiate closure well before the particular activity is due to end.

The second major purpose of closure is *to help organise the student learning*. Simply calling attention to the conclusion of the lesson is not sufficient, as a large amount of information and activity may have been covered. It is the responsibility of the teacher to tie these all together into a meaningful whole. The learner should not be left with a feeling of incompleteness and frustration. A skillful closure will recapitulate the various bits of information and place them in a coherent picture for the learner.

Finally, closure has its third purpose as *to consolidate or reinforce the major points to be learn.* The teacher should briefly refocus on the key ideas or processes presented in the lesson, after having signaled the end of the lesson. The objective is to help the students retain the important information presented in the lesson and to increase the probability of increasing their ability to recall and use the information later on.

Usage

The closure should be used in following situations:

- To end a long unit of work in the class
- To close a discussion, question and answer session
- To end a skill building activity, laboratory exercise
- To reinforce presentation of a guest speaker, usually done while proposing in formal vote of thanks
- To consolidate learning experiences after a field visit
- To organise thinking around a new concept/principle.

Techniques of Closure

A list of specific techniques of closure used by experienced teachers in different teaching situations are given below:

- Attempts to draw students' attention to a closing point in the lesson
- Reviewing major points of teacher-centered presentation
- Reviewing sequences used in learning materials during presentation
- Relating lesson to original organising principle or concept
- Providing summary of important student-oriented discussion
- Attempting to lead students to extend or develop new knowledge from previously learned concept as a link to future lessons
- Allowing students to practise what they have learned.

Thus, closure is the skill of reviewing the key points of a lesson, tying them together into a coherent whole and finally ensuring their use by anchoring them in the students' larger conceptual network. The role of the teacher in using closure is to structure each situation such that it ends in a way to promote student learning. *A useful tip for using closure in chalk and board method of lecturing is to keep a portion of the board earmarked in which the list of key points be written during the discussion.* However, due to inadequate planning of lesson by the teachers, the most common form of closure is the ringing of the bell or the presence of the teacher for the next lesson at the classroom door announcing the end of the lesson.

A teacher usually demonstrates sequentially the above mentioned three skills during his/her presentation. The other skills, which would be discussed in subsequent sections have to be integrated with those skills as applicable and are usually overlapping.

Questioning Skill

The skills of questioning are as old as teaching itself. Socrates in the 5th Century B.C. used questioning as the basis of his teaching method and almost every teacher in every classroom uses them extensively. The educators have recognised for a long time the crucial role of questions in the learning process. It may be defined as any statement that tests or creates knowledge in the learner. Questions, which test knowledge, may be described as *lower order cognitive questions.* For example, What is the definition of stress? There is usually correct single answer to this type of questions. The questions which, create new knowledge in the learner may be referred as *higher order cognitive questions*. This type of questions stimulates the thinking in students to apply the already learned knowledge to develop new knowledge. Research evidence suggests that when thought provoking, higher order questions are asked in the class, performance of students in achievement test improves. However, it has been observed that most of the questions asked by teachers in classroom belong to lower order category involving simple recall of previous knowledge from memory. Thus, there is a need for teachers to be trained in using effective questioning technique particularly for stimulating thinking among the students.

Purposes

A teacher may use the questioning technique in a classroom with various purposes. Some such are:

- To encourage students to talk
- To signal an interest in listening about students' thinking and feeling
- To stimulate interest among students
- To encourage problem solving approach
- To help student externalise and verbalise knowledge
- To encourage 'Thinking Aloud'
- To help student mutual learning
- To monitor students' learning.

The first step in effective questioning is to recognise that questions have distinct characteristics, serve various functions and stimulate different levels of thinking. Many experts in the field have made various categorisation of questions, which is beyond the scope of the present section of this book. A general classification useful for developing the questioning skill is briefly discussed below.

Categories of Teacher Questions

Type	*Order*	*Sl. No.*	*Category*	*Purpose*
		1.	Compliance	The student is expected to comply with a command worded as a question
		2.	Rhetoric	The student is not expected to answer. Teacher answers his/her own question
		3.	Recall	Can the student recall from memory what he has seen or heard?
CLOSED	LOWER	4.	Comprehension	Does the student understand what he/she recalls?
		5.	Application	Can the student apply rules and techniques learn to solve problems that have unique correct answers?
		6.	Analysis	Can the student identify intentions and causes, make interferences and give examples to support his/her statements?
OPEN	HIGHER	7.	Synthesis	Can the student make predictions, solve problems or make designs?
		8.	Evaluation	Can the student judge the quality of ideas, products, problem solutions or designs?

Sl.1 and 2 (i.e., *Compliance* and *Rhetoric* respective questions do not belong to either lower or higher order questions though used frequently by the teachers. *Compliance* questions are mostly related to the class control, e.g., a teacher says to a student 'Will you please stop talking?'. The student concerned is not expected to give any reply but he/she is directed to be silent. *Rhetoric* questions are stated by the teacher as a link during the course of presentation, e.g. a teacher states 'Now what are the main sources of water pollution?' and then starts to elaborate the list of sources. The students are not expected to give any answer and the teacher himself/herself gives answer to the question posed.

Techniques of Effective Questioning

It is not enough to only select the appropriate level of question. A teacher must know how to communicate the question effectively to the group of students. Ultimately, the questions are only as good as the answers that they evoke. This section deals with various elements of questioning technique.

Clarity and Coherence: The questions should be clear and coherent to convey an unambiguous meaning to the listener. This is particularly important for higher order questions and can be achieved only through proper planning. It is recommended that such questions be written earlier and scrutinised by the teacher, particularly those who are new to teaching. A question which appears to be clear and coherent to the teacher, who is aware the answer(s), may not be so to the students, who do not possess the knowledge and skill at the same level as the teacher. Hence, scrutiny should be made from the aspect of expected level of knowledge possessed by the students.

Distributing and Directing: Teachers usually ask questions to the handful recognised bright students who are expected to give reasonably correct answers and in the process, rest of the students are discriminated against. Thus, a teacher through this practice creates one minor group consisting of few active learners and another major group consisting of most of the students as passive learners. This passivity may change to boredom leading to deviant behaviour resulting in classroom management problems. Asking the question to the whole class, without specifying any particular student, can minimise these problems, which is called *distributing*. This may result in two alternative situations—some students may simultaneously try to give the answer or no one attempts to answer. A teacher should monitor the students, in the latter case, to identify from the body language of the students those who appear to be willing to answer. In the former case, teacher should set the rule, at the first instance, of indicating willingness to answer like raising of hand by such students and wait for further direction of the teacher.

The teacher then should direct the question to a particular student, preferably by naming him/her. If the first student directed is unable to give the answer, the teacher needs to direct the question to another student. The teacher should take care while directing that most of the students in a class get the opportunity to answer the questions.

Skilful distributing and directing questions involves students more closely and they are more likely to participate and enjoy discussion. Directing questions in non-threatening way will draw out the students who are shy or reluctant to participate in discussion. The efforts of the students who are unable to give proper answer should be acknowledged with proper reinforcement so that they are not discouraged to take part in further discussion.

Pausing and Pacing: Research study has shown that although teachers ask a large number of questions during a lesson, they generally show little tolerance in waiting (pause) for student replies. Research evidence also has shown that quality and quantity of student responses increase when teachers increase the silence time, after asking a question, from usual 1 second to 3 seconds or more to provide students more time to think. Longer 'wait time' is needed when higher order questions are asked. The length of pause also signals to the students about the extent of thinking required for answering a question. A short pause indicates that the teacher wants a prompt answer that does not involve much thinking. A long pause over 3 seconds indicates that the teacher wants the students to think deeply before answering the question. During the pause, a teacher should look for non-verbal signals from the students about their readiness to answer the questions. The failure of teachers to obtain answers to the questions asked, particularly by budding teachers, is due to lack of pauses and also due to lack of variation in their delivery of asking questions (pacing).

The pacing of questions or the speed of delivery of questions is determined partly by the nature of the question being asked. Lower order questions, particularly recall type questions, can be asked at quick pace. If more complex questions are asked at quick pace, the students become confused and are likely to remain silent and bewildered.

Prompting and Cuing: Prompting consists of helping the students to provide the correct answer. A series of prompts, followed by encouragement, help students to gain confidence in giving replies. This is done by building up on the partial answer given by a student leading towards the correct answer. For instance, a teacher may say, 'well probably you were meaning to say this (orienting the answer to the proper direction), now can you further elaborate on this.'

Cuing consists of giving hints by the teacher to help the students to find the answer. In a lesson, teacher may ask 'Can you tell the effect of force on a body?' If no response is obtained, he may demonstrate by pushing the duster on the table with finger and ask what has happened to the duster when pushed. The usual response will be it moves and gradually with further cues the correct response that the position of a body is changed under the effect of force will be reached. Cues provided should be relevant to the question and designed such that these lead the students towards the correct answer.

Probing—This consists of asking such questions as to direct the student to think more deeply about his/her initial response and to express himself/herself more clearly. They sustain thinking of the students to probe the unknown and enable the students to develop their critical thinking and communication skills. Probing may be done in various ways like asking the student to clarify his/her answer, to give evidences to support or to prove the accuracy of his/her response, to provide examples, or to involve the rest of the class to seek a degree of consensus about the response given by a student.

The skill of probing helps teachers to stimulate students to think more deeply and widely, often about the issues raised by them. Practicing this over a long period with a class will improve the students' willingness to talk, their formulation of responses and group thinking skill. The students will eventually start probing their own thought without the stimulus from teacher, which is the key to acquiring the 'learning-to-learn' skill.

Accepting Response to Questions

Continuation of the participation of students in classroom discussion depends on the manner in which the teacher accepts or rejects the responses given by the students. The principles of reinforcement skill based on praise and recognition should be integrated in the response of the teacher to the students' responses. Special care should be taken while rejecting a response to ensure that the respondent is not discouraged from giving responses on future occasions.

This possess two aspects. One is the cognitive processing of the response and response guidance, which may take the following forms:

- **Repeating the answer given by a student, for thinking and consideration by other student.**
- Modifying/rewording the responses for better precision.
- Generalising from a specific response given.
- Inferring with the help of the respondent toward the desired response.

The other aspect is to accept individual feelings and provide conditional reinforcement as follows:

- Good/correct/not exactly/thank you for the idea; let us examine the idea further.
- Good answer, it is useful in the following ways, e.g.
- Right. This is an important aspect. Let's see what others can add to it.

- Perhaps my question was not clear. Let me put it this way.
- It was intelligent thinking on your part, but can you redirect it to the proper direction?
- Good attempt. I am sure you will be able to reach the correct answer if you think further in this line.

Stimulus Variation

Boredom is a major problem in usual classroom as students sit for long hours listening and watching presentation made by the teacher. The inappropriate instructional styles of many teachers enhance the feeling of boredom of the students. One effective way to help the teacher to relieve boredom of students is to use more stimulating instructional materials and to use instructional methods based on discovery learning approach. Another way is for the teacher to change his/her behaviour patterns, stressing behaviours that he/she can perform to add more variety to his/her teaching style. This skill is arbitrarily named as 'stimulus variation' or 'teacher liveliness'.

Its purpose is to alleviate sense of boredom and monotony of students in the classroom that may lead to inattentiveness. These are achieved through various verbal and non-verbal activities performed by the teacher, as listed below.

Teacher Movement: The goal of movement training is to break the teachers' habit of delivering lecture from one spot and to encourage him/her to move freely about the classroom. The movements by the teacher compel students to make sensory adjustments so that their attention is likely to be gained. However, movements with a high frequency would lead to distraction of students.

Teacher Gesture: Gestures with hands, body and face convey meanings and are helpful in communication. The goal of gesture training is to get the teacher to be more expressive and dynamic in his/her presentations. The teacher consciously attempts to extend the range and frequency of his/her gestures, enhancing his/her oral communications with these cues. Gestures with hands may be very effectively used to indicate the size, shape, direction of movement of things etc. It should be kept in mind that too frequent gestures of any one limb would cause distraction.

Focusing: Frequently, during a lesson, occasions arise when a teacher wants to draw attention of the students to a particular point. This act of calling attention to any specific material is termed as 'focusing'. Verbal focusing is demonstrated by such statements as 'Pay special attention to this!', 'Look at the diagram in the handout!', 'Listen carefully to this!' etc. An example of focusing with gesture is the teacher pointing to a specific object or banging on the blackboard for emphasis.

Interaction style: Teacher monologues are frequently the cause of boredom and loss of attention of the students in a classroom. The purpose of the interaction training is to get the teacher to use a variety of interaction patterns. In fact, excessive use of any single interaction style can become routine and dull. A teacher in a classroom can commonly use three patterns of interaction styles.

A. *Teacher-Group:* The teacher carries on the dialogue with the entire class. When he/she asks questions, he/she asks them to the whole class group not to any specific individual. This type of interaction usually prevails for most of the duration of a class.

B. *Teacher-Student:* The teacher directs a statement or question to an individual student and engages in dialogue with him/her. Asking an individual student a question, receiving the answer and following it up with a series of questions to the same student trying to get the student to probe the issue more deeply may achieve this interaction style.

C. *Student-Student:* The teacher, after asking a question, refrains from commenting on the response by the student and seeks views of another student on the response for comment or clarification. Often the teacher is able to involve many students in dialogue between them while limiting his/her role to only directing the discussion. Once started, the interaction is primarily among the students. This style of interaction is very difficult to achieve within the limitations of a class hour. Further, if this is not planned and controlled properly it would result in chaos in the classroom. This style gives the students the sense of participation and achievement and is very effective for learning, particularly with adult learners, expecially at university departments.

***Eye Contact and Movement*:** Eye movements and contact are the key ways of conveying feelings and of controlling interaction. If the teacher has a fixed eye contact with a student while talking, it becomes difficult for the student to have his/her attention distracted. However, continuing the fixed eye contact with a particular student for long duration will cause a feeling of uneasiness in the student. As such, the eye movement is necessary to distribute the eye contact among all the students.

Furthermore, various feelings may be expressed through the eyes such as wide opening of eyes conveys interest, very wide opening of eyes expresses surprise or alarm, narrow eyes with closely knit eyebrows accompanied by frown conveys feeling of displeasure or annoyance etc.

Teachers should use the eye movements and contact to forcefully convey the meanings of their statements. However, it is not expected from a teacher to use the eyes as done by a *Bharatnatyam* or *Kathakali* dancer.

Teacher's Voice—This is probably the most essential requirement of a teacher. An attractive voice automatically draws attention of the listeners. The voice of a teacher should be loud and clear enough to be audible from all corners of a classroom. Teacher should try variation in quality of voice by changing the tone, pitch and modulation. A teacher should talk in a measured pace to make his/her voice clear. Too fast pace will make the statements unclear, while a too slow pace will make the listeners' attention to wander. Variation in the pace of talking leads to renewal of attention of the listeners. A teacher should use his/her voice to effectively convey his/her feelings of enthusiasm and interest on the topic being discussed.

Pausing—Actors and public speakers know well the value of a pregnant pause in riveting attention of the audience on them. A short pause before saying something important is an effective way of holding the attention of the listeners. A sudden pause for up to three seconds in the middle of a sentence gains attention, while a pause extended to twenty seconds can be distracting for the listeners. New teachers tend to be afraid of pauses and rush to fill them with extra questions and statements. During a lesson, a well-inserted pause can accomplish several effects - it can prepare students for an important statement or question, signal the transition from one idea to another or stop the present action to rally the students' attention to the teacher.

Shifting Sensory Channels—Training in shifting sensory channels aims at heightening the attention by systematic changing of the students' receptors. Put simply, it aims to get the teacher to switch the primary mode of communication, whether oral or visual, so that the student is forced to change their sensory receptors. For instance, when the teacher switches from oral to visual instruction, the students have to switch their primary receptor to eye from ear and thus their attention would be sharpened.

For example, a teacher, during a cognitive closure, may say 'Here are the main points of discussion till now' and draws attention of the students to writings on the blackboard or projected overhead transparency or a chart and remains silent, while the students are compelled to read the display.

Teacher may also switch between media in the same sensory channel e.g., from black board to projected transparency or slide, or from oral commentary to tape recording, etc. Number of research in Indian setting proved that Periodical shifting of sensory channels draws the attention of the students away from the teacher and when the teacher returns to the scene, his/her words and gestures are likely to be attended more closely by the students. Training in stimulus variation strengthens the ability of a teacher to attract and hold the attention of the students.

Reinforcement Skill

'Reinforcement' is the technical term used to describe any technique, which modifies or changes behaviour. Reinforcement may be positive (rewarding) or negative (punishing). The reinforcement may give the recipient feedback information about his/her actions and thus acts as a means to correct his/her behaviour. This section is concerned with positive reinforcement only through praise/recognition and corrective feedback. The educational psychologists developed the technique of changing behaviour through experimental observation and the educationists have recognised its importance in learning process. Good teachers know that encouraging the students through praise and rewards can enhance their involvement in the learning process. However, teachers frequently fail to develop their potential as 'reinforcing agents' or they get into the habit of encouraging only those students who are already doing well. The experimental evidences indicate that various aspects of praise and corrective feedback are positively correlated with students' achievements and positive attitudes.

Teachers may use three modes to provide reinforcement in classroom situation - verbal, extra-verbal and non-verbal. Examples of the verbal praise may be such comments by the teacher as 'Excellent!', 'That's splendid!', 'Very good!' etc. It may be extra-verbal with sounds such as 'Mmmmm' or Aaaah' etc., or non-verbal such as a smile, nod of the head or friendly eye contact by the teacher. Writing the response of the student on the black/green board is an effective way of rewarding the student. Usually a teacher while praising uses a mixture of these methods. The expression of praise should be such as to convey the feeling to the student that he/she has done something really worth to be praised and the teacher has to use his/her voice and gestures to express this. The practice of mechanically praising by bland expressions of 'OK or 'Good' to the students' responses, without discriminating between the quality of responses, should be avoided. Too frequent praise again results in loss of its rewarding property.

Corrective feedbacks act as reinforcement to continuation of students' participation in discussion during teacher-student or student-student interaction. This is essential to encourage the students to probe further when exact answer could not be arrived at. This may also be provided in three modes: verbal, extra-verbal and non-verbal.

Verbal feedback consists of prompts, probes and giving directions. Some examples of such feedback are:

'That's a good start, can you say a bit more about it?'
'It seems you are almost near the correct answer, can you try further?'
'Excellent, can you give an example to clarify what you have said?'
'You were probably meaning to say this' etc.

Extra-verbal feedback may be '*Mmm*' '*Aaaah*', '*acchya*', '*baria*' etc. These may be coupled with non-verbal feedbacks such as puzzled frown, raising of eyebrows, frowning, nodding of head in agreement, looking at a student in a thinking posture etc.

Lack of systematic use of reinforcement is an important reason for wide scale passivity among students in a classroom.

'Using students' ideas' is a special form of reinforcement, which is very helpful to encourage students to participate in classroom interaction. The ideas may be simply acknowledged, may be accepted with enthusiasm or restated (towards closure) or may be used as a springboard for development of further discussion.

Skillful use of reinforcement skills by successful teachers conveys the feeling of warmth and friendliness from the teacher. Such relation overcomes the barrier of fear or shyness on the part of students to make them feel free to participate in classroom interactions leading to meaningful learning by students.

Recognising and Attending Student Behaviours

This is an important survival skill of a teacher in the classroom. Students continuously provide feedback, through non-verbal behaviours, about the quality of a lecture or presentation by a teacher. Monitoring these feedbacks by the teacher is an important element in effective class control. A teacher should be skilled in attending to these behaviours and adopt suitable strategies like switching activities, take a break or change the topic of discussion etc. A checklist is suggested below for monitoring students' behaviours—

1. ***Posture***—Are the students turned *away from* or *towards the* object of the lesson?
2. ***Head orientation***—Are the students looking *at* or *away from* the object of the lesson? Are their heads *up* or *down*?
3. ***Face***—Do the students look *sleepy* or *awake*? Do they look *withdrawn* or *involved*? Do they look *interested* or *uninterested*?
4. ***Activities***—Are the students working on something related to the class? Are they furtively communicating with each other?

Silence and Non-Verbal Cue

A common criticism of classroom teaching is that the discussion is mostly teacher-centered i.e., teachers talk too much. To decrease the amount of unnecessary talking and to increase students' participation, the teachers can be trained to use silence and non-verbal cues. The goal of such training is to keep the teacher from continually interjecting himself/herself in the classroom while enabling him/her to keep the discussion moving. A related goal is to give students the opportunity to think about the teacher's or other students' statements.

A skilled teacher can use silence to control the behaviour of the students effectively.

Silence after an introductory statement stimulates students to think about what the teacher has just said.

Silence indicates that the statement is important.

Silence after a question from a student indicates that the teacher is considering the question.

Silence after a student response will encourage the student to continue talking.

Students are frequently satisfied with single statement answers. The teacher fosters an elaborated and extended answer through the use of silence.

However, silence alone is not enough to effectively control student's participation as it conveys ambiguous signals to the students. The students cannot infer from the mere silence whether the teacher is indicating acceptance, rejection or thoughtful consideration. Hence, silence is most effective when accompanied by non-verbal cues indicating pleasure, displeasure, acceptance, rejection, questioning or direction.

Non-verbal cues give students feedback about their responses without the teacher having to make comments about each response and keep the discussion moving. The teachers commonly use four broad categories of non-verbal cues in a classroom.

1. Facial—a smile, frown, a serious or quizzical look etc.
2. Body Movement—moving towards the responding student or adopting some type of thinker pose etc.
3. Head Movement—yes or no nods, shaking of the head, tilting head and ear toward the student etc.
4. Gestures—made with hands such as pointing to a student, motioning to continue or to stop, pointing from student to student etc.

The non-verbal cues should not be considered separate, discrete actions, but rather parts of a combined behaviour pattern to increase the student participation.

Teaching Skills and Learning Phases

The basic aim of teaching is to enable the students to learn. Hence, any teaching skill should be related to students' learning. Various experts have propounded different theories of learning, which is beyond the scope of discussion of this volume. This section will discuss briefly the different learning phases and their relationship with the different components of the skill to indicate the contribution of these skills towards learning.

The complex process of learning can be broken into eight phases viz.—

1. motivation phase,
2. apprehending phase,
3. acquisition phase,
4. retention phase,
5. recall phase,
6. generalisation phase,
7. performance phase, and
8. feedback phase.

Although the act of learning is continuous and seamless, an analysis of this nature enables us to identify and examine the characteristics of each phase and decide on classroom activities for enhancing the learning process. The relationship between the learning phases, the internal process, instructional events and the required skills are illustrated below.

Sl. No.	*Learning phase*	*Process*	*Instructional events*	*Major Skill Component*
1	Motivation	Expectancy	Arousing interest; stating the learning objectives; creating rewarding learning situations	Set Induction
2	Apprehending	Attention, Perception, Understanding	Exposition; directing attention to significant features; explaining	Explaining
3	Acquisition	Coding, Storage entry	Suggesting means of coding	
4	Retention	Storage	Not specific	
5	Recall	Retrieval	Stimulating recall; suggesting schemes and cues for recall; providing learning guidance	Questioning
6	Generalisation	Transfer	Promoting transfer by providing variety of contexts for retrieval cuing	
7	Performance	Responding	Instances of performance	
8	Feedback	Reinforcement	Information feedback; link to new information to be supplied in future	Closure

In nut-shell, it may be said that Various components of teaching skills have been discussed in this section. The task of a teacher in respect of acquiring the various skill components is comparatively more difficult than that of a sportsperson or an actor. The latter can develop some of the desired skill components to become a good sportsman like a good batsman/a good bowler or an actor fitting a particular role like romantic or tragic. But a teacher is expected to demonstrate all the components of skill to become an effective teacher. A teacher through experience over the years and depending on classroom situation and environment decide on the skills to be demonstrated frequently and develop the individual style of teaching. A word of caution for new teachers is *that teaching techniques cannot be prescribed*, as it would vary depending on the characteristics of students, subject and the topic to be discussed and the teacher. It should be kept in mind that whatever has been discussed in this unit is only to provide a guideline to help the teachers in finding the answer to the question " how to teach?" Finally keep in mind that the classroom-platform is not a stage and the teacher is not mere an actor, rather, a teacher.

ACTIVITIES

Activity-A

Prepare the list of the usual activities performed by a teacher during a classroom lecture.

Activity-B

Relate the activities and the attributes identified in activities A with the components of teaching skill.

Activity-C

Identify what the underlying purpose would be for each of the following ideas, procedures or processes that require an explanation. The four underlying purposes are

(A) To show a direct cause and effect relationship.
(B) To show that a particular action is governed by a general rule of law.
(C) To illustrate a procedure or a process.
(D) To show the intent of an action or a process.

Please write A, B, C or D, whichever is applicable within the ( ) sign on the left of the ideas/procedures/processes given below:

( ) 1. Internal Combustion.
( ) 2. The purpose of incineration of hospital wastes.
( ) 3. The effects of stress on teacher's job satisfaction.
( ) 4. The use of question mark in English language.
( ) 5. Firing of clay pottery.
( ) 6. The ill effects of an improper diet.
( ) 7. Writing algorithm for a computer programme.
( ) 8. The use of traffic sign/symbol.

Activity-D

I. Examples that require explanations where underlying purpose is to show a cause-effect relationship:
(a) The effect of heat in changing a liquid to gas.
(b) The result of inaccurate measurement in scoring answer booklet.
(c) The effect of unclear communication.
(d) The effect of pollutants in air.

Write 3 examples from the subject you teach that require an explanation, where underlying purpose is to show a direct cause-effect relationship.

II. Examples that require explanations where underlying purpose is to show that a particular action is governed by a general rule or law:
(a) The reason for sterilising procedures in a hospital operating room.
(b) The need for a particular type of clothing in varied weather condition.
(c) The need for protective tests when using personality tests.

Write three examples from the subject you teach that require an explanation where underlying purpose is to show that a particular action is governed by a general rule or law.

III. Examples that require explanations where underlying purpose is to illustrate a procedure or a process:
(a) Sampling for conducting a cross-sectional Research.
(b) Preparation of a standardized achievement test.
(c) Making entries of transactions in a book of accounts.

Write three examples from the subject you teach that require an explanations where underlying purpose is to illustrate a procedure or a process

IV. Examples that require explanations where underlying purpose is to show the intent of an action or process:
(a) The motivation for a character's behaviour in a story.
(b) Why we fire pottery.
(c) The use of a particular procedure in employee recruitment.
(d) The function of sand in stowing of underground mines.

Write 3 examples from the subject you teach that require an explanation where underlying purpose is to show the intent of an action or a process.

Activity-E

Please respond by indicating 'T' next to the true statement and by indicating

'F' next to the false statement, from among the statements given below:

1. Closure, as a lesson presentation skill is a natural complement to set induction. ☐
2. Closure is less important than set induction because students can tell by their watch when the class period ends. ☐
3. Closure helps students to know when they have achieved lesson objectives. ☐
4. One of the purposes of closure is to draw attention to the end of presentation. ☐
5. Closure gives the opportunity to students to review what they are supposed to have learned. ☐
6. One of the purposes of closure is to help organise students' learning. ☐
7. Closure helps to get your lesson off in right note. ☐
8. One of the purposes of closure is to consolidate or reinforce the major points to be learned in a presentation. ☐

13
Development of Teaching Skill

Strategies for Development of Teaching Skills

The process of acquisition of any complex skill may be divided in three stages—Cognitive Understanding, Practice and Knowledge of Result (KOR). The learner first forms a cognitive map of skills to be learnt and gains knowledge about the purpose of the skills and how it will benefit him. This phase helps the learner to isolate various elements of the skills, their sequencing and nature of final performance. Practice is an essential phase in learning a skill and skill cannot be acquired unless it is practiced. But practice alone will not enable a learner to demonstrate the skill perfectly unless s/he receives feedback about the level of perfection demonstrated through s/he performance. In fact, any effective skill training programme will involve a repetitive continuous cycle of the second and third phases simultaneously till the desired level of perfection is achieved.

The traditional method of teacher training, called 'School Practice', better to say, practice teaching, consisted of the 'sitting with Nellie approach', whereby trainee teachers were sent to the institutions to observe teachers in the classroom, with the implications being that the trainee should 'model the master teacher' and was called the 'school practice'. The modified approach to this or 'apprenticeship approach' is still adopted in many institutions, particularly in higher education system. A newly recruited teacher is attached with an experienced teacher as his/her mentor and the trainee teacher accompanies the experienced teacher into the classroom to observe the experienced teacher and also help him/her in various classroom activities.

The major problem with both the approaches is that these assume that teachers encountered by the teacher trainees would be highly competent which are not true on many occasions. The technique of modeling a 'master teacher' would be acceptable if all teachers always display ideal teaching behaviours and are widely experienced. But the number of highly competent teachers is insufficient to cope with the demands of the teacher training institutions. Further, difficulties are increased, as the teacher trainees are often not trained in methods of observation prior to being sent to the classroom. The difficulty in adoption of these approaches is further complicated by the fact that the institutions may not be in a position to spare the new recruits to act as apprentice teachers for a period lasting over at least one semester. Thus the technique of modeling was not found to be satisfactory approach for teacher training.

As a result of recognition of many complexities involved in classroom teaching, the teacher educators of one of the prominent university, i.e. Stanford University concluded that any attempt to train a teacher should take place in a simplified situation. The group then turned its attention to other professions and analysis of the training methods used indicated that in many cases complicated skills were taught by being 'broken down' into simpler skill areas. It was also found that such training often occurred in a simulated situation rather than in the real situation. Actors have always had their rehearsals, prior to the presentation of a play, when various scenes are practiced in isolation until adjudged to be satisfactory. Similarly, athletes and other sports players have always attempted to identify the crucial areas, which affect performance and then practice these areas separately before 'putting them all together' when it matters most. The Stanford team, therefore, devised a programme of training, which composed of teaching a number of teaching skills in a scaled down encounter termed 'microteaching'. In the initial phase of development, a simulated traumatic environmental condition of a classroom situation was used for practice teaching by trainees involving four student volunteers each assigned to play a typical pre-situation. One was called 'Eager', who responded positively and vigorously irrespective of the teaching performance. One was called 'Slow Poke', who never did quite catch on. Another was 'Know-It-All', who anticipated the teacher's strategies and examples and from time to time offered alternative approaches to the instructional procedures. Finally, there was 'Couldn't Care Less', who engaged in various destructive manoeuvres, from talking to noise making and so. The result was disastrous as the teacher trainees failed miserably as revealed by the four students during feedback discussion of their performance on the next day. The technique was abandoned as both trainees and supervisors felt that this did not contribute towards development of teaching skills.

Consequently, formal technique of *microteaching* was developed wherein trainees practiced before students who displayed natural behaviours. The next unit discusses details of this technique.

A Model for Teacher Training

The business of learning to teach is more complex than that of teaching. A teacher trainee has twofold intentions- that his/her students learn while s/he learns to teach. S/he has to develop the Learning skill, to use and extend

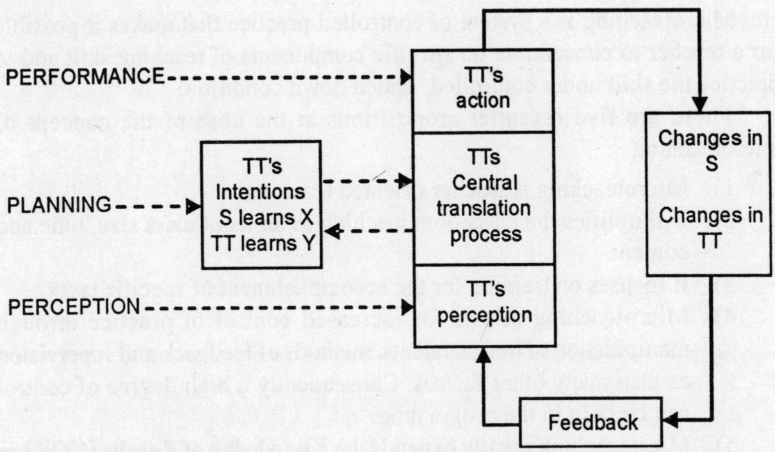

his/her teaching repertoire, to monitor changes in his/her students and modify his/her behaviour accordingly. The simplified model of teacher training developed on the basis of social skill model of teaching is shown below.

In the above model, the following abbreviations have been used.

T T = Teacher Trainee S = Student

X = Material to be learnt Y = Skills that Teacher Trainee wants to learn.

Three constituents of a teacher training programme can be extracted from this model—PLANNING, PERFORMANCE and PERCEPTION. The microteaching format satisfies the requirements of teacher training model. Rules of planning are given in lectures preceding practice and teacher trainees have to plan the micro lesson. Performance is split into its component of teaching skill and are demonstrated, opportunities for practice are given in controlled conditions. Feedback in the form of video recordings is given and trainees are taught what cues to look for in their interaction with students. The system is augmented by use of systematic observation schedules, which focus the attention of the trainee and supervisor upon the skill under review. As such, it is expected that the microteaching is more efficient than other methods of acquiring teaching skills and experimental evidences support this contention.

Concepts of Microteaching

Microteaching may be defined as 'a *simulated* classroom situation for *practice* by a teacher with different components of *teaching skill*, wherein s/he *obtains feedback* about his/her performance'. It is a scaled down teaching encounter designed to develop in a teacher new skills and refine old skills. It is somewhat analogous to the net practice adopted in the game of cricket where cricketers practice different components of cricketing skill like batting, bowling, fielding etc. Microteaching is a system of controlled practice that makes it possible for a teacher to concentrate on specific components of teaching skill and to practice the skill under controlled, scaled down condition.

There are five essential propositions at the core of the concept of microteaching

1) Microteaching is teacher-oriented teaching.
2) It simplifies the classroom teaching in terms of class size, time and content.
3) It focuses on training for the accomplishment of specific tasks.
4) Microteaching allows for increased control of practice through manipulation of time, students, methods of feedback and supervision as also many other factors. Consequently a high degree of control can be built in the programme.
5) Microteaching greatly expands the Knowledge of Results (KOR) or feedback dimension. Immediately after a microteaching session, the teacher trainee gets feedback about his/her performance and several sources of feedback may be used.

Microteaching greatly reduces the complexities of the teaching situation in terms of (i) number of students to be taught, (ii) duration of the lesson, (iii) subject matter to be taught. This enables the trainee to concentrate on a particular component of teaching skill, before attempting to perform effectively the complicated task of teaching at micro level in classroom situation.

Methods of Microteaching

The complete steps of a microteaching model is diagrammatically shown below.

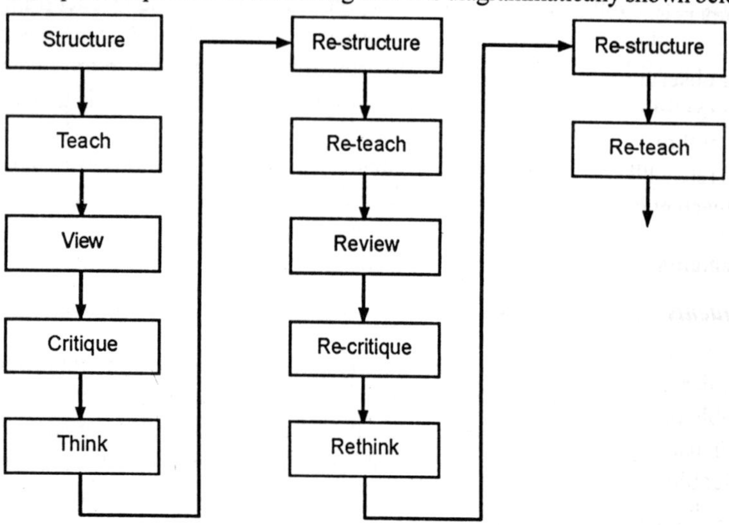

The original microteaching cycle, developed at Stanford University, consisted of the sequence PLAN→TEACH→OBSERVE (Critique)→ REPLAN→RETEACH→REOBSERVE. In this model, in a microteaching session, a teacher trainee taught a small group of students between five and ten for a short period of time (five to ten minutes duration) in presence of tutor/supervisor. During the period, s/he is to focus specifically on one particular skill of teaching. After the micro lesson was completed, the trainee was immediately provided feedback, usually in the form of tutorial guidance and in most cases in the form of a video replay of his/her 'teach' focusing on the particular skill displayed. Each teaching skill was practiced for two teaching sessions. The first practice session was given after the trainee had been informed as to what skill s/he was expected to acquire, was given adequate training in the use of an observation schedule and was shown 'model tapes' of teachers using the skill in a teaching situation. This was referred to as 'teach' of the skill. The trainee was then given the above-mentioned tutorial guidance and video feedback and was given some time (usually a minimum duration of one hour) to consider how s/he might improve the use of the skill. S/he then taught the same micro lesson, incorporating the feasible improvements to a different group of students. Each cycle is devoted to practice of one component skill.

There are now many variations in the original model. The modified model used at the New University of Ulster is PLAN→TEACH→OBSERVE. Emphasis is given to planning and perception as well as performance skill. The programme is carried out in teams of three or four trainees working with a supervisor. This is more economical than the Stanford model. The loss of the immediate reteach is offset by the gain through planning the lessons together and observing each other's teaching. A study in the same university showed that the trainees disliked the reteach sessions. In a National Research Institute, the author used to follow a model, a combination of the approaches is used and reteach cycle was adopted specially for those trainees whose performance in teach cycle is found unsatisfactory.

Elements of Microteaching

Students

Actual school student volunteers, on payment basis, were used as the students in microteaching sessions. However, in Ulster model, due to organisational problems, this was modified and the peer group of student–teachers have been used as students in subsequent models. One study indicated that it was a valuable learning experience for peers, in terms of improving their own teaching performance, to participate as simulated students in microteaching. However in the training programmes offered by the author, the trainee teachers other than the presenter act as simulated students during the presentation by one trainee.

Duration

Another feature of microteaching is the notion of reducing the length of time spent in actual teaching. This helps reduce the complexity and gives the teacher-trainees a greater opportunity to concentrate on the actual skill for which s/he is being trained, without having to worry too much about the subject matter involved. Usually the length of micro lesson in microteaching is between 5 and 10 minutes. The researchers found at Stanford University that 5 minutes was sufficient and that indeed length was not a major factor in skill learning. In many institutions, including University of Ulster, the length of lesson had been increased gradually as the teacher trainee progresses. Through the author's own programmes, microteaching programme with more than one skill integrated for practice. In the original concept of Stanford model of practicing one skill at a time was adopted; however, the supervisors take the opportunity of pointing out the presence or absence of other overlapping skills as these occur during presentation.

Feedback

Feedback tutorial is an important feature on which the effectiveness of the microteaching programme depends. Three variations are possible in relation to this.

1. *Tutorial feedback only*—The teacher trainee receives feedback from an experienced tutor/supervisor but his/her performance is not taped.
2. *Audio-visual feedback only*—The teacher trainee receives feedback in the form of replay of his/her delivery of the lesson performed on a video recorder but does not receive any tutorial suggestions.
3. *Tutorial and Audio-visual feedback*—This is a combination of the previous alternatives. The trainee and tutor/supervisor view a video recording of the trainee's lesson and the tutor/supervisor offers advice and **constructive** criticism.

Feedback may be given in individual tutorials or in group tutorials with a number of peers. The feedback may be given as general comment or in the form of counts or ratings on observation schedule. There is an evidence to suggest that without such additional information the changes in the teaching performance may be minimal.

In a highly organised microteaching framework, where teacher trainees are presented with model tapes linked with theoretical lectures, they can demonstrate a high level of skill competence and the role of the supervisor become supportive rather than instructive. On the other hand, in less well-organised microteaching framework quite often trainees will approach the practice element with a low level of skill competence and, in such cases, the role of the supervisor becomes an instructive one.

In Stanford model, feedback is provided as the audio-visual feedback with video replay of performance and feedback with specific comments by the supervisors along with guided structured feedback from the peer group of teacher trainees. The peer group who acted as simulated students during skill demonstration act as supervisors during feedback session. The performer trainee is also asked to give his/her feedback about his/her performance from the self-perception. This practice helps in developing the skill of receiving and giving feedback among the teacher trainees and also the training for conducting microteaching sessions in their respective institutions.

Advantages and Limitations of Microteaching

The main advantages of microteaching are that this is methodological and logistical.

- Trainees are faced with less complicated learning environment than they encounter in conventional classroom as the lessons are much shorter and students are few in number.
- Most of the variables can be controlled since the learning environment is simplified and a wide variety of teaching environments and purposes can be conveniently generated.
- There is greater opportunity for practice by the trainees and the demonstration is teacher oriented only.
- Trainees and supervisors can focus their attention on strengths and weaknesses of a trainee while demonstrating a specific skill.
- More KOR can be obtained, as there is scope for systematic analysis of performance on the basis of viewing and the assessment is more reliable and can be done jointly in different cases.
- The main limitation of microteaching is that it is skill oriented rather than content oriented. But the content, which forms the most important component of the teaching-learning process, is not paid adequate attention during microteaching sessions.
- In microteaching emphasis is laid on specific skills. leaving integration of skills to natural consequences
- The scope of microteaching is narrow, as the entire process of teaching is not covered.
- Further limitations arise from inappropriately conducting of the sessions due to inability on the part of supervisors to provide feedback

properly and the inability on the part of the trainee to properly receive feedback. The unwillingness of the peer group to criticise a trainee and also the unwillingness of the trainee to listen to critique may make the microteaching session ineffective. This limitation can be overcome through adequate orientation of the supervisors and the trainees in giving and receiving feedback, which are dealt with in a subsequent section.

- The simulated condition of presenting before the peer group and in front of the video camera also restrains to some extent the natural performance of the trainees.

Despite the evidences of improvement of teaching as a result of microteaching training, the critiques often argue, on one hand, that the microteaching will produce homogenised teachers with standard similarities and, procedures and, on the other hand, that the skills may not be internalised. The former rests on the assumption that the microteaching is too effective, while the latter assume that it is not at all effective. In fact, the middle ground is held in practice.

Microteaching sharpens and develops the teaching skills, helps eliminate gross errors and builds up the confidence of teachers, particularly of newly recruited ones.

In spite of these limitations, microteaching has been established as the only effective and economic method for adequately preparing the teachers to teach effectively in the actual classroom situation. Various research studies have been conducted on different aspects of microteaching, which are discussed in subsequent sections.

Role of Supervisors in Microteaching

The microteaching supervisor plays an important role towards the effectiveness of the training session as:

- a resource person
- an advisor
- an interpreter
- an assessor
- a general morale booster.

It has been suggested that a supervisor must have clarity in mind the behaviour s/he wants to influence, so that feedback can be specific and the trainees will know what or how to change as a result of the feedback. If a supervisor focuses on a few selected aspects of teaching skill and does not destructively criticise the trainee, a useful purpose would be served especially if aided by a videotape recording.

The role of the supervisor basically is to help a trainee to improve his/her own teaching. In the early stages of training, the supervisor needs to be particularly encouraging and supportive. Towards the end of the programme, the support is gradually withdrawn and the student should be able to analyse and suggest improvements with virtually no help from supervisor.

Some guidelines are suggested below for effective supervision of microteaching session-

- It should be kept in mind that the main objective of the session is to make the programme a rewarding experience for the trainees and *not an exercise in fault finding.*
- A supervisor should ask the trainees to comment on both strengths and weaknesses of the performance of the skill immediately after viewing the lesson.
- The trainees should be asked about their suggestions to improve the skill.
- Only one or two main points related to the skill being practiced should be discussed.
- Detailed discussion of other aspects of the lesson should be avoided unless they are absolutely crucial.
- Focus should be on the group to suggest ways of improving performance.
- Supervisor should summarise including his/her views.

Giving and Receiving Feedback

A microteaching session is an opportunity to teach in front of colleagues and friends and hear constructive feedback. The feedback one receives will tell him/her what s/he is doing that is effective, as well as what s/he can do to strengthen his/her performance.

The manner in which feedback is given and received contributes to the learning process. Feedback that is vague, judgmental, ill timed, or unusable is not as valuable as feedback that is specific, descriptive, timely, and practical. Similarly, although being criticised is often not pleasant, being open to well-intentioned, well-crafted feedback can only further the professional development.

Some suggestions for giving and receiving feedback in a microteaching session are given below:

Giving Feedback

The feedback provided should be always constructive. The characteristics of constructive feedback are:

1. It is descriptive, rather than evaluative
2. It is specific, rather than general
3. It focuses on behaviour, rather than on the person
4. It is directed toward behaviour that the receiver can do something about
5. It emphasises sharing information, rather than giving advice
6. It comes in amounts that the receiver can use, rather than everything that could possibly be said
7. It is checked to ensure clear communication

When giving feedback, one should try to:

- ***Be specific rather than general.*** The more concrete the feedback is, the more useful it will be to the person receiving it. Thus, rather than saying, " sometimes you weren't clear in your explanations.," the trainee should be told exactly where s/he was vague and describe why one had trouble understanding him/her. Similarly, it's nice but not very helpful to say, " I thought you did an excellent job." Rather specific things that the trainee did well should be listed. For example, s/he might have motivated the problem effectively, used transitions advantageously, or communicated interest and enthusiasm. The trainee should be told how these techniques contributed to the success of her performance.
- ***Be descriptive, not evaluative.*** Focus should be on the effect the performance had on one, rather than on how good or bad one perceives it to be. For example, saying, "It's wrong to call on students when they don't have their hands up," is a generalisation that may or may not be true in all cases. However, saying "I felt uncomfortable because you called on me when I didn't have my hand up," can help the person realise that students may have the same reaction. It should be remembered, too, that some of the responses will come from one's own perceptions (for example, not everyone feels uncomfortable when called on). Thus it's good practice to begin most feedback with, "In my opinion. " or "In my experience."
- ***Describe something the person can act upon.*** Commenting on the vocal quality of someone whose voice is naturally high pitched is

only likely to discourage him/her. However, if the person's voice had a squeaky quality to it because s/he was nervous, it might be said, " you might want to breath more deeply to relax yourself, and that will help lower the pitch of your voice as well."

- ***Choose one or two things the person can concentrate on.*** People can usually act on only a few pieces of feedback at a time. If they are overwhelmed with too many suggestions, they are likely to become frustrated. When giving feedback, attention should be called to those areas that need more improvement.
- ***Avoid inferences about motives, intentions, or feelings.*** To say, "You don't seem very enthusiastic about this lesson" is to imply something about the person her/himself. A better comment might be, "Varying your rate and volume of speaking would give you a more animated style."

Receiving Feedback

While receiving feedback, one should try to

- ***Be open to what one is hearing.*** Being told that one needs to improve him/herself is not always easy, but, as it has been pointed out, it's an important part of the learning process. Although one might feel hurt in response to criticism, it should be tried not to let those feelings deter one from using the feedback to his/her best advantage.
- Take notes, if possible, while listening to the other people's comments. Then one will have a record to refer to, and it might be discovered that the comments that seemed very harsh when they were being said were actually the most insightful and useful.
- Ask for specific examples if one needs to. If the feedback one is receiving is vague or unfocused, the critique should be asked to give several specific examples of the point s/he is trying to make.
- Judge the feedback by the person who is giving it. One does not have to agree with every comment. One should think about the person's credibility when assessing the validity of her/his statements. Other people may be asked if they agree with the person's critique. In sum, one should be practical, tactful, and upbeat when giving and receiving feedback—both in the microteaching session and in actual classes as well.

Annexure A

DEVELOPMENT OF TEACHING SKILLS

Supervision Checklist for the Skill of 'SET INDUCTION' (Introducing the Lesson)

Behaviour	Minutes				
	1	2	3	4	5
1. a) Establish pre-Instructional set b) Say 'Hello' and recognise students					
2. a) Elecite Interest of students and/or provide related interesting activities b) Begin with known facts and ideas c) Begin with anticipatory questions d) Relate lesson to other experiences of students e) Link the known facts with the lesson					
3. Review previous lesson					
4. a) Make clear the purposes of the lesson b) State the objectives c) Explain students' role in the lesson					
5. a) Present facts b) Be very general rather than specific in the presentation					

Supervision Checklist for the Skill of 'CLOSURE' (Concluding a Lesson)

Behaviour	Minutes				
	1	2	3	4	5
1. Stress and review major points					
2. Itemise the points focused					
3. Repeat key points					
4. Evaluate by asking thought-provoking questions					
5. Provide feedback and reinforce					
6. Relate to the next lesson/laboratory/ workshop activities					
7. Provide out-of-class assignments					
8. Estimate student growth in learning in taking the lesson					
9. Estimate utility of learning that has taken place (Transfer of Learning)					
10. Boost by say encouraging words					

Supervision Checklist for the Skill of 'ASKING QUESTIONS'

Behaviour	Minutes				
	1	2	3	4	5
1. Ask question to the whole class					
2. Encourage all students to participate					
3. Pause for a moment					
4. Designate respondent					
5. Elicit response from students/Redirect					
6. Reinforce by KR (Complete, satisfying answers)					
7. Ask thought-provoking questions					
8. Pose questions for students to discuss					
9. Ask questions to evaluate students' understanding					
10. Ask questions which are clearly understood by students					
11. Express questions coherently					
12. Pause after asking a question					
13. Vary the pace at which you ask questions					
14. Direct some questions to individual students					
15. Distribute your questions among the whole group					
16. Prompt to help students formulate their answers					
17. Use probing technique to help students think more deeply about their answers					

Supervision Checklist for the Skill of 'EXPLAINING'

Behaviour	Minutes				
	1	2	3	4	5
1. Present sequentially					
2. Emphasis Key concepts					
3. Employ analogy in lecture					
4. Elaborate ideas					
5. Illustrate by use of examples					
6. Use "Rule-e.g.-Rule"					
7. State fact or generalisations					
8. Relate lecture to previous learning					

Supervision Checklist for the Skill of 'VARYING THE STIMULUS'

Behaviour	Minutes				
	1	2	3	4	5
1. Change tone of voice					
2. Rearrange physical setting					
3. Use Chalkboard					
4. Use other aids					
5. Read directly from notes/texts					
6. Change pattern of student participation					
7. Move around					
8. Use silence					

Annexure B

SAMPLE MICRO LESSON PLAN

1. (a) Name of Presenter:
   (b) Designation:
   (c) Institution:
2. Skill to be presented: SET INDUCTION
3. (a) Course: Physical Science
   (b) Topic: Water Treatment
   (c) Sub topic of discussion: Coagulation
   (d) Level: Ist Semester Physics, U.G. Class
   (e) Date:
4. Objectives:
   - To arouse curiosity among students about the subtopic by relating it to common day-to-day experiences.
   - To assess the level of understanding by students about the basic concepts discussed in related previous lesson.
   - To motivate the students to learn by relating the subtopic to the field practices.
   - To make students aware of the contents to be discussed relating to the subtopic.
5. Expected previous knowledge of students (related to the subtopic)
   - The principles and methods of removal of suspended particles by the 'Plain sedimentation' process of water treatment.
   - Limitations of the Plain sedimentation process in respect of removal of finely suspended colloidal particles.
6. Plan Outline

Sl.	*Key points*	*Teacher activities*	*Remarks*
1.	Interaction with students	Say "Hello" etc.	Ice-breaking
2.	Introduction of term 'Paneer'	Linking with some sweets from usual experience of students through appropriate interaction	Arousal of curiosity by sudden change of focus from water treatment
3.	Method of preparation of paneer in kitchen	Teacher asks probing questions with prompts to develop the method from student responses.	Illustration of analogy from daily experiences

Sl.	*Key points*	*Teacher activities*	*Remarks*
4.	Separation of milk colloidal particles and their settling during paneer preparation	The teacher asks probing questions to derive the principle	Linking of analogy to the subtopic of discussion
5.	Identification of chemical agent used in paneer preparation	Teacher attempts to lead to 'Alum' through probing and prompting	
6.	Size of suspended particles removed by plain sedimentation	Asking simple questions about the basic principles of plain sedimentation and cause of the problem focusing on the particle size.	Recapitulation and assessing previous knowledge
7.	Problems faced with removal of colloidal suspended particles		
8.	Introduction of the term 'Coagulation'	Teacher announces the topic of discussion and writes on the chalk board	Announcement of lecture topic
9.	Content to be discussed during the lecture presentation and expected outcome from students after attending the lecture.	Teacher describes	Advanced Organiser.

Note: The actual script of the lesson is given in Annexure-C.

Annexure C

SCRIPT OF MICRO LESSON FOR PRESENTATION OF SET INDUCTION SKILL

T: Teacher S: Student

T: "Good Morning, Students"
Sumit, you are a Bengali from Calcutta, is it not?

S: Yes, Sir.

T: Can you tell why are there abundance of sweetmeat shops in Calcutta? There is practically one shop at every street corner.

S: Well sir, Bengalis are very fond of sweets.

T: Very good, You have identified the basic reason.
Gurbachan, Can you name the sweet for which Bengal is famous? *(Pause)*
It is of round shape, white colour and is soft by nature.

S: Sir, it is called Rasgoolla.

T: Sumit, would you please tell from which milk product Rasgoolla is made?

S: Sir, it is made from Paneer.

T: Excellent, yes we call it in Bengali as 'Chhana'
Well, Surekha, you must have seen your mother making paneer in her kitchen.

S: Yes, Sir.

T: Well, would you please describe how she makes it?

S: She boils milk in a pan, adds some lemon juice and stirs with a spoon and after some time milk turns into paneer and coloured water.

T: Is the paneer floating on milk surface?

S: Initially it floats in granular form on surface in scattered fashion, but after cooling these form an accumulated mass and fall down to the bottom of pan.

T: Excellent, it shows you are also interested in cooking apart from becoming a civil engineer. Thank you.
Well any- one else who has seen your mother making paneer. *(Pause and Directing)*

T: Sarfaraz, can you name any substitute that is used when lemon is not available?

S: Sir, calcium citrate is used by my mother.

T: Good, can you name any other chemical, which is very common? It looks solid and was also used in your grandfathers' time as substitute of shaving lotion after shaving.

S: Yes sir, it is called alum, this is also used for making paneer.

T: Excellent, thank you very much.

Now, Joshef, I heard from your Chemistry teacher that you were very strong in that subject. Can you tell us when milk powder is added to water to make milk what do we get - a solution or suspension of milk in water?

S: Sir, it is a suspension of colloidal milk particles.

T: Excellent, you really have a sound knowledge of Chemistry. I shall take your help often during our discussion. Thank you.

Now, where were we stuck up in last class during the discussion on removal of suspended particles by plain sedimentation? Rajesh, do you remember?

S: Yes Sir, we could not remove the finely suspended colloidal particles by plain sedimentation.

T: Very good, can you also tell why this was happening?

S: Due to small size, these suspended particles have very large settling time and as such cannot be removed by plain sedimentation.

T: Splendid, you have rightly answered but only you have to add that these cannot be removed within a reasonable time by plain sedimentation.

Now, Sumitra, can you guess what is happening to the milk colloidal particles during paneer making such that the paneer is found lying at the bottom of the pan.

S: Sir, the milk colloidal particles are joining together to become bigger in size and as such they settle down quickly.

T: Excellent, you have just found the solution to our problem.

T: So, we shall borrow this simple principle of paneer making in mother's kitchen and use it for removal of colloidal particles from water by using the principles of settling.

Today we shall discuss this process, which is called Coagulation. We shall try to understand the physical and chemical principles underlying the process of coagulation and also discuss how the plain sedimentation process is modified to adopt this. We shall also discuss the laboratory experiment related to this topic that you will have to perform in the laboratory class. So at the end of our discussion, you will be able to explain the coagulation process and describe the treatment units required for adopting this process and also determine the type and amount of chemicals required for the process.

SECTION E

Measurement, Evaluation and Measuring Devices

14
Basics of Measurement, Evaluation and Allied Devices

By evaluation we mean a systematic process of collecting and analysing data in order to make decisions, toned with judgemental comments.

Evaluation is something more than measurement because it is both qualitative and quantitative. Performance evaluation is a process that determines the achievement of learning outcomes. It is a means of monitoring learning progress and diagnosing learning difficulties. From an instructional standpoint, evaluation may be defined as a systematic process of determining the extent to which instructional objectives are achieved by learning.

Evaluation is the determination of a thing's value. In education, it is the formal determination of the quality, effectiveness, or value of a programme, product, project, process, objective, or curriculum. The process of evaluation holds an important place in the entire educational system.

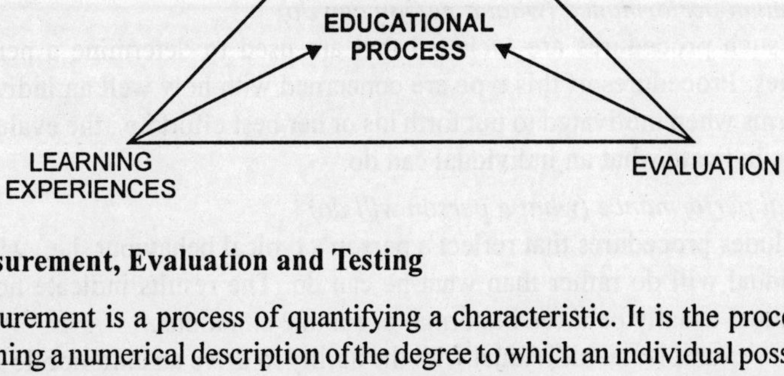

Measurement, Evaluation and Testing

Measurement is a process of quantifying a characteristic. It is the process of obtaining a numerical description of the degree to which an individual possesses a particular characteristic. It determines the quantity, i.e., "how much?"

Measurement and evaluation are closely related terms and quite different at the same time. Evaluation is a more comprehensive term and measurement is only a part of it. Whereas measurement is making a statement or stating a fact, evaluation is passing a verdict or making a judgment.

Measurement answers how much but evaluation tells about how good. Evaluation may also include the non-measurement techniques when the description is beyond quantitative domain. Thus evaluation is not always based on measurement, it includes even some non-measurement parameters plus value judgment (good or bad etc.), as shown in following Fig.

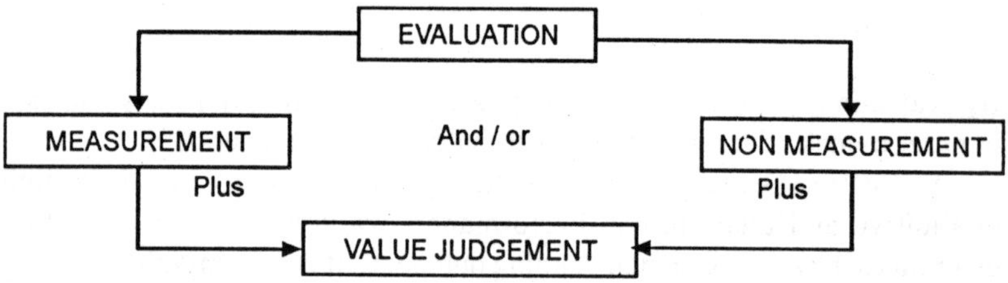

Testing is the process of obtaining a measurement of whether or not the learners learnt what was intended.

Testing can be carried out both orally as well as written or combining both and there are several types of tests that can be employed based on what needs to be tested. Teachers, as evaluators should be very clear about what to be tested and how to test.

The Evaluation Procedure—Broad Classification

The vast array of evaluation procedures used in educational institutions can be classified and described in many different ways. Some major ones are listed below:

Based on the Nature of the Measurement

Maximum performance (what a person can do)

Here such procedures are included that are used to determine a person's abilities. Procedures of this type are concerned with how well an individual performs when motivated to put forth his or her best effort i.e., the evaluation results indicate what an individual can do.

Typical performance (what a person will do)

It includes procedures that reflect a person's typical behaviour, i.e., what an individual will do rather than what he can do. The results indicate how an individual usually behaves in normal or routine situations.

For example, an individual with the ability to drive an automobile safely may typically drive in an unsafe manner. A student with considerable aptitude for mathematics may show little interest in the pursuit of mathematics.

Based on the use in Classroom Instruction

Placement evaluation

Evaluation of learner's entry performance in a sequence of instruction. (determines entry behaviour).

Formative evaluation

Evaluation of learner's progress during instruction. (determines learning progress).

Diagnostic evaluation

Evaluation of learner's learning difficulties during instruction (determines causes of learning problems).

Summative evaluation

Evaluation of learner's achievement at the end of instruction (determines end-of-course achievement).

Based on the Method of Interpreting the Results

Criteria Referenced

The specific performance of the learner that was evaluated is interpreted directly (e.g. X calculated 10 problems in 30 minutes without error).

The result describes learner's performance in terms of a specific domain of instructionally relevant tasks.

Norm referenced

Norm referenced testing is the process of comparing the test scores of individual students. The specific performance of the learner that was evaluated is interpreted in terms of the relative position held in some group (e.g. Y calculated more accurately than 80 per cent of the class members did).

The result describes learner's performance in terms of the relative position held in some known group.

Criterion

Referenced interpretations enable us to describe what an individual can do, without reference to the performance of others. Norm—referenced interpretations enable us to determine how an individual's performance compared to that of others. The current trend is for the criterion—referenced testing. Here it is assessed whether the performance of the learners is up to a standard or not, i.e., their progress towards the criterion can be reliably measured.

Glaser (1963) has advocated norms that indicate the attainment of a particular level of skill or competence. The definitions of a task attainment or expert judgment is used to determine particular standards of performance.

Tools for Evaluation

Evaluation requires some means to serve its purpose, the different types of tests act as the tools. They must be used appropriately to be helpful. The tests help the teacher to measure the different aspects of the learners' behaviour. In the hands of a good teacher, the tests become valuable tools for the diagnosis of individual strengths and limitations. The tests may be available in the market or even teacher made. Tests can measure the learner's achievement. Some of the commonly used teacher made tests are objective tests, short answer and essay tests, renamed as Short Response Type Question (SRQ), Restricted response type questions (RRQ) and Extended Response type Questions (ERQ), respectively.

Role of Teacher

A teacher holds a key role in appraising the worthwhileness of the educational experiences, at least for his/her class, i.e., the extent to which the learners achieve the instructional objectives. The teacher's job as an evaluator has essentially two important aspects. One has its orientation in the group instructional programme and the extent to which the class, as a whole, is achieving its goals, the other has its orientation in the study of individual students—in diagnosis of their growth lags and finding out the important causal factors for such lags. Both aspects are indispensable to good teaching. A teacher must take care of evaluating both the knowledge and skill of the students. It has been found that the latter part is often neglected, thus the passouts face a difficulty in transferring their knowledge to the actual job situation. Hence, teachers should equally emphasise upon the evaluation of student performance in the skill outcomes also.

A good teacher always keeps him/her informed of the learners' performance and hence finds evaluation an indispensable part of the teaching—learning process. Therefore, such a teacher always tries to involve a continuous and interrelated series of instructional decisions concerning ways to enhance learning.

The main purpose of evaluation may broadly be stated to help learners achieve a set of intended learning outcomes. These outcomes would typically include all desired changes in the intellectual, emotional and skill aspects. The intended learning outcomes are established by the instructional objectives, the desired changes in learners are brought about by the planned learning activities and the learners' learning progress is periodically evaluated by the various tools of evaluation. Thus evaluation is an integral part of the instructional programme and provides basic information for a variety of educational decisions.

Evaluation is a process by which changes in the behaviour of learners are studied and guided towards the goals set. An evaluation cannot be done adequately using a single tool. A comprehensive evaluation requires use of many techniques. [Achievement tests, observation, oral test etc.]. Teaching and testing are teachers' roles. Teaching covers objectives, strategies and evaluation.

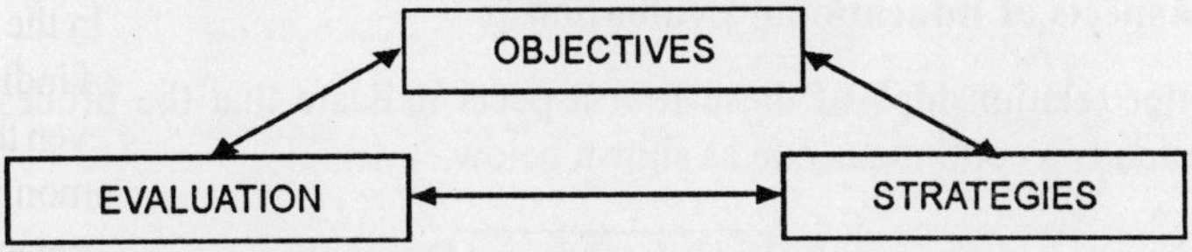

Objectives give purpose to activities and experiences. The term evaluation includes measurement, assessment and testing. It is a continuous process in the teaching—learning situation and is the broadest concept.

Measurement *Verses* Evaluation

Measurement refers to observations that are expressed quantitatively. This is obtained through achievement tests i.e., how much a learner has scored in a subject.

Evaluation proceeds beyond measurement and involves both quantitative and qualitative description of events, behaviours as well as value judgement of events described. Evaluation is passing a verdict making a judgement.

Evaluation = Measurement + value judgement

Evaluation concerns itself of 'what value' i.e., how best? Evaluation serves to answer both students and teachers, what progress they are making.

In terms of education, evaluation involves estimating the probable worth of the activities involved in the teaching—learning relationships.

Measurement is quantitative and tells how much a learner has scored on a given test.

Assessment implies value judgment. Assessment is defined as the practical application of measurement. Assessment is inherent in the classroom as the classroom is a social environment.

Evaluation is a comprehensive concept. The main objective of evaluation is making decision, but it is not an end in itself, but a means to effective instruction. Evaluation covers all the means of collecting evidences on learner's behaviour.

Classroom Measurement Model

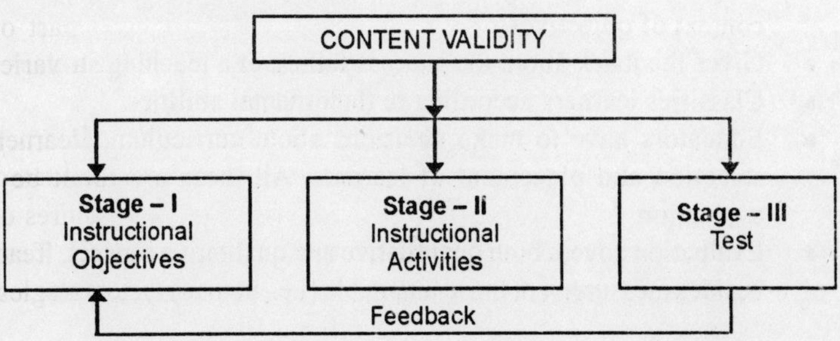

Four Aspects of Educational Evaluation

The inter relationships of these four aspects indicate that the process of evaluation is a continuous one as shown below.

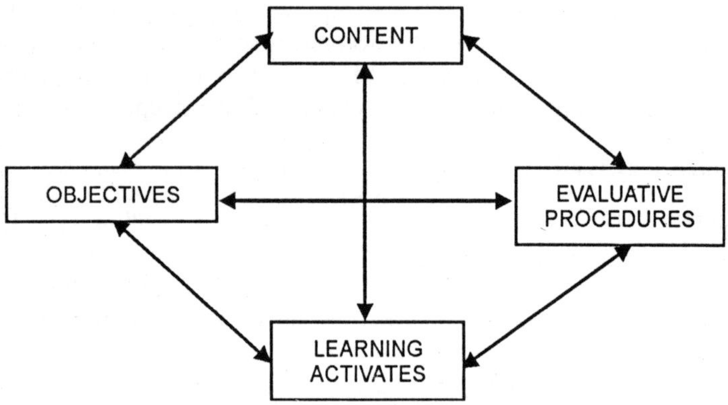

At the higher education level the major goal is to assess the learners' achievement of instructional objectives. The commonly used methods to assess the educational progress of students are practical, the oral/viva-voce and teacher made test [Achievement test].

Achievement Tests

Achievement tests are used to measure the present level of attainment of a student in a particular subject—their knowledge, skill, competence. Achievement tests measure learning outcome.

In order to evaluate, teachers have to construct test items that are valid, reliable, objective, practical and discriminating.

Purposes of Evaluation

- Useful to improve the quality of instruction.
- Motivates learners to be active and alert in their studies.
- Helpful in measuring the capacities and abilities of learners in the context of objectives.
- Gives feedback about the success/failure of a teaching strategy
- Classifies learners according to their mental abilities.
- Educators have to make decisions about curriculum, instruction, selection and placement of learners. All these are facilitated by evaluation.
- Evaluation covers both quantitative and qualitative aspects. It covers besides measurement those intangible (i.e., human) factors not subject

to quantitative measurements i.e., appraisal of the learner as a whole. In short, evaluation is useful to assess learner's knowledge, skills acquired and behavioural changes as a result of instruction.

- Evaluation is diagnostic. It helps a teacher to identify a learner's strength, limitations and interest in the subject.

Practical Test

Ability to design and conduct experiments require theoretical knowledge of the subject and manipulative skills of scientific apparatus. Further skills in observation and the ability to report and interpret data are to be developed through several practical experiences.

Point to be considered in constructing test items:

- Requires the learner to make a comparison—write a description or explain certain points. The student is allowed freedom of expression in analysing, comparing, describing, explaining or reasoning.
- Determine definite specifications for marking.
- Follow a definite procedure in marking.
- Call for specific answers.

Points to be noted in test construction:

- Make the test comprehensive.
- Make each item independent of others.
- It is not possible to measure all outcomes with one type of test.
- State questions clearly. Eliminate ambiguous questions.
- Make sure the directions are clear and complete.
- Word the items in the simplest possible manner.
- Do not lift statements directly from books and use them as test items.
- Make sure that no item can be answered simply by referring to other items.

In order to evaluate achievement, teachers have to construct tests that are valid, reliable, objective, practical and discriminating.

The goal of evaluation is to enable the learner to acquire the desired knowledge, skills, attitudes, habits and values. The traditional system of examinations is designed to measure memorisation of facts. The concept of evaluation in modern times is gradually replacing the concept of examination.

Teacher constructed tests are mostly paper- pencil tests. But occasionally performance tests are also used in which learners have to demonstrate their proficiency in a skill.

On principle, it is assumed that irrespective of type of questions, may be it SRQ, RRQ or ERQ, it should be objective in nature. However our pre-conceived notion denotes the SRQs as only form of objective questions.

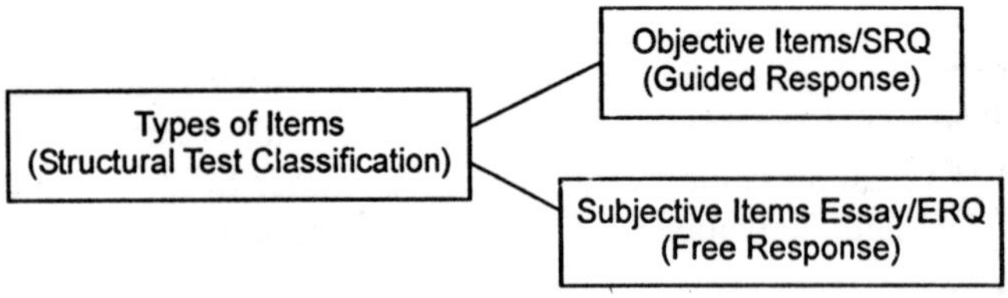

Objective items include (a) True/False (b) Matching (c) Very short answer (d) multiple choice and (e) completion type items. In this process preparing a table of specifications is helpful as it gives the weightage assigned to each area covered in the test.

Teachers are evaluators and all of them are involved in evaluation process.

Evaluation is to be stressed from the beginning of instruction. Evaluation is related to all components of the educative process.

R.C. Branch (1996) says that "instructional evaluation initiates, permeates and concludes the instructional design, development and utilisation process."

An Evaluation cannot be adequately done by a single tool. Complete evaluation requires using many techniques.

At times the affective and cognitive questions are given in examinations as performance items. When written tests cannot measure all abilities. Project work, group discussion, interview and observation can also be used to measure achievement.

Norm–Referenced and Criterion Referenced Testing

In Norm-Referenced testing, a learner's performance is compared with the performance of a specific group of students. A norm provides an indication of average or typical performance of the specified group.

Criterion Referenced testing is used to identify a learner's status with respect to an established standard of performance. Learners are compared to some established criterion rather than to other learners. This approach measures levels of mastery.

In evaluation, learner is appraised as a whole whereas measurement appraisal is quantitative only. In evaluation, the focus is on intangible factors i.e., judging adequacy and desirability of the changes in learners.

For any purposeful evaluation, especially of a large number of learners over a variety of subjects it is necessary to adopt scientific procedures to convert raw scores in to standards scores. (Z. Scores, T. Score, percentiles etc.). Raw scores are to be converted into standards scores for comparison. No comparison should be made based on raw scores.

All the 3 domains contribute to better teaching-learning process.

Tools and Techniques of Evaluation

Testing Techniques
- Oral Test
- Written Test
- Practical Test
- Performance Test

Non-Testing Techniques
- Observation
- Rating Scale
- Interest inventory etc.

In the examinations, we generally do not go beyond achievement tests. (i.e., aptitude, creativity and intelligence, tests can also be used). In professional education, achievement tests have written, oral and performance tests.

Observation in the class is also useful for evaluation.

Still in most examination Norm-referenced testing is followed in India.

Formative and Summative Evaluation

Evaluation is an integral part of teaching-learning system. It serves as a basis for improvement. Besides providing information as to how a course helped in meeting the needs of the learners, evaluation also suggests on how the course can be improved further because the needs and demands may change with time. Based on the use in classroom instruction or a course as a whole, evaluation can be broadly classified in two categories, such as formative and summative. Both the types of evaluation can add valuable information on teaching principles and practice that could have a much wider application.

Formative Evaluation

It is carried out during the process of teaching learning or while the course is proceeding with the intent to improve the programme (process or product). This will ensure the attainment of the goals of the instruction. While evaluating the course, formative evaluation measures the outputs specifically so as to modify the form of the course or change either its structure or the processes which go on. Formative evaluation takes place during the course as well as at the end of the course. It is designed to produce feedback which modifies the course or the inputs to the course.

The Role of Formative Evaluation

Evaluation provides learners with the information as to what they have learnt well or mastered and also the content part where they need to spend more time to learn. For this we mainly depend on the formative type.

The formative tests help the learners in identifying the important elements in the instruction giving them the idea as to how well they have learnt those elements. After taking a formative test, the learners should be able to realise if their preparations for the class have been adequate or not.

The nature of the feedback provided will depend in part upon the format of the formative test. e.g., If the formative test is made up of objective type of items, the feedback it provides may be simply a record of which items were answered correctly and which ones were missed. Knowing that each item is designed to assess learning of a particular concept or objective, students can immediately turn to corrective activities that focus on the concepts or objectives they have not yet mastered. If the formative test includes essay items, students will need a clear and precise description of what was lacking in their response and how it can be improved.

In order to provide this description, specific criteria for evaluating students' responses should be developed, together with ways of communicating these criteria to students. Similarly, if the formative test involves a skill demonstration, criteria for evaluating students' performance are essential if the feedback is to be prescriptive and useful.

Summative Evaluation

As the name suggests, summative evaluation sums up the results or outputs of a course; normally conducted at the end of the course. In case of classroom teaching, summative evaluation finds out how well a group did on a learning task so that both the learning materials and learning process can be evaluated.

Summative evaluation includes all types—written, practical and oral examinations. The results of summative evaluation may be useful in the evaluation of learning programmes, the learning environment or teacher performance. It provides information on what a student has achieved at the beginning or at the end of a unit, programme or course so that the final grade can be awarded.

In nut-shell, it may be said that the tools that have been described here would be helpful both for formative and summative evaluation. The two kinds of evaluation can provide sufficient input in determining teaching effectiveness by giving information on the quality of the design and delivery of teaching-learning system. Formative evaluation gives immediate feedback on the effectiveness of one's teaching.

Specification Table

Any classroom teacher is also an evaluator. Teachers conduct tests in order to measure their learners' progress during the course and to motivate them in their studies. It is worthnoting to mention that an unit-question is termed as an 'item'.

In any examination, the teacher has to design the question paper taking into consideration the learners' ability, content to be covered, level of questions and the type of items. A balanced question paper should be thought of giving weightage to all the units. In this, a detailed course outline or scheme of work would be helpful in delineating the area of coverage of a test *vis-a-vis* the test objectives. In this way, the scope of coverage is delimited and a table of specification is evolved.

Definition of Specification Table

A table of specification is a matrix in the form of a two-dimensional table relating the behavioural objectives to content area(s). It is a way to depict the framework of a representative sample of the desired behaviour. A table of specification, also called a 'test blueprint', is a plan of a test constructed to examine the major and important sections of a course of study. The learning outcomes should cover all instructional objectives that can be tested, and the subject matter content should include all of the major topics that were considered during the course.

The Dimensions

Any teacher has to prepare the list of questions reflecting the objectives of the subject studied. A table of specification accommodates the following:

- All units based on their importance.
- Number of questions and the time required to answer them.
- The degree of complexity of test items (All the questions normally test students' cognitive abilities in terms of knowledge, comprehension application as also skill, this refers to the objectives to be fulfilled.)
- Specification of course objectives.
- Specification of course content area.
- Specification of test item number on the basis of course objectives vis-a-vis course content section.
- Specification of the relative importance to be given to the course objectives.
- Specification of the relative importance to be attached to the various sections of the course.
- Specification of the total number of test-items intended for the test.

While preparing a table of specification, the following steps may be borne in mind:

- Identifying the learning outcomes and content areas to be measured by the test.
- Weighing the learning outcomes and content areas in terms of their relative importance.
- Developing the table in accordance with the above weights by

Table of Sameple Specifications

Class: 1st Semester
Sub: Chemistry
Sub Area: Metallurgy
Units: Five

Time: 2 Hrs.
MM: 100

No.	Units	Knowledge			Comprehension			Application			Skill			Total			Total
		Ob*	SA*	E*	Ob*	SA*	E*	Ob*	SA*	E*	Ob*	SA*	E*	Ob*	SA*	E*	
1	Iron	1(1)	—	—	1(1)	1(4)	—	—	—	1(10)	—	—	1(10)	2(2)	1(4)	2(20)	5(26)
2	Steel	1(1)	—	—	1(1)	1(4)	—	—	—	1(10)	—	—	—	2(2)	1(4)	1(10)	4(16)
3	Copper	1(1)	—	—	1(1)	1(4)	—	—	—	1(10)	—	—	1(10)	2(2)	1(4)	2(20)	5(26)
4	Lead	1(1)	—	—	1(1)	—	—	—	—	1(10)	—	—	—	2(2)	—	1(10)	3(12)
5	Aluminum	1(1)	—	—	1(1)	2(8)	—	—	—		—	—	1(10)	2(2)	2(8)	1(10)	5(20)
Total		5(5)	—	—	5(5)	5(20)	—	—	—	4(40)	—	—	3(30)	10(10)	5(20)	7(70)	22(100)

Figure in bracket indicates the marks. Ob: Objective Type, SA: Short Answer Type, E: Essay Type

Weightage to Units	
Iron	26%
Steel	16%
Copper	26%
Lead	12%
Aluminum	20%
Total	100%

Weightage to Test/Type of Item	
Objective	10%
Short Answer	20%
Essay Type (Application + Skill)	70%
Total	100%

Weightage to Objectives	
K	5%
C	25%
Ap	40%
Sk	30%
Total	100%

distributing the test items proportionately among the relevant cells of the table.

A table of specification makes the task of an evaluator (teacher) easier and simpler by specifying each of the following:

- Weightage to each of the learning outcomes.
- Weightage of units.
- Weightage of the item-types.
- Sample of items to be used.
- Nature of each item in the test.
- Distribution of marks.

Given here is a table of specification for a question paper on chemistry.

After arriving at the matrix, the teacher should proceed to prepare the question paper. This process ensures that the questions cover all the chapters completed.

The questions should be given in clear unambiguous terms. In Essay items, if sub questions are given then it is desirable to give the marks allotted to each of them.

A sample question paper covering five units in Metallurgy under the subject chemistry is given on previous page. Here, in order to explain the steps involved in designing a test paper, five units from Metallurgy have been chosen. But actually teachers should cover all the units e.g. 8 to 10 prescribed for the course and each chapter title should be given. The weightage to each unit is decided depending upon the importance of the unit, applications involved and objectives to be fulfilled.

15

Questions: Types and Characteristics

The Purpose of Classroom Testing

Classroom tests can be used for a variety of instructional purposes. These can be tests described in terms of their location in the instructional process.

Tests may be given at the beginning of an instruction (pre-testing) to determine—

- Whether the learners have the pre-requisite skills needed for the instruction i.e., to determine readiness.
- To what extent the learners have already achieved the objectives of the planned instruction i.e., to measure entry behaviour.

Tests given during instruction are used to note the errors and provide feedback to learners as well as teachers. Such tests are called formative tests. Persistent learning difficulties may require the use of diagnostic tests. For this type of testing, a number of test items are needed in each specific area with slight variation from item to item.

Tests may also be administered at the end of an instruction. Here the main intention is to measure the extent to which the intended learning outcomes have been achieved. These end-of-instruction tests are called summative tests. They also serve to provide feedback to learners, assigning of remedial work and evaluating instruction. End-of-Instruction testing can serve the functions of both formative and summative testing and in some cases serve as pre-test for the next/following instruction/unit.

Test Items

Broadly the test items can be categorised as —

a) Objective Item and
(b) Descriptive/Subjective question.

Objective item is highly structured and requires the learner to supply a word or two or to select the correct answer from a number of alternatives. The descriptive/Subjective item permits the learner to select, organise and present the answer in essay form.

The Objective Test Item

This includes different types and can be classified into those items that require the learner to supply the answer and those that require the learner to select the answer from a given number of alternatives.

Some basic types of objective test items are as given below which mainly test for the knowledge objectives.

Supply Type

In this type, the responder (examinee) is provided with alternatives (choices) from which s/he has to select the best alternative.

The simplest form of the supply type is the completion item.

e.g., Boyle's law establishes the relation between ________ and ________ of gases.

Another supply type may be the *very short answer type question or answering in one word.*

e.g. What is the formula for common salt?

Selection Types

True -False or alternative Response Items

e.g.In the equation $2x + 5 = 9$, 'x' equals 3 (T/F)

Matching Items

The learner has to match items of one column with that of the other.

e.g.,Match the items of column A with those of column B

A	B
Iron	8
Copper	1
Aluminium	29
Hydrogen	26
Oxygen	7
Nitrogen	13

Multiple - Choice

This is the commonest of objective type tests.

A statement is given with four options, the learner has to choose the best alternative or the option nearest to the right one.

Example—Which of the following metal is mostly used as a conductor?

a) iron
b) copper
c) aluminium
d) zinc

All these objective test items have one feature in common, i.e., they present the learners with a highly structured task that limits the type of response they can make. The learners have to demonstrate the specific knowledge or understanding called for in the item.

The Subjective Type Item

This is commonly viewed as a single item type. As the examinee has to supply his/her own answer to each item, this is also a supply-response type of item.

Example,

(a) Answer the following questions:

(i) Explain the process of extracting iron from any of its ores.

(ii) State five properties of iron.

A classification is based on the amount of freedom of response allowed to the learner.

This includes

a) The extended response type in which the learners are given almost complete freedom in making their responses and

b) The restricted response type in which the nature, length or organisation of the response is limited.

Both these types have their own limitations and advantages. There is a third category of test item called the short answer type item, quite similar to the restricted response of essay type item. This item requires the learner to respond in limited words or sentences.

Advantages and Limitations of Objective Items

Advantages: It is useful for measuring knowledge of facts. Multiple choice items can also measure understanding, thinking skills and provide an extensive sampling of course content because of the large number of questions that can be included in a test.

Scoring is quick, easy and consistent. The learners are also encouraged to develop a comprehensive knowledge of specific facts and the ability to make fine discriminations among them.

Limitations: Objective tests are inappropriate for measuring ability to select and organise ideas, creative abilities, and some types of problem - solving. Preparing the tests is also time consuming.

Advantages and Limitations of Descriptive Items

Advantages: Essay type items are especially useful to measure originality of response. They are appropriate for measuring ability to select and organise ideas, writing abilities, problem-solving skills requiring originality and creativity. Such tests encourage learners to concentrate on larger units of subject matter, with special emphasis on the ability to organise, integrate and express ideas effectively.

The preparation of items is relatively easy.

Limitations: The scoring is time consuming, difficult and inconsistent.

The items are less reliable because of inconsistent scoring. Sampling of course content is usually limited because of the small number of questions that can be included in a test.

It may be noted that despite their limitations and advantages, each type should be used where most appropriate, with appropriateness determined by the learning outcomes to be measured. Objective test items are the new pattern of items and subjective or descriptive tests are based on traditional pattern of examination. Once the authorities decide to have both types in examination, the respective weightage for these two types is to be determined. If objective items are included, learners are to be given practice by a good number of items by the teachers concerned. Objective items may be given for a maximum of one hour out of the normal duration of examination. Normally in academic setting, the students are not discouraged or penalized for wrong answers in objective items.

Different Types of Test Items

There are two types of items used in classroom tests

(i) Objectives item: It is highly structured and requires the learners to supply a word or two or to select the correct answer from a number of alternatives.

(ii) Essay question: It permits the learners to select, organise and present the answer in essay form.

Different Types of Objective Test Items

The different forms of objectives test items are

i) Short answer item
ii) True-false or alternative response item
iii) Matching exercise
iv) Multiple-choice item.

Short Answer Item

The short–answer item and the completion item both are supply –type test items that can be answered by a word, number or symbol.

The short–answer item uses a direct question, where- as the completion item consists of an incomplete statement.

Examples

Short Answer: What is the name of the person who discovered the law of gravitation? (Isaac Newton)

Completion: The name of the man who discovered the law of gravitation is (Isaac Newton).

The short answer test items is suitable for measuring a wide variety of relatively simple learning outcomes.

Examples:

i) Knowledge of terminology. If a machine tool operates in a semiautomatic or automatic cycle as per instructions transmitted to it in a coded form is said to be numerically controlled.

ii) Knowledge of specific facts. During the operation of a machine tool, a majority of its structures are subjected to compound loading.

iii) Knowledge of principles.
If temperature of a gas is held constant while the pressure applied to it is increased. What will happen to its volume? (It will decrease.)

iv) Knowledge of method or procedures. What device is used to detect whether an electric charge is positive or negative? (electroscope)

v) Simple interpretation of data.In an equilateral triangle, what is the number of degrees in each angle of the triangle? (60)

vi) Ability to solve numerical problems?

vii) Skill in manipulating mathematical symbols.

$$\text{If } \frac{x}{b} = \frac{3}{b-1} \text{ then, } x = \frac{(3b)}{b-1}$$

viii) Ability to complete and balance chemical equations.
$Mg + (2)\, HCl \rightarrow (MgCl_2 + H_2)$
$(2)\, Al + (6)\, HCl \rightarrow (2AlCl_3 + 3H_2)$

Advantages of Short-Answer Items: Short answer item is easy to construct, partly because of the relatively simple learning outcomes. Except for the problem- solving outcomes measured in mathematics and science, the short-answer item is used almost exclusively to measure the recall of memorised information.

Pupils supply the answer, which reduces the possibility that the pupils will obtain the correct answer by guessing.

Limitations of Short-Answer Item: It is unsuitable for measuring complex learning outcomes.

Difficulty of scoring unless the question is very carefully prepared, many answers of varying degrees of correctness must be considered for total or partial credit.

Suggestions for Constructing Short Answers Items

(i) Word the item so that the required answer is both brief and specific. The answer to an item should be a word, phrase, number or symbol.

Example:

Poor: An animal that eats the flesh of other animals is (carnivorous)

Better: An animal that east the flesh of other animals is classified as (carnivorous).

The first version of this item could be completed with answers such as " The Wolf", " a meat eater", etc. But asking the pupils to classify this type of animal, as called in the improved version.

ii) Do not take statements directly from text books to use a basis for short- answer items:—When taken out of context, text books statements are frequently too general and ambiguous to serve as good short item answer items.

Example:

Poor: Chlorine is a (halogen).

Better: Chlorine belongs to a group of elements that combine with metals to form salt. It is therefore called a (halogen).

iii) A direct question is more desirable then an incomplete statement:– Direct question is more natural to the pupils, as this is the usual method of phrasing questions in daily classroom discussions. The direct question usually better structures the situation and prevents much of the ambiguity that creeps into items.

Examples:

Poor: Johan Glenn made his first orbital flight round the earth in (1962).

Better: When did Johan Glenn make his first orbital flight around the earth?

Best: In which year did John Glenn make his first orbital flight around the earth ?(1962)

The first version of the item could, of course, be completed with "a space capsule", "Friend Ship seven", "Space". etc.

The second version in question form forces us to indicate whether it is in the time, place, or method we are interested in knowing. The last version is merely a refinement that makes the questions even more specific and that naturally evolves from a consideration of the "when" aspect of the previous question.

iv) If the answer is to be expressed in numerical units, indicate the type of answer wanted—For computational problems, it is usually preferable to indicate the units in which the answer is to be expressed.

Examples:

Poor: If oranges weigh $5\frac{2}{3}$ 0z. each, how much will a dozen oranges weigh ? Answer (4 lb, 4.0z)

Better: If oranges weigh $5\frac{2}{3}$ 0z. each, how much will a dozen oranges weigh? Answer ((4) lb. 4.0z)

Unless the type of unit is specified, as in the revised version, correct answers will include 680z. $4\frac{1}{4}$ Lb, 4.25 lb, and 4 lb 4.0z. This adds unnecessary confusion to the scoring.

It is also helpful to indicate the degree of precision expected in the answers. For, example, specifying that the answers should "carried out to two decimal place" or " rounded "off to the nearest tenth of a percent", makes clear to the pupils how far to carry their calculation.

i) Blanks for answers should be equal in length and in a column to the right of the question: If blanks for answers are kept equal in length; the length of the blank spaces does not supply a clue to the answer.

Example:

Poor: What is the name of the parts of speech that corrects words, clauses, and sentences? (*Conjunctions*)

What is the name of the part of speech that declares, asserts, or predicts something? (*verb*)

Better: What is the name of the part of speech that connects words, clauses and sentences? (*Conjunction*)

What is the name of the part of speech that declares, asserts, or predicts something ? (*verb*)

ii) When completion items are used, do not include too many blanks—If a statement is over mutilated, the meaning will be lost, and the pupil usually must resort to guessing what the teacher had in mind.

Example

Poor: (*Warm-blooded*) animal that are born (*alive*) and (*suckle*) their young are called (*mammals*).

Better: Warm-blooded animals that are born alive and suckle their young are called (*mammals*)

Checklist For Reviewing Short Answer Items

Review Questions	Yes	No
i) Is this the most appropriate type of item to use for the intended learning outcomes ?	☐	☐
ii) Can the items be answered with a number, symbol, word, or brief phrase?	☐	☐
iii) Has textbook language been avoided?	☐	☐
iv) Have the items been stated so that only one response is correct?	☐	☐

v) Are the answer blanks equal in length? ☐ ☐
vi) Are the answer blanks at the end of the items? ☐ ☐
vii) Are the items free of clues (such as a or an)? ☐ ☐
viii) Has the degree of precision been indicated for numerical answers? ☐ ☐
ix) Have the units been indicated when numerical answers are expressed in units? ☐ ☐
x) Have the items been phrased so as to minimise spelling errors? ☐ ☐
xi) If revised, are the items still revel vent to the intended learning outcomes? ☐ ☐
xii) Have the items been set aside for a time before reviewing them? ☐ ☐

True-False or Alternative –Response Items

Characteristics

- This test items consists of a declarative statement that the pupil is asked to mark true or false, right or wrong, correct or incorrect, yes or no, fact or opinion, agree or disagree, and the like.
- This type of item is commonly used in measuring the ability to identify the correctness of statements of fact, definitions of terms, statements of principles, and the like.

For measuring such relatively simple learning outcomes, a single declarative statement is used with any one of the several methods of responding.

Advantages

- It is easy to construct true-false item. But to construct unambiguous true-false items requires much skill.
- A wide sampling of course material can be obtained.

Limitations

- True-false item is not useful in measuring the learning outcomes beyond knowledge area.
- True-false item is susceptible of guessing. With only two alternatives, a pupil has a fifty-fifty chance of selecting the correct answer.

Common Suggestions for Constructing True-False Items

(i) Avoid broad general statement if they are to be judged true or false.
(ii) Avoid trivial statements.
(iii) Avoid the use of negative statements, especially double negatives.
(iv) Avoid long, complex sentences.
(v) Avoid including two ideas in one statement, unless cause-effect relationships are being measured.

(vi) If opinion is used, attributes it to some source, unless the ability to identify opinion, is being specifically measured.

(vii) True statements and false statements should be approximately equal in length: As the true statements are precisely phased to meet the criteria of absolute truth become longer, which gives a clue to correct answer.

(viii) The number of true statements and false statements should be approximately equal.

Checklist for Reviewing True-false Items

Review Questions	**Yes**	**No**
i) Is this the most appropriate type of item to use?		
ii) Can each statement be clearly judged true or false?		
iii) Have specific determiners (e.g. usually, always) been avoided?		
iv) Have trivial statements been avoided?		
v) Have negative statements (especially double negative) been avoided?		
vi) Have the items been stated in simple, clear language?		
vii) Are opinion statements attributed to some source?		
viii) Are the true and false items approximately equal in length?		
ix) Is there an approximately equal number of true and false items?		
x) Has a detectable pattern of answers (e.g. T, F) been avoided ?		
xi) If revised, are the items will be relevant to the intended learning outcomes?		
xii) Have the items been set aside for at time before reviewing them?		

Characteristics of Matching Exercises

A matching exercise consists of two parallel columns, with each word, number or symbol in one column being matched to a word, sentence, or phrase in the other column.

The items in the column for which a match is sought are called premises, and the items in the column from which the selection is made are called responses.

Example:

On the line to the left of each United States space event in column A, write the letter of the astronaut in column B who achieved that honour. Each name in column may be used once, more than once, or not at all.

Column A	Column B
(C) 1. First United States astronaut to ride in a space capsule	A. Edwin Aldrin.
(E) 2. First United States astronaut to orbit the earth.	B. Neil Armstrong.
(H) 3. First United State astronaut to walk in space.	C. Frenk Barrman.
(B) 4. First United States astronaut to step on the moon.	D. Scott Capenter
	E. John Glenn
	F. Wally Shirra.
	G. Alan Shephard
	H. Edward White

- The items in the list of premises in column A are homogenous as they all are concerned with important space events. Such homogeneity is necessary if a matching exercises is to function properly.
- For each premises in Column A there are several plausible responses in Column B. Thus, the incorrect responses serve as attractive choices for these pupils who are in doubt about the correct answers.

Advantages

- It is compact and makes it possible to measure a large amount of related factual material in a relatively short time.
- Erase of construction, but good items require a high degree of skill. Much of the difficulty is because the correct response for each premise must also serve as a plausible response for the other premises.

Limitations

- It is restricted to the measurement of factual information based on rote learning and that it is highly susceptible to the presence of irrelevant clues.
- Difficulty of finding homogenous material that is significant from the viewpoint of the objectives and learning outcomes.

Considerations While Constructing Matching Exercises

- Use only homogeneous material in a single matching exercise.
- Include an unequal number of responses and premises, and instruct the pupil that responses may be use once, more than once, or not at all.
- Keep the list of items to be matched brief, and place the shorter response on the right.
- Arrange the list of responses in logical order Place words in alphabetical order and numbers in sequence.
- Indicate in the directions the basis for matching the responses and premises.
- Place all the items for one matching exercises on the same page.

Check List for Reviewing Matching Items

Review Questions	Yes	No
i) Is this the most appropriate type of item to use?		
ii) Is the material in the two lists homogenous?		
iii) Is the list of responses longer or shorter than the list premises?		
iv) Are the response brief and on the right hand side?		
v) Have the responses been placed in alphabetical or numerical order?		
vi) Do the directions indicate the basis for matching?		
vii) Do the directions indicate that each response may be used more than once?		
viii) Is all of each matching item on the same page?		
ix) If revised, are the items still relevant to the intended learning outcomes?		
x) Have the items been set aside for a time before reviewing them ?		

Multiple-Choice Items

Characteristics

- A multiple choice item consists of a problem and a list of suggested solutions.
- The problem may be stated as a direct question or an incomplete statement and is called the stem of the item.
- The list of suggested solutions may include words, numbers, symbols, or phrases and are called alternatives. The correct alternative in each item is called key, and the remaining alternatives are called distractors.
- The stems can be direct question type or incomplete statement type.

Uses of Multiple Choice Items

i) Knowledge of knowledge outcome
   (a) Knowledge of terminology
   (b) Knowledge of specific facts
   (c) Knowledge of principles
   (d) Knowledge of methods and procedures

   This includes such diverse areas as knowledge of laboratory procedures, knowledge of methods underlying communication, computational, and performance skills, knowledge of methods used in problem solving; knowledge of governmental procedures; knowledge of common social practices.

(ii) Measuring outcomes at the understanding and application levels
   (a) Ability to identify application of facts and principles

(b) Ability to interpret cause-and-effect relationships
(c) Ability to justify methods and procedures

Uses of Multiple Choice Items

It can effectively measure various types of knowledge and complex learning outcomes.

The ambiguity and vagueness that frequently are present in the short—answer item are avoided because the alternatives better structure the situation.

One advantage of multiple –choice item than the true –false item is that pupils cannot receive credit for simply knowing that a statement is incorrect; they must also know what is correct.

Multiple-choice item has greater reliability than true—false item because the opportunity for guessing the correct answer is reduced.

Using the best-answer type of multiple choice item also circumvents a difficulty associated with the true-false item-obtaining statement that are true or false without qualification, where the problems are not absolutely true or false but vary in degree of opportunities.

An advantage of the multiple-choice item over the the matching exercises is that the need for homogenous material is avoided.

Limitations of Multiple Choice Items

It is limited to learning outcomes at the verbal level i.e. it measures whether the pupil knows or understands what to do when confronted with a problem situation, but it can- not determine how the pupil actually will perform in that situation.

It requires selection of correct answer and therefore it is not well adapted in measuring some problem—solving skills in mathematics and science or in measuring the ability to organise and present ideas.

It has the difficulty of finding a sufficient number of incorrect but plausible distractors.

Suggestions for Consulting Multiple Choice Items

- The stem of the item should be meaningful by itself and should present a definite problem.
- The item stem should include as much of the item as possible and should be free of irrelevant material.
- Use a negatively stated item stem only when significant learning outcomes require it.
- All the alternatives should be grammatically consistent with stem of the item.
- An item should contain only one correct or clearly the best answer.
- Items used to measure understanding should contain some novelty, but beware of too much-The problem of too much novelty usually

can be avoided by selecting situations of the pupils' everyday experiences, by including in the stem of the item any factual information needed, and by phrasing the item so that the type of application or interpretation called for is clear.

- All distractors should be plausible.
- Verbal associations between the stem and the correct answer should be avoided.
- The relative length of the alternatives should not provide a clue to the answer.
- The correct answer should appear in each of the alternative positions in approximately equal number of items but in random order.
- Avoid using special alternatives such as "none of the above" or "all of the above"
- Do not use multiple-choice items when other items are more appropriate.
- Break any of these rules when you have a good reason for doing so.

Checklist for Reviewing Multiple Choice Items

Review Questions	**Yes**	**No**
i) Is this the most appropriate type of item to use?		
ii) Does each item stem present meaningful problem?		
iii) Are the item stems free of irrelevant material?		
iv) Are the item stems stated in positive terms (if possible)		
v) If used, has negative wording been given special emphasis (e.g., capitalised)		
vi) Are the distractors grammatically consistent with item stem?		
vii) Are the alternative answers brief and free of unnecessary words?		
viii) Are the alternatives similar in length and form?		
ix) Is there only one correct or clearly best answer?		
x) Are the distracters plausible to non- achievers ?		
xi) Are the items free of verbal clues to the answer?		
xii) Are verbal alternatives in alphabetical order?		
xiii) Are the numerical alternatives in numerical order?		
xiv) Have "none of the above" and "all of the above" been avoided (or used sparingly and appropriately)?		
xv) If revised, are the items still relevant to the intended learning outcomes?		
xvi) Have the items been set-aside for a time before reviewing them?		

Essay Tests

Features

- Freedom of response i.e. pupils are free to select, relate, and present ideas in their own words.
- Essay questions are used to measure complex achievement. They are suitable to measure the abilities to select, organise, integrate, relate and evaluate ideas which require the freedom of response and the originally provided by essay questions.

Classification of the Essay Type Questions

Essay questions can be conveniently classified into two types of as following,

(a) *Restricted response questions*
- The content is usually restricted by the scope of the topic to be discussed.
- Limitations on the form of response are generally indicated in the questions.
- They are useful for measuring learning outcomes requiring the interpretation and application of data in a specific area.
  Examples:
  Why is the barometer one of the most useful instruments for forecasting weather? Answer in a brief paragraph.
  Describe two situations that demonstrate the application of the law of supply and demand.

(b) *Extended response questions:*
- This type of question allows pupils to select any factual information that they think is pertinent, to organise the answer in accordance with their best judgment, and to integrate and evaluate ideas as they deem appropriate.
- This freedom enables them to demonstrate their ability to select, organise, integrate, and evaluate ideas.
- They are inefficient for measuring mere specific learning outcomes and introduce scoring difficulties.

Example 1: Describe the influence of Mendel's law of heredity on the development of biology as a science.

Example 2: Write a scientific evaluation of the Copernican theory of the solar system. Include scientific observations that support your statements.

Advantages of Essay Questions

1. It measures complex learning outcomes that cannot be measured by other means.

2. The advantage of extended response question is its emphasis on the integration and application of thinking and problem—solving skills.

Limitations of Essay Test

1. Unreliability of the scoring. Answers to essay questions are scored differently by different teachers and that even the same teacher score the answers differently at different times. One teacher may stress factual content, one organisation of ideas, and another writing skill.
2. Essay questions require more time for scoring the answers.
3. Essay questions provide limited sampling.
4. Few questions can be included in a given test that some areas are measured thoroughly, but many others are neglected.

Suggestions for Constructing Essay Questions

1. Restrict the use of essay questions to those learning outcomes that cannot be satisfactorily measured by objectives items.
2. Formulate questions that will put forth the behaviour specified in the learning outcomes.
3. Phrase each question so that the pupil's task is clearly indicated.
4. Indicate an approximate time limit for each question.
5. Avoid the use of optional questions.

Suggestions to Score Essay Questions

1. Prepare an outline of the expected answer in advance.
2. Use the scoring method that is most appropriate.—There are two common methods namely point method and rating method. With the point method, each answer is compared with the ideal answer in the scoring key, and a given number of points is assigned according to the adequacy of the answer.
3. With the rating method, each paper is placed in one of a number of piles, as the answer is read. These piles represent degrees of a quality and determine the credit assigned to each answer. If eight points are allotted to the question, for example, nine piles might be used ranging in value from eight points to none. Usually between five and ten categories are used with the rating method.
4. Decide how to handle factors that are irrelevant to the learning outcomes being measured—Several factors (such as legibility of hand writing, spelling, sentence structure, punctuation, and neatness) influence our evaluations of answers to essay questions that are not directly pertinent to the purpose of the measurement.
5. Evaluate all answer to one question before going on to the next one—One factor that contributes to unreliable scoring of essay questions is shifting of standards from one paper to the next. A paper with

average answers may appear to be of much higher quality when it follows a failing paper than when it follow one with near –perfect answers. One way to minimise this is to score all answers to the first question, shuffle the papers, then score all answers to the second question, and so on, until all the answers have been scored.

6. Evaluate the answers without looking at the pupils' name.
7. If especially important decisions are to be based on the results, obtain two or more independent ratings.
8. Some- times essay questions are included in tests to select pupils for awards, scholarships, special training, and the like. In such cases, two or more competent persons should score the papers independently, and their ratings should be compared.

Characteristics of Evaluation Tools

Evaluation tools will not be of much use if they cannot provide consistent result. An evaluation tool should also measure what it intends to measure. Moreover it should be economical both in terms of time and money, besides ensuring coverage of all study units. These are some of the essential attributes of a good evaluation tool. These characteristics or attributes are variously named as reliability, validity, practicability, etc., which are being described as follows:

Important Characteristics

Validity: The validity of a test is the extent to how well it fulfills the function for which it is being used.

Reliability: Reliability of a test is its consistency with which it measures what it claims to be measuring. Reliability is necessary but not a sufficient condition for validity.

Practicability: This is the one of the important attributes of a good test besides validity and reliability. It includes all practical considerations like availability of a test, cost, mode of administration, etc., that are taken in to account in order to use a particular test.

Comprehensiveness: A test should cover all possible units of study i.e., items/questions should be framed from every unit in order to make it comprehensive.

Types of Validity: In determining the validity of an evaluation tool, the different types of validity may be required to be considered that are being discussed here.

Face Validity: Face validity answers the question "how do the test items look like in the light of the objective of the test?" This means it answers the reasonableness of the items of a test in context to the background of the testers that the test is meant for. This is determined by assuring the relevance, adequacy and coverage that the test item stands for.

A test is said to have face validity if on first impression it appears to measure the intended content or trait.

Content Validity: Content validity determines the degree of relationship between the curriculum course content or units of study and the items of the test. This is usually done by developing table of specification. A test which is said to have been content validated ensures a high degree of correlation between the course content and the test items. Content validity answers the question, "To what extent does the test require demonstration by the student of the achievements which constitute the objectives of instruction in that area?" The content validity of a test must always be viewed in relation to the particular objectives to be assessed.

Predictive Validity: Predictive validity predicts some subsequent measure of performance i.e., the results of a test with predictive validity can be used for predicting some future outcomes. When we are interested in finding out how the results of a test can be used for predicting a future outcome, we expect a high degree of relationship between the test scores and the criterion measure of success for the future task, predictive validity ensures this.

The higher the degree of correlation between the test scores and the future criterion measures, the more effective the test is as a predictor. As a future criterion is used in the determination of predictive validity and due to the empirical nature of such an exercise, predictive validity is sometimes also referred to as an empirical or criterion related validity. Some experts consider predictive validity as a subclass of criterion-related validity.

Construct Validity: When a test is used to describe the degree to which a tester manifests an abstract psychological trait or ability, construct validity is taken into consideration.

Construct validity of a test informs something meaningful about a person's trait such as introversion, interest, attitude, etc. (constructs). The term construct refers to non-observable, postulated variables that have evolved either informally or from psychological theory. Construct validation is an analysis of the meaning of test scores in terms of psychological constructs. There are more than one criterion used in construct validation.

Types of Reliability: In this unit, the three important types of reliability that may be of use to a classroom teacher as an evaluator have been described.

Scorer Reliability: Scorer reliability refers to the degree of agreement between two scorers scoring the same test-answer script, hence it is also called "inter-scorers' reliability". Scorer reliability also refers to the degree of consistency in grading the same test-answer script by the same scorer on two different occasions, in such a case it is also called as "intra-scorers' reliability".

Content Reliability: The ability of all the items of a test to measure competencies in the same general content area is determined by content reliability. A content reliable test is one whose items focus on related content area such that they will be capable of measuring similar or related traits. This means that content reliability concerns itself with the internal consistency measures of the items of a test.

Temporal Reliability: Temporal reliability is related to the stability of the results of a test over time. This is the third major dimension of reliability. Temporal reliability is assessed by giving the same test twice (test-retest method) to the same sample at two different times and by correlating the results derived from such tests.

Practicability

Also referred to as usability by some, it is determined only after the reliability and validity of a test have been determined. Convenience of administering a test and scoring the answer scripts, economy of use, and interpretability of test scores all determine the practicability of a test.

In sum, The two characteristics, namely reliability and validity are the most important and essential attributes of a good evaluation tool. The validity of a test is the accuracy with which meaningful and relevant measurements can be made, and it actually measures the traits it was intended to measure. A reliable test should measure consistently (time and again) the parameter of interest to the evaluator every time s/he uses it. Reliability is usually expressed in the form of a coefficient of correlation.

16
Skill Evaluation

Teachers as assessors are often suppose to evaluate skill-sets of students. It is more so far an institution, dealing with developing teaching skills of the trainees.

Skill shall be used to refer to actions (intellectual or physical and now-days with growing concept of soft-skill, affective-skill too) and indeed 'reactions' (to ideas, things or people) which a person performs in a competent way in order to achieve a goal. In practicing a skill, one uses certain items to knowledge that are stored in the mind. Any skilled action may have four component activities—perception, planning, recall of pre-requisite knowledge, and finally the execution, or performance, of the action. Skill develops with experience and practice.

Categories of Skill

Main Skill Category	*Types of Knowledge Content*	
	Reproductive Skills (Applying procedures i.e., algorithm)	*Productive Skills (Applying principles and strategies)*
Cognitive Skills (Decision-making, problem solving, logical thinking etc.)	Applying a known procedure to a known category of 'problem' e.g., dividing numbers, writing a grammatically correct sentence	Solving 'new' problems, 'Investing' a new procedure, e.g., providing a theorem, writing creatively
Psychomotor Skills (Physical action, perceptual acuity etc.)	Sensor—motor skills, repetitive or automated action, e.g., typewriting changing gear, running fast.	'Strategy' skills or 'planning' skills, arts and crafts e.g., page layout design 'road sense' playing football.
Reactive Skills (Dealing with oneself, attitudes, feelings, habits, self-control)	Conditioned habits and attitudes, e.g., 'attending responding and valuing', 'approach/avoid behaviours'.	'Personal control', skills, developing a 'mental set' or a value system 'self-actualisation'.
Interactive Skills (Dealing with others)	Social habits, conditioned responses, e.g., good manners, pleasant tone, verbal habits.	'Interpersonal control' skills, e.g., leadership, supervision, persuasion, discussion, salesmanship.

Guideline to Evaluate Learner's Progress in the Development of a Skill

One can check the learner's observed progress against the list of stages in skill development

i) Has s/he got the necessary pre-requisites—the knowledge of what should be done, why and how, any essential basic skills, requisite perceptual acuity etc.

ii) Is s/he applying what s/he knows correctly—i.e., performing all the necessary steps and in the correct sequence?

iii) Is his/her performance still jumpy and very step-by-step, or has s/he commenced to transfer control to other senses than the edges and achieve a smoother, more integrated pattern of work?

iv) Does s/he still require to concentrate on the execution of the skilled work to the exclusion of all else, or has s/he commenced to 'automatise' the skill?

To what extent is s/he already capable of handling variety? Can s/he generalise the newly learnt skills to other similar situations? To what extent is s/he being creative in his/her execution of the skilled activity? How well is s/he planning the execution of the skilled activity?

How to Select Tasks for Skill Test?

i) The following guidelines for selecting tasks for a skill test improve test validity and efficiency of measurement (per unit of testing time).

ii) Choose tasks that are representative of the significant skills emphasised in the course.

iii) Choose tasks, or aspects of tasks, that are reasonably difficult for students. Since performance testing is time consuming, eliminate tasks, or parts of tasks, that almost everyone can do, say for example, in testing driving skill, a student would do parallel rather than angle parking.

iv) Plan a test that involves a minimum of repetition of identical procedures. Example: A test of driving skills should be planned so that the student spends little time repeating right turns and other routine tasks.

v) Choose tasks that are crucial to success on the job as a whole. The test should provide opportunities to make those mistakes that are frequently responsible for failure in the total task or for failure to progress to higher levels of proficiency.

Example – 1: A bandmaster would want to 4test students for accurate music reading and ability to come in at the proper place after a rest.

Example 2: A swimming teacher would place considerable weight on the students ability to synchronise his breathing with the pattern of his crawl stroke, as well as those characteristics of swimming form that minimise water resistance.

i) If feasible, choose tasks that do not require too much time to perform, so that one can include a larger sampling of different tasks.

Example: A student of statistics might complete several problems in which the easier, time-consuming work had been done for him.

ii) Choose tasks in which the conditions of work can be made standard for all students and the performance can be judged with considerable objectivity.

Example: The student's skill in backing a car down a market lane can be judged more objectively than his ability in parallel parking. If possible, choose tasks that involve materials and equipment commonly used in the course, and of which there are sufficient sets available to permit a number of students to be tested at one time.

Difficulties in Performance (Skill) Tests

The difficulties are:

i) the amount of time required in administration, since only a few students can usually be tested at a time;

ii) the need for planning constructive activities for students not being tested at any given time;

iii) the fact that such tests are difficult to construct and to administer; and

iv) that fact that such tests tend to penalise students who cannot work well under pressure.

Basis of Scoring Students' Performance in Skill Development

The scoring of student performance in work samples or simulated situation tests may be based on

i) The performance in process.

ii) The product of the performance, together.

iii) The product and process of performance.

Writing Objectives on Process

In stating and defining performance objectives, the focus should be on the performance itself (e.g., the process) when:

- the act of performing is the main outcome, or there is no product.
- a diagnosis of the performance is needed to improve learning.
- the performance is based on a collection of elements or series of steps that can be identified.

For any particular performance there are number of elements, or procedures, that are crucial to a successful performance. Thus, in writing objectives in this area, it is necessary to analyse the performance to identify those elements or procedural steps that define a satisfactory performance.

Example 1: Using laboratory equipment properly.

Here the student:

- Selects appropriate equipment for an experiment.
- Assembles equipment correctly for an experiment.
- Manipulates equipment as needed during the experiment.
- Measures accurately with proper measuring devices.
- Follows safety rules in conducting experiment.
- Uses materials without wasting any.
- Completes experiment within time limits.
- Clears equipment and returns to proper place.

It is to be noted that all the skill-set need to be performed sequentially.

Example 2: Applies varnish correctly.

Here the performer:

- Sands and prepares surface properly.
- Wipes dust from surface with appropriate cloth.
- Selects appropriate brush.
- Selects varnish and checks varnish flow.
- Pours needed amount of varnish into clean container.
- Puts brush properly into varnish (one—third of bristle length).
- Wipes excess varnish from brush on inside edge of container.
- Applies varnish to surface with smooth strokes.
- Works from centre of surface toward the edges.
- Brushes with the grain of the wood.

- Uses light strokes to smooth the varnish.
- Checks surface for completeness.
- Cleans brush with appropriate cleaner.
- Does not pour excess varnish back into can.
- Cleans work area.

Writing Objectives on Product Outcomes

Performance objectives should focus on the product from the performance when:

- The product is the main outcome of the performance.
- The product has identifiable characteristics that can be used in evaluating the quality of the product.
- There is considerable variation in the process that can be used in producing the product, or the procedures are not observable to the instructor (e.g., out-of-class work).

If the objective indicates a product and the characteristics of the product can be identified and clearly defined, the specific learning are stated as criteria that describes a high-quality as follows:

i) Constructs a bar graph

1. Uses a separate bar for each measure.
2. Matches length of each bar to data
3. Arranges bars in some logical order.
4. Makes bars wider than spaces between them.
5. Uses scale and guide lines that make bars easy to interpret.
6. Identifies each bar with a label.
7. Uses title clearly to indicate the nature of the graph.

ii) Writes an effective composition

1. Expresses ideas clearly.
2. Uses ideas that are logical
3. Relates ideas to the main thesis.
4. Organises the thesis to fit the topic.
5. Writes well structured, relevant paragraphs.
6. Uses parts of speech correctly.
7. Uses words that effectively convey meaning.
8. Spells all words correctly.
9. Uses correct punctuation.

Writing Objectives on both Process and Product Outcome

Performance objectives should include both procedure and product outcomes when:

- There is a clear set of procedures for producing the product (e.g., cooking recipe, steps for constructing a wood working project).
- Learning is at an early stage and the product can be improved by correcting procedural errors.
- Both the process and the product have identifiable elements that can be described and observed.

Here the aim is to learn the proper procedures and to obtain a satisfactory level of performance, rather than a high degree of proficiency. Thus, wherever feasible, focus should be directed toward both the procedures used and the product.

Why Evaluation of products tends to be more reliable than evaluation of process?

The reasons are as follows:

i) More time is available for judging products, while performance in process must be judged "on the wing".
ii) Independent judgment of products, made by different evaluators, can be obtained, checked for inter-scorer reliability, and combined.
iii) We can develop a scale of products (representing approximately equal differences in quality) to aid in objective scoring.
iv) We can train persons in the use of product scales, we can check their reliability in grading and the extent to which their judgments agree with those of adjudged experts.

Use of Ranking Processes and Products Checklists and Rating Scales

When a teacher grades students in such performance skills as swimming or playing tennis, or when he grades their products, he is presumably ranking the performances or products on some continuum of quality. Too often the characteristics used as a basis for grading differ from teacher to teacher, and also differ as the same teacher observes and evaluates the work of different students. One advantage of using checklists and rating scales is to minimise these differences with respect to selective attention and recall.

Another problem in grading is differences in generosity (from teacher to teacher, and from time to time with the same teacher). If all teachers rank students' work, differences in generosity do not affect students' scores. No teacher can place an unusually large number in the top 10 per cent; whereas he could be very generous in assigning A's. Moreover, the ranking process requires the teacher to make a more careful study of inter-individual differences than is usually considered necessary in the assignment of marks.

Use of Checklist to Evaluate a Process

When specific learning outcomes are properly stated, they can be easily converted to a checklist by simply adding a place to check "yes" or "no" for each procedure. A checklist is an aid to the observer in recording information regarding sequence of acts or use of approved methods. The person using the checklist might simply check the actions that occur or the methods used. A checklist might be used to record those elements in a complex task that had been satisfactorily completed.

Example of Checklist Scoring for use of laboratory equipment by a student:

		Yes	No
a.	Is appropriate equipment for the experiment selected?	☐	☐
b.	Is s/he able to assemble equipment correctly for the experiment?	☐	☐
c.	Is s/he able to manipulate the equipment as needed during the experiment?	☐	☐
d.	Is s/he able to measure accurately with proper measuring device?	☐	☐
e.	Does s/he follow safety rules in conducting experiment?	☐	☐
f.	Does s/he use materials without any wastage?	☐	☐
g.	Is he able to complete experiment within time limits?	☐	☐
h.	Does s/he clean equipment and return to proper place?	☐	☐

Using a Rating Scale to Evaluate a Process

When specific learning outcomes are properly stated they can be easily converted to a rating scale by adding a place to rate each procedure as it is performed

Rating scale requires a qualitative evaluation of aspects of a total performance or of steps or subtasks within a series.

The first step in constructing a rating scale is to break down the process into components. Decisions may also be made concerning the relative importance of different components.

Example:

TO SAW TO A LINE WITH A RIP AND CROSS-CUT SAW

Tools and materials: Sharp rip saw and cross-cut saw, bench, wood vise, and piece of wood.

Directions: Observe learner as s/he works, and rate him/her on the following points.

	1	2	3	4	5
1. CLAMPING STOCK Stock should be so held that it will not be loosened or cracked, and that its position will facilitate sawing. 2. STARTING CUT With thumb at line, saw should be placed against the thumb. Saw should be pulled back slowly a few times to make a groove, than pushed forward. 3. HOLDING SAW Saw should be held firmly. For cross-cut saw, angle should be 45 degrees, for rip saw, 60 degrees. 4. STROKE Stroke should be long and even, not too fast. Proper angle should be kept during sawing. Line should be followed. 5. ENDING CUT The piece being out off should be held with the free hand. Saw strokes should be slow and with little pressure so as to prevent breaking off the end.					

Using a Checklist to Evaluate a Product

To devise a checklist for products compare good and poor products and identify those characteristics that differentiate between poor and good products and in the checklist.

Example:

SCORING FOR STUDENTS FOR CONSTRUCTION OF A BAR GRAPH

	Yes	No
a. Does s/he use a separate bar for each measure?	☐	☐
b. Does length of each bar match to data?	☐	☐
c. Does s/he arrange bars in some logical order?	☐	☐
d. Are the bars wider than spaces between them?	☐	☐
e. Does s/he use scale and guidelines that make bars easy to interpret?	☐	☐
f. Does s/he identify each bar with a label?	☐	☐
g. Does s/he use title that clearly indicate the nature of the graph?	☐	☐

Rating Scale to Evaluate a Product

The list of specific statements defining a product can be easily converted in to a rating scale for use in performance assessment.

A product scale is a graded series of products (usually five or more) carefully chosen to represent successive levels of quality along an interior superior continuum. In the evaluation of hand writing and composition skills, product scales have been used for many years.

Example:

Point Scale Rating Form for "fastening" in wood working:

	1	2	3	4	5
a. NAILS					
i) Straightness Are sales driven straight, heads square with wood, no evidence of bending?					
ii) Hammer marks Is wood free of hammer marks around nails?					
iii) Splitting Is wood free of splits radiating from nail holes?					
iv) Depth Are depths of nails uniform and of pleasing appearance?					
v) Spacing Are nails spaced too close or too far apart?					
vi) Utility Will the nails hold?					
b) SCREWS					
i) Slots Are slots free of splitting and other evidence of driving strains?					
ii) Straightness Are screws straight, heads parallel with surface?					
iii) Splitting Is wood free of splits in the area of screws?					
iv) Screw driver marks Is wood free of screw driver marks near screws?					
v) Countersinking Is countersinking neat and of satisfactory depth?					
vi) Spacing Are screws spaced too close or too far apart?					
vii) Utility Will the screws hold?					

Evaluating Product and Process Outcome

- By adequately describing the procedures, we can provide guidelines for diagnosing and improving those elements of the performance that will result in a better product.
- Description of the product provides a means for evaluating the effect of the improved procedures on the quality of the product and the level of proficiency attained.

Evaluation Proforma

Project Type: Design and implementation based

Student's name:
Roll no/Regd. no:
Title:

Mark the project report as 'excellent','satisfactory' or 'unsatisfactory ' according to the criteria given below. Use the intermediate columns as needed.

Criteria	*Excellent*	*Satisfactory*	*Unsatisfactory*
Background Reading General understanding of the subject area			
Report organization and structure			
Reasonable and well justified conclusions Critical appraisal of the work			
Key problems identified and solved			
Documentation (user/System manuals, design documents etc. as appropriate)			
Completeness (Objectives achieved fully)			
Overall system design			
Appropriate use of data structures and algorithms			
Appropriate use of tools, libraries, existing codes etc.			
Well-structured and readable implementation			
System testing and/or verification			
Count the ticks in each column			
Multiply each count by these weights	X8	X4	X1
Add weighted counts together			
Multiply total weighted count by 25/24 to yield agreed mark.		%	

Evaluation Proforma

Project Type: Design based
Student's name:
Roll no/Regd. no:
Title:

Mark the project report as 'excellent', 'satisfactory' or 'unsatisfactory' according to the criteria given below. Use the intermediate columns as needed.

Criteria	*Excellent*	*Satisfactory*	*Unsatisfactory*
Background Reading. General understanding of the subject area			
Report organization and structure			
Reasonable and well justified conclusions Critical appraisal of the work			
Key problems identified and solved			
Documentation (user/System manuals, design documents etc. as appropriate)			
Completeness. (Objectives achieved fully)			
Requirements and objectives well understood and presented			
Appropriate use of design methodology			
Overall quality of the final design			
Evaluation and/or verification of the design (e.g. by prototyping)			
Practicality of the design			
Count the ticks in each column			
Multiply each count by these weights	X 8	X 4	X 1
Add weighted counts together			
Multiply total weighted count by 25/24 to yield agreed mark		%	

Apart from the above mentioned two assessment proforma, the student may be asked to make his course assessment, after all the material connected with his/her project/dissertation has been submitted. His/her replies will not be analysed until the final evaluation is over.

COURSE EVALUATION BY THE STUDENT

Department: Education	Supervisor (s):
Course code:	Group or Individual work (G, I) ———

(1) PREPARATION AND TRAINING		-2	-1	0	+1	+2	
The aims of the project were	Unclear						Clear
Preparation for practical aspects of the project was	Poor						good
The training in presentation skills was	Poor						good
The preparation for data interpretation was	Poor						good
The training in time management was	Poor						good
The quality of supervision was	Poor						good
The amount of supervision was	too little						too much
(2) CONTENT AND FACILITIES		-2	-1	0	+1	+2	
The project workload was	Too low						too high
Your interest in the project was	low						high
The required report length was	too short						Too long
Library facilities were	poor						good
Computing facilities were	poor						good
Laboratory facilities were	poor						good
(3) OVERALL ASSESSMENT		-2	-1	0	+1	+2	
Overall my view of the project was that it was	Very poor						Very good

In nut shell, a project can be described as offering unique learning opportunity where students can demonstrate project management skills in a time bound domain. The project work is clearly a student–centered learning experience which requires the supervisor to take role of a facilitator. Further, supervisor's management and interpersonal skills can also be tested through the process. In project work, students are offered with a range of planning tools. The supervisor must extend support for the student (to take the role of a facilitator), prompt and encourage, supervises to move forward with innovative ideas.

17

Instructional Plan for Laboratory

Laboratory experiences for the students serve as a powerful tool in making the teaching learning process more effective. Many of the instructional objectives, pertaining to certain skills and attitudes, can be better developed through laboratory work rather than through classroom teaching.

Types of Skill-Sets

- *Cognitive or intellectual skills*—thinking or reasoning. The skills of 'using one's head'.
- *Psychomotor or physical skills*—Sports and practical tasks. The sills of 'using one's body'.
- *Reactive or personal skills*—Personal behaviour. The skills or 'Controlling oneself'.
- *Interactive or interpersonal skills*—Interacting with others, leading, selling, persuading. The skills of 'controlling others'.

Classification of Skills according to Degree of Creativity

- ***Reproductive skills***—Executed in totally automated manner, involving no analytical thinking, planning or evaluation of alternatives. Depend on the application of previously learned algorithms.
- ***Productive skills***—Executed in a non-automated manner, involving the analysis and evaluation of alternatives and planning of appropriate strategies of problem solving. Depend on the application of concepts and general principles.

How Skills are Learned?

- Reproductive skills are learned through practice.
- Productive or creative skills cannot be learned by mere practice. Once 'threshold' learning is reached through practice, the perfection can be reached through practice in the intellectual, planning, sub-skills which are used for creative decision.

Classification of skilled performance

Skill Specification	*Reproductive Skills*	*Productive Skills*
Cognitive or intellectual Skills	Division, multiplication, reading a circuit diagram	Solving geometry problems, designing a novel circuit.
Psychomotor or physical skills	Typing, writing by hand, kicking a ball straight, running	Playing piano artistically, playing football, strategically.
Reactive or personal skills	Personal habits, punctuality, hygiene, truthfulness, etc.	Personal life style–living in accordance with a set of values or beliefs.
Interactive or interpersonal skills	Interpersonal habits, good manners, tone or voice, listening skills	Leadership, persuasion, selling, supervision, negotiation, teaching and similar complex/creative skills.

Nature of Learning Process in the Laboratory

a) The Stimulus Situation

- Listening is minimised, reading is simplified and observation is maximised.
- Arrange the stimulus situation so as to make it most appropriate and intelligible to the group.
- The teacher arranges the environment, suggests ways of acting on it and devices controls to keep the students attentive on specifics in the environment.
- Environment should be attractive to the students and stimulus should be challenging for each of them.

b) The Response Situation

- Response in motor activities follows immediately after every observed or perceived stimulus.
- To ensure proper response, the control should be situational, and distractive influences of irrelevant cues should be reduced to minimum.

c) The Interaction Situation

- The student learns best when he gets direct help from the teacher the least.
- The relevant learning skill in the contrived situation has to be imparted at stages so that the student gradually becomes Independent of the teacher.

How Skills are Taught?

Actually skill can't be taught, rather those needs to be imbibed.

- For perfection of reproductive skills, practice should be done. Practice makes a man perfect.

- In productive skills, one must provide opportunities for self- analysis, reflection and exchange of ideas with other equally or more skilled practitioners.
- For productive skill development, briefing and debriefing sessions should be included in instructional designs.
- For most skills, combine the instruction of new knowledge with its skilled application in the same lesson.
- The skilled performance of a task is usually enjoyable, so the sooner that some results are seen by the learner, the higher the level of interest and motivation to continue learning.

Aims of Laboratory Work

- Understand concepts
- Understand principles
- Discover rules and relationships
- Solve problems
- Develop ability to observe and measure
- Identify sources of errors and methods for minimising equipment/ instrument/material
- Develop manipulative skills such as setting, adjusting and handling of equipment
- Follow standard procedure of testing
- Write formal and informal reports
- Work in groups (team work) successfully
- Develop habit of enquiry
- Observe safety precautions
- Interpret the results/data
- Locate fault in equipment/instrument/circuits
- Judge magnitude without actual measurement.

Different Categories of Laboratory Experiments

1. Conventional Type Experiment

In conventional type of experiment, all the information regarding the performance of each experiment are provided to the student. Information is either provided to the student verbally or by way of work sheet or laboratory manual.

Experiments are teacher centered i.e. there is not much scope for the student to think on his/her own. Students attempt to verify certain known relationship, principles or determine some physical quantity. In most cases, the interpretation, conclusion or the outcome is already known to the students.

Merits

- Instructions help less able students
- It can precede or replace class room instructions
- Develops ability to follow instructions.

Limitations

- Less freedom to students
- Little scope for student initiative
- Limits the conclusions to be drawn
- Monotonous.

2. Discovery Type Experiment

It is designed to guide/encourage student to discover for himself certain facts, concepts, principles, laws, relationships etc. instead of directly telling him. Interwoven questions should be built into the procedure which will facilitate thinking and lead the student to the discovery of the intended fact, concept, or some standard relationship. The procedure should be in greater detail so that discovery takes place.

Merits

- Better understanding and retention
- Suitable for fault location/measurement skills/Instrument handling
- Habit of enquiry
- It can precede or replace classroom instruction.

Limitations

- Thinking is canalised
- Limited freedom of expression
- Less challenging for able students.

3. Investigative Type Experiment

It is at slightly higher level than the discovery type. It is so designed that the decision-making abilities of the student and the application of rules, concepts, etc. should be more than that which occurs in the discovery type. Investigative experiments utilises various laws, rules, principles and the skills the student has already acquired. Complete procedural instructions need not be provided, they can be partially structured and partially open-ended. Some kind of directions/information is provided with regard to tools, equipment, materials etc. Students are free to think of alternative strategies, instruments and methods. They are required to plan their own experimental strategy, collect experimental data and draw conclusions. In this type teachers activity become lesser in comparison to the discovery type.

Merits

- Scope for students' initiative and interest
- Develops ability to select suitable equipment and materials among the students.

- Error identification and reduction is possible.
- Helps among the students the ability to interpret results and to draw conclusions.

Limitations

- Difficult for less abled students
- Takes more time
- Pre-requisites are must before students take up this type of experiment.

4. Problem Solving Type Experiment

Student presented with problem solving experiences in his/her discipline to develop problem solving abilities and inculcate the confidence to face such situations.Once the problem statement/specification is given student is made to think, plan, generate alternative solutions, evaluate them and execute the best alternative.The student decides what data is to be collected, choose the requisite instruments/tools and decides how to carry out the method selected.

Merit

- Develops higher experimental skills -selection, planning, designing
- Develops confidence in solving problem
- Encourages initiative and interest
- Challenging for abled students.

Limitations

- Difficult for less abled students
- Adequate resources and time is required
- Constant supervision and interaction by teacher is required
- Tactful guidance by teachers is required.

5. Project Type Experiment

Here Student is asked to choose any type of laboratory or field exercise s/he prefers. This is intended to integrate the knowledge, skills and attitude, which the student should have acquired over the entire period of a programme. It should have a measureable and achievable outcome, a realistic time-frame; an action plan and persons identified for each activity. The work involved for initial background and investigation may involve use of facilities in different laboratories and workshop.

Merits

- Develops decision making skills
- Extends freedom to students to design and in writing reports
- Enhance creative abilities
- Encourages initiative and interest
- Develop confidence and skills to solve problems.

Limitations

- Students' background restricts variety
- Organization and evaluation is difficult
- More resources are required
- Time consuming.

Components of Laboratory' Instruction

1. ***Short title of the test/experiment:*** It must carry the theme of the experiment/test in the shortest possible words.
2. ***Aim of the test/experiment:*** What do students finally determine in a test/experiment.
3. ***Performance Objectives:*** These are the objectives to be achieved by students during testing/experimentation.
4. ***Theory:*** This includes
   - Fundamental definitions
   - The basic formulae to be expressed
   - Meaning of symbols and units used
   - No derivation of formula.
5. ***Necessary instruments/equipment used:*** List them with specifications/dimensions.
6. ***Specimen used (as supplied):*** A brief description of the specimen used.
7. ***Outline of the laboratory set -up, if any:*** Name all the items in a set-up in the form of a neat sketch.
8. ***Recommended procedure:***
   - A standard/accepted procedure is to be followed, using codes of practice.
   - It should be written down in the form of instruction using appropriate action verbs, briefly, clearly and sequentially.
9. ***Precautions:***
   - Students should follow the precautions side by side with steps and procedure.
   - In some experiments, measures of precautions are so vital that without precautions some procedural steps are found to be prone to accidents.
10. ***Observations:***
    - Prepare appropriate observation table to match with the formula being used.
    - Columns in the observation table must have their symbols to be so selected as to have the relevance with the adjacent columns.
    - Carefully recorded observations are to be filied up in this table.
11. ***Sample Calculations:*** A few sample calculations are to be presented

so as to let teachers know about the adequate proof of students' ability to use the formula already employed.

12. ***Results:***
    - Test results should be presented in the form of summary table and or curves.
    - Students should show their competency of using formula and or plotting curves as to how to arrive precisely at correct results.
13. ***Discussions/Conclusions:*** Students should mention the followings during submission of a laboratory report in order to generate their independent power of thinking regarding a laboratory experiment/ test just performed.
    - Discuss any difficulty experience or inaccuracy introduced while performing the test.
    - Suggest any improvement in the employed procedure.
    - Account for any unusual or unexpected results.
    - Make a clear statement concerning probable accuracy of results due to errors in instruments used.
    - Compare the results obtained with those for other specimen.
    - Mention different areas/field of application of results.
    - Analyse the plotted curves/results so obtained.
    - Interpret/discuss results if plotted in natural scales, semi-log scales, log-log scales etc.
14. ***Objective-type/short Answer-type Test Items:***
    - Include four options multiple choice/true-false/short answer type test items.
    - Students should answer them and submit them along with the report.
15. ***Bibliography/Reference:*** A series of concerned books, journals etc. are to be mentioned as referred while preparation/submission of report of tests/experiments performed. The reference should follow appropriate referencing style.

Evaluation of Laboratory Performances

Laboratory performances are assessed by considering the following domains which help to develop continuous evaluation:

- Cognitive domain (related to knowledge, comprehension, application and analysis)
- Psychomotor domain (skills)
- Affective domain (general attitudes by learners while dealing with laboratory activities).

Laboratory Performances Cognitive/Psychomotor Domain

Sl. No.	*Specification evaluation criteria*	*Credit 25*	*Poor 0*	*Below Avg. 1*	*Avg. 2*	*Above Avg. 3*	*Excell 4*	*Total 100*
1	Ability to state the definition/ formula	2						
2	Ability to list materials/instruments	1						
3	Ability to draw sketches of equipment/test set–up	2						
4	Ability to mention steps of procedure adopted in the experiment/test							
5	Ability to state sources of error and precaution taken/to be taken in the experiment/test	3						
6	Ability to record observations correctly	2						
7	Ability to draw graph(s) to calculate results	2						
8	Ability to compare results with those of standard ones	2						
9	Ability to draw conclusions	2						
10	Ability to mention areas of application	2						
11	Ability to submit the report as per instruction	3						

Sl. No.	*Specific features of evaluation criteria*	*Rating*
	Interest	
1	Ability to complete the work with tenacity without waste of time	Excell Fair Poor
2	Ability to undertake worthwhile work even though it is difficult	Excell Fair Poor
3	Ability to work independently (only necessary help will be provided)	Excell Fair Poor
4	Learning by self- discovery	Excell Fair Poor
5	Ability to enquire matters related to experiments/ tests	Excell Fair Poor
	Co–operation	
6	Ability to help others whenever they need	Excell Good Fair Poor
7	Ability to accept help from others in case of need	Excell Good Fair Poor
8	Ability to work in a group of persons	Excell Good Fair Poor

Laboratory Performances: Affective Domain

Sl. No.	*Specific features of evaluation criteria*	*Rating*		
	Punctuality			
1.	Entry to the laboratory on time	Excellent	Fair	Poor
2.	Date and time of submission of Laboratory report as per instruction	Excellent	Fair	Poor
	Attitudes			
3.	To issue and to return instruments by counting them and by cleaning them and by cleaning them and by cleaning them after works being over.	Serious	Casual	Indifferent
4.	To submit number of experiments set by the Institute in a particular discipline in a session	100%	> 75%	< 50%
5.	To learn required skills in each experiment	100%	> 75%	> 50%
6.	To learn by self-regarding preparation of report	Self-written	Contribution of self-written and copying	Totally copied
7.	Recording laboratory observations	Honestly	Partially Honest	Dishonestly
8.	Joint venture of laboratory work	Jointly done as required	Partially committed	Not done at All
9.	Ability of doing work with care and safety	Excellent	Fair	Poor
10.	Assuming responsibility for the issued instruments	Fully Responsible	Partially Responsible	Irresponsible
11.	Habit of neat dress	Good	Fair	Poor
12.	Ability of doing neat work	Good	Fair	Poor

SECTION F

Psychopedagogy and Teaching

18

Interface of Psychology, Education and Guidance

Etymologically, 'Psychology' means the study of soul as it is derived from the two Greek words *psyche*, meaning soul and logos signifying a rational course of study. Problem to study 'soul' leads to the other definition, which connotes the study of 'mind'. The failure to define the terms soul and mind persuaded to define psychology as... "The description and explanation of state of 'consciousness (of mind)". During nineteenth century the accepted definition reads, *"Psychology may be best and most comprehensively defined as the positive science of the conduct of living creatures"*.

Later the definition was modified in the following way:

> *Psychology is a science, which aims to give us better understanding and control of behaviour of the organism as a whole.* It is the investigation of human and animal behaviour and of the mental and psychological processes associated with behaviour.
>
> Woodworth, the famous western psychologist opines, "...*First psychology lost its soul, then its mind, then it lost its consciousness. It still has behaviour of a sort*".

Psychology is the science of behaviour. The term behaviour includes all the motor or conative (or psychomotor) activities like walking, speaking, writing; cognitive activities, say for example, thinking, reasoning, etc.; and affective activities like feeling happy, sad, angry and so on.

Psychology includes conscious, subconscious and unconscious behaviour—both overt and convert. Psychology refers to the behaviour of all living organism—that means his or her entire life activities and experiences.

Psychology is a positive science of behaviour and not a normative science. It is a behavioural—i.e., social science. Basic two branches of Psychology are Pure and Applied psychology. The sub-brances of psychology are presented as follows:

Psychology

Pure	*Applied*
General	Educational
Abnormal	Clinical
Social	Industrial
Experimental	Legal
Physiological	Military
Para (Extra Sensory Perception)	Political
Geo	Developmental
	Training

Psychology helps human being to learn the art of understanding their own behaviour, seeking adjustment with themselves and with others and enhancing as well as actualising their potentialities to the full.

Psychology is quite scientific in nature. It believes in the relationship of cause and effect, uses observation, experimentation and other scientific methods of study, possesses a universally accepted body of facts and believes in modification and alteration in its principles through future researches and findings. However, it is not as perfect and developed a science as the other natural and physical sciences. In fact, it is a developing behavioural science, which is in the process of becoming as objective, exact and accurate as possible to come at per with the developed sciences. Therefore, it is termed as a *"Developing positive science of behaviour"* which may be categorised as a subject under social sciences.

Educational Psychology for Students' Guidance

Educational psychology is one of the applied branches of psychology, mainly dealing with the problems, processes and products of education. It is that branch of psychology, which studies the behaviour of the learner in relation to his educational needs, in particular, and educational environment, in general.

According to *B.F. Skinner (1958),* 'Educational psychology is that branch of psychology which deals with teaching and learning'.

To *L.D. Crow and Alice Crow (1973)*, 'Educational psychology describes and explains the learning experiences of an individual from birth through old age'. *E.A. Peel (1956)* says, Educational psychology is the science of education.

In fact, educational psychology concerns itself with suggesting ways and means to improve the processes and products of education, enabling the teacher to teach effectively and the learners to learn effective by putting in the minimum effort. Therefore, it is called as 'science of education'. It simplify the task and improve the efficiency of the teacher or all there connected with the processes and products of education in the way of acquainting them with the essential knowledge and skills in much the same way as science and technology is helping to maximise output through minimum input in terms of time and labour in our day to day activities.

It provides knowledge and skill to the teacher to realise objectives of education in general and objectives of the respective lessons in particular, apart from scientific skill, technological expertise.

While in psychology, the scope of study and the field of operation are extended to cover the behaviour of all living organisms, related to all their life activities, in educational psychology, the scope of such behavioural study has to be limited within the confines of the teaching—learning process—that is—studying the behaviour of the learners in relation to their educational environment, specifically for the satisfaction of their educational needs and all-round development of their personality.

The basic questions which center round the process of teaching learning are:

a) Who is to be taught/educated?
b) By whom is s/he to be taught/educated?
c) Why to be taught?
d) What is to be taught? Or,
e) What learning experiences are to be imparted to the learner to achieve the desired educational/instructional objectives?

All these questions may be answered to realise the need and significance of educational psychology.

Who is to be Educated?

Obviously, the learner. Teacher should know the psychological make- up, his intrinsic and innate abilities, learned or acquired abilities, extent of interest, aptitudes, attitudes, level of intelligence, creativity and critical thinking ability of the student along with his growth and development pattern.

By Whom?

By the teacher. Much depends on the competency and capability of the teacher for carrying out the desired task. The task is crucial to modify the behaviour or to develop the personality along with achieving desired instructional objectives for a number of students attending a class. The teacher must be aware about the tasks, s/he is supposed to perform.

What is to be Taught?

Educational Psychology plays its role to decide over the type of learning experiences suitable for the students at each developmental stage, keeping in view the differences in their potentialities, apart from the subject matter. Presentation of subject matter (which is usually referred to as content) should be at per with the students motive, attitude, aptitude, interest and allied affective attributes. Their age is also to be taken into account. Educational psychology encompass the essential knowledge and skills for equipping the teacher to plan, select and arrange learning experiences to the students suitable for their age, grade and also meeting their specific individual potentialities.

What Learning Experiences are to be Imparted?

A teacher with sound knowledge in educational psychology is competent enough to decide what learning experiences are to be imparted among the learners considering the following factors.

a) Nature, Laws and theories of learning and cognition
b) Remembering and forgetting
c) Means of effective learning and motivation
d) Formation of concepts
e) Dealing with facts, procedures and principles.
f) Interest and attitude formation, thinking, reasoning and problem solving behaviour.

How, When and Where are the Learning Experiences to be Provided?

The 'How' of the question is linked with the philosophical perspective. The effectiveness of a teaching-learning programme depends largely on the suitability of the teaching-learning situation in terms of time, place and other environmental factors. Knowledge of educational psychology helps the teacher to modify the environment.

Educational psychology helps the teacher in following ways:

1. To know the learner.
2. Help the teacher to know his self, his strengths and limitation, and also to acquire essential teaching skills.
3. Selection and organisation of proper learning experiences suited to the individuality and developmental stages of the learner.
4. Suggest suitable methods and techniques for providing the desired learning experiences obviously.
5. In arranging proper learning situations.

And all these are to be known by the teacher, if s/he is really interested to extend proper guidance and counseling services to the student, irrespective of the dimension—may it be educational, vocational or social.

Individual Difference: The Basic Factor of Guidance

Members of same species are not alike in all aspects. Human beings are not exception. Students of a class or semester differs in terms of their family background, extra-institutional environment, ability, aptitude, intelligence, physical capabilities and so on. These differences are termed as individual differences. Individual differences stands for those differences, which in their totality, distinguish one individual from others. It is the variations or deviations among individuals in regard to single characteristics or a number of characteristics.

Whatever differences or variations exist among the human beings may commonly be grouped into two broad categories. These are—

i) Physiological/Physical differences and
ii) Psychological differences.

Specific individual differences may be observed under following aspects:

a) ***Physical Differences:*** Such as height, weight, colour of skin, eyes, hair; size of limbs, structure and functioning of internal organs and other native or acquired physical characteristics.
b) ***Mental Differences:*** Such as abilities and capacities like reasoning and thinking, power of imagination, creative expression, intelligence etc.
c) ***Differences in Motor Ability:*** Such as reaction time, speed of action, steadiness, rate of muscular momentum.
d) ***Differences in Achievement:*** i.e., achievement and knowledge among the students with same entry knowledge, level of intelligence etc.
e) ***Emotional Differences:*** Individual differs in terms of their positive emotions like love, affection, amusement etc. and negative emotions like anger, dissatisfaction etc. Individual also differ in terms of their manner following which they express their emotions. Some are emotionally stabled and mature where as others are unstable and immature. These causes the emotional differences among the individuals.
f) ***Differences in Interest and Aptitudes:*** Individuals differ in terms of their interest in meeting social gatherings and group activities where as other are not. In similar way people express difference in their aptitudes.
g) ***Differences in Attitudes, Beliefs and Opinions:*** Such as attitude towards, some object, individual, things, ideas, political philosophy etc.
h) ***Learning Differences:*** Say, some learn more easily and are able to

make use of their learning more, compared to others; where as some can't. For somebody, one method of learning or memorisation is more suitable while for some others, a different method suits. In same way suitability of learning environment also depends upon the individual nature of the learner.)

i) ***Difference in Social and Moral Development:*** For example, some are found to be adjustable properly in the social situations and led a happy social life while others are socially handicapped, unsocial or asocial. Similarly people are found to differ in respect of ethical and moral sense.

Distribution of such individual differences among human beings follows the pattern of *normal probability curve.* As a consequence, majority (almost 70%; exactly 68.26%) is quite average in terms of possession of one or the other personality attributes. A very few deviate too much from the average value, making themselves exceptional individuals among the total population.

While extending guidance to individual students, all the aforesaid factors need to be taken into consideration.

Determinants of Individual Differences

Both heredity and environmental forces are said to be the sole determinants of the wide individual differences found in human beings.

The features which individual acquire from the environment (i.e., physical, social, cultural and educational opportunities) are termed as acquired abilities.

The features, which the individual receive from his parents at the time of birth, are termed as innate abilities.

The knowledge of the existing wide individual differences among the learners carries quite significant educational, guidance and counseling implication. It has helped the learners to know themselves in terms of their potentialities and teachers and parents to realise that they have to teach and care for their wards in terms of their individualities. It has led to the individualisation of instruction and educational programmes to suit needs, interests and potentialities of individual learners. Even after completion of study, proper vocational or career guidance can only be extended to the individual student if the guide or the counselor is well acquainted with the individual traits of the students. Otherwise, all the effort of guidance and counseling will go in vain.

Scope of Educational Psychology for Guidance

Educational psychology possess an influential role in the process of learning. It equip the teachers to know the learners in varied ways, which leads to proper planning of teaching and effective learning for the students. It covers the following aspects:

- The nature, potentialities and mental health of the learner
- The impact of social environment over the learning
- The general nature of learning
- Learning to deal with one's social and physical needs
- Helps to develop the personality.

General Content of Educational Psychology

Educational Psychology deals with the principles, which contribute for better learning and good teaching. It covers the following content areas:

I. Scientific study of human (learner) behaviour in ***pedagogical*** setting.
II. The 'WH' questions of education.
III. Learned with learning situation and the process by which learner can be made more efficient and effective.
IV. Evaluation of the outcomes of educational process.
V. Educational Psychology is concerned with study of human behaviour involved in teaching-learning situation.

Why Teacher should Learn Educational Psychology?

The new teacher or the person newly inducted in teaching should learn education psychology. Because,

a) It equips the teacher to increase their effectiveness in helping the learner to enhance their progress.
b) Teachers become familiar with various teaching techniques and strategies through educational psychology, which they can apply for effective teaching and better learning.
c) It helps the teacher to understand his/her students and further helps to deliver content in such a way which match the learners requirements.
d) Educational Psychology helps the teacher to understand the individual differences among the learners.
e) The teacher can acquaint himself with the various stages of development of human learner, as well as the various needs (emotional, physical, psychological, social etc.) of different stages; and can satisfy the needs of students accordingly.
f) Knowledge of educational psychology helps teacher to perform his role as a therapist, instructor, ***counselor and above all a guide.***

Task of a Teacher: Teacher should be able to

- Direct learning

- Guide learner
- Motivate learners
- Help learners to develop desirable attitudes
- Continuously improve teaching techniques
- Acquire the qualities that are conducive to successful teaching.

Contribution of Psychology to Education

1) Experimental Psychology helps in construction, use and application of achievement tests.
2) Educational psychology explains the nature of general intelligence and show how to apply intelligence testing.
3) It acquaints the teachers about the individual differences among the learners.
4) Research in educational psychology helps to develop appropriate method of teaching for exceptional learners, viz. first learners and slow learners.
5) Maintenance of cumulative record cards (a type of learners performance report maintained for an extended period of time) can be best done with the knowledge of educational psychology.

Psychological Factors Influencing Learning of the Learners

Following are the major psychological factors, which contribute for the learning.

a) *Intelligence*
b) *Memory—Remembering and forgetting*
c) *Motivation*
d) *Attention*
e) *Emotion*
f) *Creativity*
g) *Aptitude*
h) *Attitude*
i) *Capacity of adaptation*
j) *Personality*
k) *Individual differences*
l) *Learning Style*, etc.

All these psychological factors play a pivotal role in the process of learning, apart from the social factors. Until the teacher is acquaint enough with all these psycho educational attributes and can trace the level of the learner over those attributes, proper guidance and counseling is not only difficult but may result to dangerous impact over the student's future life.

Psychoeducational Attributes

a) Intelligence: Intelligence is the mental energy, which enable an individual to cope up with his environment in terms of adaptation and dealing with novel situations as effectively as possible. Intelligence can't be observed directly. We can only observe the effects of intelligence as shown or reflected in behaviour. It is the ability to think, reason or to solve problems.

b) Memory: Memory is a special faculty of the mind to conserve or retain what has been previously experienced or acquired through learning and, then, at some later stage, to revive or reproduce. It is the form of recall or recognition to enable us to utilise such learning in different situation.

c) Motivation: Motivation is a psychological factor, which compels, prompts and energies one to engage in a particular behaviour. The activating forces for the motivation may be termed as needs, drives or motives.

d) Attention: Attention is a deliberate and conscious effort on the part of an individual to select one out of the various stimuli present in the environment and bring it to the center of his consciousness in order to perceive it clearly to achieve a desired result.

e) Emotion: Emotion is a complex affective experience, which involves diffuse psychological changes and can be expressed overtly in characteristic behaviour patterns. It is a dynamic internal adjustment, which operates for the satisfaction, protection and welfare of the individual.

f) Creativity: It is the ability of an individual to think in divergent ways.

g) Aptitude: It is a special ability, different from general intelligence which leads the individual towards the probable success in a particular field after receiving appropriate opportunity for learning or training.

h) Attitude: Attitude is the expression of a person that manifests or shows how individual feels about some object, issue, individual, situation or the like.

i) Adaptation: Adaptation is the inner capacity of the individual, which helps him to accommodate or to sit himself in a new situation.

j) Personality: It is a stable system of complex characteristics by which the life pattern of an individual may be identified.

k) Individual Differences: It indicates the differences among individuals that distinguish or separate them from one another.

Interface between Heredity and Environment and Their Impact over Human Psyche

A teacher who is well aware about the abilities and potentialities of his learners is in a more advantageous position to make the teaching learning process more effective, compared to those who are not (well aware). This requires the knowledge of growth and development. Growth and development are very much influenced by heredity and developmental factors, which take place within the environment.

Growth: The word indicates positive change in size of various parts of a body all over. This happens in terms of height and weight of an individual, which is measurable and observable. Growth is a quantitative connotation.

Development: Development means the changes in the shape of the parts of the body and the integration of the various parts into functional units as growth goes on. The development is observable by noting changes in the shape of a part as they occur. Development is qualitative in nature.

Heredity: The word heredity is the process or system following which the characteristic features flow from parents to the offsprings'.

Environment: The word environment refers to the external situation, which is the commutation of number of factors, and that influence the growth and development of an individual—i.e., the physical, social and cultural environment. In the other words, environment is the very thing that affects the individual to accept his jeans.

Different environmental forces have a desirable impact over the physical, social, emotional, intellectual, moral and aesthetic development of the individual. Their influence is a continuous one, which begins with the emergence of life and follows till death. Heredity and environment, both possess a tremendous impact over the development of an individual. Psychologist ***Watson's*** comment is worth noting in this context. He says—

> *"Give me a dozen healthy infants, well infants, well informed and my own specified world to bring them up in and I will guarantee to take any one at random and train him to become any type of specialist I might select—doctor, lawyer, artist, merchant chief and yes, even beggarman and thief, regardless of his talents, penchants, tendencies, abilities, vocations and race of his ancestors".*

Being a behaviourist, what ***J.B. Watson*** wanted to mean that it is the environment, which is more influential then heredity. Though it is debatable, however no one can deny the impact of environment, in the process of education. What actually Watson wanted to mean is that there are no hereditary characteristics which can't be modified to an extent at hands of the environment and none such characteristics are completely transformed or substituted, however effective like the environment. Environmental factors only begin to work on biologically hereditary mechanism. A better way to express the relationship between heredity and environment is by considering the amount of a change in behaviour, which can bring about by manipulations of environment. From this viewpoint, it can be said that hereditary traits are those, which are inherent and omnipresent in individual; where- as environment is changeable. Almost all the trait characteristics of an individual are affected by both heredity and environment.

Growth, in all living species, is a biological factor related to heredity but the environment furnishes the situation for the manifestation of development. It is, therefore, crystal clear that both heredity and environment are inseparable regarding their influence on the growth and development of any individual.

In fact personality of an individual is the product of heredity and environment and the learners' maximum development is to some extent, (not absolutely) influenced by his/her heredity. It is worth noting in this context that though learning environment can be manipulated for better learning, however nobody can control the heredity, the inheriting potentialities with proper environment.

19

Psychopedagogy for Guiding Adolescent Students

The responsibility of the teacher is to provide appropriate learning environment to the learner, which includes all the required physical facilities to enable the learner to learn, including a healthy teacher-student relationship. To do so, teacher requires professional skills, which are termed as teaching skills. The teacher should provide such an environment, which will help the learner for their overall development. The emphasis should also be given over the need of adjustment according to the environment. Thus the student can develop a positive attitude towards the learning environment and will be motivated to learn.

Adolescent Characteristics

The students who normally attend the age of 13 to 21 years are neither young, nor fully matured. They differ from both the young and adults in terms of behavioural pattern apart from their social, emotional and physical needs. Mostly they are adolescents.

The etymological meaning of the word 'adolescent' is 'to grow', which is derived from the word '*adolescere*'. In human development, after infancy (0-2 years) and childhood (2-14 years) the third phase appears which is termed as adolescence, when one attains puberty (i.e., sexual maturity) and is capable of reproduction. In true sense, it is the transition phase between childhood and adulthood. This phase lasts for 5-7 years. Often this phase of development is termed as 'period of storm and stress'—because individuals, in this stage, are erratic, unstable and unpredictable. The phase is normally divided in two phases—early adolescents and late adolescents.

- Early—Persons between $12^+ - 16^+/17$ years
- Late—$17/17^+ - 20^+/21$ years

These phases are also known as teenager and youths, respectively. In the combined phase of adolescents individual require special support so far their intellectual, physical, emotional and social development are concerned.

Intellectual Development

Intellectual development raise to its extreme during adolescents, compared to the already crossed levels of human development. In this stage, the level of abstract thinking increases. Retention and recall improves. There is an increased ability to generalise facts. Language development, vocabulary and depth of understanding are also increased at this phase.

Physical Development

During adolescence, physical development enhanced to its extreme among the humans. The body shape, voice, limbs and organs exhibit sudden change in this stage. The growth of physic, though rapid, but uneven, results in lack of balance.

Emotional Development

At this stage, family and educational institutions influence emotional development. When they have an increased interest in peer group activity, it results in clash with parents and teachers. This causes anxiety and tensions. Society, as it appears to them, set a high standard of morality.

Social Development

The adolescent become quite conscious about their prestige, especially among the peers and wants to be independent and self-sufficient. There remains a wide gap between what they think and parents expect from them. They want social recognition and autonomy. Individuality is also prominent at this level of development. Adolescents suffer from the conflict between identity and identity-confusion.

Problems at the Stage

Adolescents are often confused with their social standing. As they want to become self-sufficient, there appears a tendency to earn, through job. They are confused with vocational-career. Therefore, proper career guidance is necessary. Though who got absorption in job without proper guidance, become frustrated which results to tension and unhappiness. They are also become sensitive towards the verdicts of the seniors, which goes against their acceptance. This creates confusion about their own moral structure. Guidance is, therefore, inevitable to resolve the conflicts arising from different social expectation.

Developmental Tasks

Social scientist says, society expects individual to exhibit certain behaviour patterns at various stages in their life. These they termed as developmental tasks. Fulfilling 'developmental tasks' at appropriate stages leads to happiness and success, where- as, failure leads to unhappiness and difficulty with later tasks. The developmental tasks at adolescent stage are:

a) Accepting ones physique and using the body effectively.
b) Desiring and achieving socially responsible behaviours.
c) Selecting and preparing for an occupation.
d) Having emotional independence from parents and other adults.
e) Emotional stability.

Teacher's Responsibility

The responsibility of the teacher is to enhance the ability of the adolescents and further to transform their learning from one situation to other. The teacher should take initiatives so that their academic excellence can be properly placed to job situations. To do so the following techniques may be helpful:

a) Group discussion and seminars.
b) Project work (Especially group projects).
c) Laboratory work based on discovery method.
d) Frequent visit to the places of actual activities.

The most important task of the teacher in this context is to deal with them with love, affection and sympathy. When adolescents behave in an undesirable manner, the teacher should deal the situation pragmatically and in the best interests of learners and organisations.

A democratic approach of the teacher will create good links between teachers and students. This will in turn, be a congenial learning atmosphere. For the proper development of adolescents into adults, teachers and parents play a pivotal role. They should therefore be sympathetic and try to understand the nature and unique problems of the adolescents.

Psychological Characteristics of Adolescent Student

In our education system, specially at college level, we deal with students who are psychophysically at their developmental stage, known as adolescent. During this stage, the boys and girls are no more children but they are at the door step of mature individuals. During adolescence, boys and girls move from childhood to adulthood physically, mentally, emotionally and socially. In Indian condition, the period of adolescence is generally between 12 years to 20 year of age.

Several changes occur in boys and girls at this stage. In the physical side, there is sudden change in height and bodily proportion. The change of voice along with change of certain secondary sex characteristics also occurs at this state. There is increase in ability in motor performance, growth in intelligence, growth in creative expression, change in emotional attitude, change in social perception and self-concept.

Self-concept

Self-concept is the individual's perceptions of her/himself, and his evaluation of his interaction with the physical and social environment. Changes in the self-concept during adolescence are an important event. Social interactions are the mirror in which the adolescents see themselves and build self-esteem. The opinions, reactions and attitudes of others contribute greatly in building up self-confidence. Strong self-confidence together with high self- esteem build up a healthy, positive self- identity.

Changes of self-concept may take place through the following dimensions.

1. Bodily sense (what is me?)
2. Self-identity (what am I?)
3. Self-image (who am I?)
4. Self-interest (what is good for me?)
5. Self-ideal (what do I strive to be?)

As self-identity is one of the important dimensions of personality, teachers have important roles here. They need to act as a facilitator in developing self-image, identifying self-interest, inculcating self-ideal and developing self-confidence in students.

Cognitive Characteristics and Needs

The development of knowledge and thinking process is known as cognitive development. Intellectual abilities come under cognitive process. Some functional abilities such as attending, perceiving, observing, remembering, imagining, using language also come under cognitive process. Cognitive development is sometimes described as extending the intellectual horizon of the individual. It is the sum total of processes of all mental abilities. During the adolescent stage, the thinking process becomes systematic (period of formal operation). Adolescents develop thinking and reasoning beyond the objects. They can solve the problem in a systematic way, which are within their reach. They are competent to transfer understanding from one situation to another situation. Several other cognitive developmental characteristics are also observed in the adolescence period.

These are as follows:

- Increased ability to generalise the facts
- Increased ability of understanding
- Increased ability to deal with abstraction
- Development of memory and imagination
- Ability of problem solving

- Increased ability to communicate with other persons
- Identification with conditions and characters in the larger world
- Ability to make decision
- Understanding of moral concepts.

Emotional Characteristics and Needs

One of the major characteristics of adolescence is heightened emotionality. The under lying causes of this heightened emotionality is the acceleration of secretion from certain specific glands and some social variables. At times, adolescents lose control over emotions.

Intense emotions and their inhibition cause intense moods. At extreme mood the adolescent may become introvert and even may commit suicide. The causes may be failure in love, failure in institutional work, maladjustment with parents or peers and the like. Emotional guidance by teachers assists the individual to understand the emotional problems and find out ways to resolve those.

Controlled emotion is the most significant characteristic of mentally healthy adolescent. An adolescent having control over emotions when threatened with conflicts and frustrations try to strike a balance by working against the stress. It has been observed that tension in the form of anxiety or frustration, causes neural disturbances. This may intensify prolonged emotional tension. At the later adolescent period when insecurities, tensions and indecisions are readily recognised by adolescents, emotional disequilibrium becomes heightened. This, of course, depends largely on environmental circumstances of adolescent's life. Not all adolescents experience the same strain and stress. But, all experience emotional instability from time to time.

Several emotional patterns of special significance have been identified during adolescence. These are fear, anger, hostility, jealousy and anxiety. These emotions have adverse effect on the individual. The role of the teacher is to create an environment where adolescent feels comfortable and can share their emotion in a healthy way.

Not all emotions have harmful effects. Like biological drives, emotions, may arouse, sustain and direct activity and as such play an energising role in behaviour. Emotions may also serve as emergency sources of power. For example, in stress situations where habitual reaction patterns are not adequate, strong emotions make maximum energy resources available and thus help the organism for meeting such emergencies. The emotions like, joy, pleasure, delight, affection, etc. are mostly helpful in overcoming the stress situation and thus protect the self from crisis and frustration. The energy resources emotions may be nurtured by teachers and parents so that emotional needs of the adolescents are fulfilled.

Emotional Intelligence

Fulfillment of emotional needs helps the individual to become emotionally mature. Further, emotional maturity contributes towards emotional intelligence (EI). EI refers to an assessment of affective domain skills, capabilities and competencies that influence a person's ability to succeed in coping with environmental demands and pressures. EI includes empathy, self-control, self-awareness, sensitivity to the feelings of others, persistence and self-motivation.

The purpose of education is to produce employable human resources and for which colleges and educational institutions should take suitable steps for the development of affective domain characteristics in students. EI constitutes one of the important dimensions of affective domain. Moderate to high level of EI empowers the individual in:

- self-awareness
- self-control
- solving intrapersonal conflicts
- solving interpersonal conflicts
- self- motivation
- decision making and
- dealing deviant work place behaviour

Social Characteristics and Needs

On the onset of puberty, the adolescents become increasingly socially conscious. This consciousness brings radical changes towards self. This demands change of social behaviour.

There is a fundamental social characteristic for the adolescents to belong to a group. It may be in home, in school or in the playground. When an adolescent feels that s/he is part of the group s/he feels secure and happy. On the other hand, in the process of belongingness, if some gap is created the adolescent starts to feel insecure.

Many adolescents feel that they are misunderstood or unfairly treated in the family or by their friends. Strict discipline in the family, too little independence, and lack of understanding of adolescents' interests get them disturbed. Sarcastic remarks, unwelcome advice, unjust behaviour by superior and so create conflict among adolescents.

During the period of adolescence they want to adjust with the opposite sex. Sometimes, vague fear, social restrictions, lack of communication ability, shyness etc. come on the way of mixing with the opposite gender.

Due to acceleration in the developmental process during adolescence, they try to find out new meaning of life. Their attitudes are in the process of rapid change. This is the time when life philosophy is to be formed which guides the individual throughout the later life.

Three groups of social needs have been identified in adolescents, which are vital for social and emotional wellbeing of the individual.

These are:

1. The need for interpersonal satisfaction
2. The need for group status
3. The need for self-development

Adolescent seek love and affection from the persons whom they think important. If the need for love and affection are fulfilled they feel warm and wanted, and their internal strength to fight with the life's problem increases. These are the feelings which make youngsters secure.

Status in a group gives an adolescent assurance that s/he is an acceptable being. Without the group membership s/he becomes lonely, loses self-confidence and starts to question his/her own adequacy. It has been observed experimentally that when adolescents are cut off from social and perceptual stimulation for a long time, normal adolescents experience intellectual deterioration, hallucination and impairment of problem solving abilities and the power of concentration.

During adolescence, due to awareness of potentialities and capacities, they feel a compelling urge to test and use these powers. They pursue self-initiated and self-directed activities, which give them feeling of personal worth. If these self-development needs like achievement, independence, personal recognition, adequacy, self- respect are not properly fulfilled that may cause sociopathic personality disorder.

The implications of various developments during adolescence have tremendous importance. It is the time when personality becomes increasingly differentiated and hierarchically organised. If the developmental needs are not properly fulfilled, the results are maladjustment. The adolescent losses the sense of identity, the self-concept is derailed and the acquisition of a set of values is impaired. The teachers can help the adolescent to meet their growing needs: cognitive, emotional and social.

20

Psycho-pedagogical Tests and Inventories in Career Guidance vis-a-vis Emotional Intelligence

Concept

Psychological tests are the devices through which it is possible to measure empirically, the characteristic traits of the individual including his mental potentialities. It helps to draw quantitative and qualitative conclusions on the relative importance of the particular feature in the individual. It was primarily devised for the determination and analysis of individual differences in intelligence, aptitude, educational achievement, career fitness and several personality traits

Classification

Psychological tests may be classified under non-projective tests and projective tests. Various performance tests and rating scales come under non projective tests.

A performance test provide a perceptual situation in which the subject manipulates items such as form boards, blocks, pictures and disassembled objects. These may also include other nonverbal materials such as printed geometric forms, substituting digits or symbols and the like.

Rating scale is the device in which the individual compares a limited number of his traits with reference to a set of situations with predetermined degrees.

In projective test, undefined stimulus situations are presented before the subject. This stimulus may be in the form of pictures, inkblots, words or incomplete sentences.

The subject's reaction to the stimulus is noted. Thus individual's covert response pattern can be known by administering the projective tests.

Inventories are self-rating questionnaires which deal with overt behaviour as well as feelings about oneself, other persons and his environment. The inventories are mostly based upon the principles that behaviour and characteristic traits are in part manifestable. A set of situations are given for a particular inventory and the individual is asked to respond to his degree of consistency with the given situations.

Purpose

Psychological tests may be used for multiple purposes. Some of the major areas where psychological tests and inventories are used are clinics, schools and colleges, industries, and in defence services for various types of service selection.

Psychological tests and inventories have wider use in career guidance and selection of career. Some of the purposes served by psychological tests and inventories in career guidance are as follows:

- Psychological tests and inventories may be used for career selection
- It helps in understanding the specific abilities present in an individual
- It helps teachers to design special activities for students
- It prevents mismatching between man and machine and thus reduce work alienation

Types

Psychological tests and inventories cover a broader canvas of human behaviour, both covert and overt. For career guidance, generally a few characteristics like aptitude, interest, intelligence and personality, need to be known.

Aptitude: Aptitude is the potential capacity of an individual to acquire some specific knowledge or to perform. This implies that if necessary training is given in a particular area in which the person has aptitude, he/she will perform quite successfully in the area after this training.

It is a set of characteristics which may be considered as symptomatic of an individual's ability which if properly nourished will fit him appropriately in a particular job or profession.

Aptitude Tests: Aptitude tests are designed to measure the degree of presence of characteristics required to perform specific tasks. This capacity is measured through aptitude tests. Generally, the existing aptitude tests may be classified under two categories. The first category comprises of multiple aptitude batteries and the second category comprises of special aptitude tests.

Multiple Aptitude Batteries: Among the best known examples of multiple aptitude batteries are Differential Aptitude Tests (DAT), Multiple Aptitude Tests (MAT), Guilford-Zimmerman Aptitude Survey, Flanagan Aptitude Classification Tests (FACT).

Differential Aptitude tests have been constructed by covering the areas of verbal reasoning, numerical ability, abstract reasoning, space relations, mechanical reasoning, clerical speed and accuracy, and language usage (Part I and II).

Multiple aptitude tests comprises of nine tests and yield scores in verbal comprehension, perceptual speed, numerical reasoning and spatial visualisation. It serves the similar purpose of DAT.

The Guilford-Zimmerman Aptitude survey is a battery of tests which provides tests for seven factors which are verbal comprehension, general reasoning, numerical operations, perceptual speed, spatial orientation, spatial visualisation and mechanical knowledge.

Flanagan Aptitude Classification Tests (FACT) was the outgrowth of the research in the development of Air force classification test during World War II. This battery is oriented towards counselling and selection of employees.

Special Aptitude Tests: Among the special Aptitude tests, the best known are Mechanical Aptitude Test battery, Stromberg Dexterity Test, Minnesota spatial Relations Test, Minnesota Paper form Board Test, Macquarie Test for Mechanical Ability etc.

Special Aptitude tests are designed to measure more 'concrete' or 'Practical' abilities. Through special aptitude tests, it is possible to cover the areas like vision, hearing, motor dexterity, artistic talents, mechanical comprehension, musical talents, literary ability, reasoning, creativity and so on.

The career counsellors/classroom teachers can make use of the aptitude tests for guidance regarding employment. Now a days a few standard tests of the kind possess Indian adaptations, which may be used.

Intelligence

Intelligence is the ability which is required for understanding and solving problems, performing different kind of simple and complex tasks and even adapting one-self in a social situation. It is the 'Global Capacity' of the individual to act purposefully, to think rationally and to deal effectively with the environment.

Intelligence tests are useful to measure intelligence. Intelligence tests may be verbal or performance. Certain intelligence tests may be administered on group or individually. But some intelligence tests can be administered only individually. A few intelligence tests which has wider use are as follows:

- Standard Progressive Matrices (SPM)
- Wechsler Adult performance Intelligence Scale (WAPIS)–Revised.
- Group Test of General Mental Ability
- Bhatia's Battery of Performance Tests of Intelligence
- Catell's Culture Fair Performance Intelligence Test

Standard Progressive Matrices (SPM)

The culture fair and culture free SPM consists of 60 problems in the order of increasing difficulty divided into five sets of 12 each. On every page, one problem is given which is a pattern with a missing bit. The subject is to decide each time the correct missing bit among the given alternatives. A person's score on the scale is the total number of problems s/he solves correctly.

Weschler Adult Performance Intelligence Scale (WAPIS)

The WAPIS contains five sub tests. These are Picture completion test, Block design tests, Picture arrangement test, Object assembly test, Digit symbol test. Total score is obtained by converting each sub test score to scaled score and then adding.

Group Test of General Mental Ability

The Group test of General Mental ability is to appoint scale for adults and can be used on educated individual of the age 15 years and above. The test consists of 100 items besides 10 items for practice in the beginning. The test consists of 9 sub tests namely Number Series, Mathematical Instructions, Following Instructions, Vocabulary Similar, Vocabulary Opposites, Classifications, Analogies, Best Answers and Reasoning. The total score is counted with addition of right answers.

Bhatia's Battery of Job Performance Tests and Job Intelligence

This test can be used for eleven to sixteen years age group. There are five sub tests namely Koh's Block Design Test, Pass along test, Pattern Drawing test, Picture construction test and Immediate Memory test. Scoring is done with the help of manual. The score obtained in each test is added and transformed to IQ.

Catell's Culture Fair Performance Test of Intelligence

This test can be used for 11 to 16 years age group. There are five sub tests namely Kohl's Block Design Test, Pass along test, Pattern Drawing test, Picture construction test and Immediate Memory test. Scoring is done with the help of manual. The score obtained in each test is added and transformed to IQ.

Uses of Intelligences Tests

- It helps to group the student according to different mental abilities
- It helps in diagnosing the difficulties of the students
- It can be widely used in career guidance

Interest

Eysinck *et al.* (1972) have defined interest as 'A tendency or behaviour oriented towards certain objects, activities or experience, which varies in intensity (and generality) from individual to individual'. An interest is generally conceptualised as being a feeling towards activity. The interests of the adolescents are very much diversified in nature. Their interests changes from time to time. Due to acceleration in various developmental processes, the interest of adolescents reflects adult like flavour rather than child- like. The social background and other related factors are important in development of interest.

Success in any career partially depends on interest. It has been observed that there is a wide variation in career interests among boys and girls. Knowledge of individual's interest provides a sound basis for education and career guidance,. By understanding the interest of the individual, s/he can be suggested to develop certain hobbies. For planning and organising placement, the knowledge about the interest of the group or individual is needed. By measuring interest, one can be suggested to select his occupation. The result of the interest inventories may help the classroom teacher/counsellor to guide students in desirable direction.

There are various methods of identification of interest. It may be as simple as observation. It may also be found out by administering some psychological inventories and tests.

Checklists are used to see the individual's liking and disliking. One such checklist is the Thurston Interest Schedule which can be used at the secondary school level and above. These interest schedules consist of a single sheet of paper in the form of four page folder. The inside page is printed with small rectangular boxes, hundred in number and each box which contains a pair of occupations. The subject is required to mark his preference in each box containing a pair of occupations. The subject is required to mark his preference in each pair. The scores are obtained for 10 occupational fields viz.

Physical Science,
Biological Science,
Computer,
Business,
Executive,
Persuasion,
Linguistics,
Humanitarian,
Arts and Music.

Several standardised inventories are available. One such widely used inventory is Strong Campbell Interest Inventory. This inventory has 325 items to most of which the respondent answers by filling in either 'Like', 'Indifferent' or 'Dislike'.

There are seven sections in the inventory booklet which are as follows:

1. Occupations
2. School subjects
3. Activities
4. Amusements
5. Types of people
6. Preference between 2 activities
7. Personal characteristics

A profile can be drawn from the scores obtained by the respondents.

Personality Appraisal

Appraisal of personality is a very broad field in psychological testing. Numerous tests, inventories, rating scales, checklists are available for appraisal of personality.

Personality tests are those devices through which it is possible to measure empirically the personality structure of the individual, including characteristic traits. These help to draw quantitative conclusions on the relative importance of the particular personality feature in the individual.

Personality Inventories

Personality inventories consist of a set of statements reflecting the attributes of personality. Generally the answers are restricted to certain category, for example, 'Yes' or 'No' types. The subject is to rate himself on the extent to which he confirms certain ways of behaviour by responding to a set of statements given in the inventory. The statements and responses are tried out before standardisation on a representative sample so as to represent a particular attribute of personality. The scoring of the inventories is usually very easy. For example, one score is given for 'Yes' and zero score for 'No' provided the inventory is not negatively oriented. Some of the popular personality inventories are:

Allport Ascendance—Submission Inventory, Minnesota Multiphase Personality Inventory, Edwards Personal Preference Schedule, the Eysenck's Personality Inventory, Multivariable Personality Inventory, Kundu's Intraversion Extraversion Inventory.

Rating Scale: A greater freedom of responses is available in rating scale, when compared with inventories. Here the subject is presented with a set of items reflecting certain personality traits for which he has to respond by rating the traits. It is a device for obtaining judgements of the degree to which an individual possesses certain traits and attributes. In order that the obtained ratings about the traits of an individual are reliable, before standardisation it is advantageous to have the ratings carried out by a number of judges and then a composite rating being arrived at.

Rating scales also include Checklist, Forced Checklist, Sorting Techniques, Graphic Rating Scale, and Semantic Differential Techniques.

Check List: A check list consists of some items, the presence or absence of which are to be indicated by checking each item with a tick or cross mark. Sometimes the response against each item may be indicated by using some appropriate word or number. For example, +1 may be scored for a favourable item, -1 for an unfavourable item and zero for a neutral one.

Scores on a check list has little meaning except it gives some gross indication. These checklists are generally used as self- rating. Counselors also can use it to get some information about the individual, such as adjustment difficulties or the like.

Apart from psychological tests and inventories, at times observation techniques are used for personality appraisal.

Projective Tests: In personality appraisal, application of projective tests is quite important. The concept of projective tests has been derived from depth psychology. Here, a series of undefined stimulus/situations are presented before the subject. This stimulus may be in the form of pictures, inkblots, words, incomplete sentences and the like. The individual projects himself into the test situation. In such projection he reveals his motives, attitudes, aspiration, apprehensions etc. The individual gets the free scope to response. There are wide variations in the responses among different individuals. This is because the subjects interpret the situation depending on his personality structure.

Interview: Interview is one of the useful methods in appraising the personality of the individual. Interview is the personal meeting between at least two individuals with predetermined objectives. In personality assessment interview, the interviewer may be one person or more than one person.

The interview may be two types. The first type is called 'Structured Interview' and the second type is called 'Un Structured Interview'. In structured Interview, the interviewer plans the questions well in advance for exploring the personality structure of the individual and in interview sessions s/he poses the questions systematically. In unstructured interview, the interviewer has the objective in mind, and in actual situation s/he puts the questions as per the demand of the situation. Of course, s/he is to regulate the question-response or discussion situation in such a way that leads to achieving the objective.

The interviewee is given a chance to talk in a non-threatening atmosphere where s/he is expected to let out what s/he really thinks and believes. The degree of success of interview depends on the establishment of relationship or rapport by the interviewer as well as the skill eliciting information from the interviewee.

In the proceeding paragraphs, several standardised tests and inventories, which are widely used in India are presented.

Multivariable Personality Inventory

This inventory is used to assess personality attributes of adolescents and adults for leadership traits.

Description: Multivariable Personality Inventory (MPI) consists of 50 items on nine variables viz., Dominance, Neuroticism, Empathy, Need Achievement, Ego Ideal, Introversion, Self Confidence, Dogmatism and Pessimism. There are five items on empathy, five items on ego ideal, six items on pessimism, seven items on neuroticism, six items on introversion, five items on need achievement, five items on self- confidence, five items on dogmatism and six items on dominance.

Administration: The inventory sheet is given to the subject and s/he is asked to read the directions carefully. The doubts are clarified. The subject is asked to start answering. The response sheet is collected at the end of the test. The scoring of the inventory is done on the basis of the manual.

Kundu's Introversion Extroversion Inventory

Kundu's Introversion Extroversion Inventory (KIEI) is used to obtain a reliable measure of introversion-extroversion dimension of behaviour. The inventory can be used with adolescents and adults with a minimum of high school qualification.

Description: The inventory consists of 70 items arranged in five blocks. Block 'A' has 11 items, the response choices for each being some objective situations or activities. There are 17 items in block 'B'. All these items in this block are mostly introspective type. There are 14 items in block 'C'. The response for each item here requires one activity over the others. Block 'D' has 14 items which are the activities of the individual for himself. There are 14 items in Block 'E'. The test has a separate scoring sheet.

Administration: The inventory is self- administering in nature. No separate instructions are necessary. The KIEI can be administered on group also. There is no time limit for the test. Scoring and interpretation is done as per the instructions given in the test manual.

16 Personality Factor Questionnaire

16 Personality Factor (16PF) Questionnaire is used to measure personality traits. The 16 PF can be used on the individual who are sixteen years of age and above.

Description: The test consists of ten to thirteen items for each scale of Form A and Form B. In form C and Form D, there are eight items for the Factor B scale, seven items for the motivational distortion scale and six items for each of the remaining scales. The questions are arranged in the roughly cyclic order determined by a plan to give maximum convenience in scoring by stencil. There are in all 187 items in Form A of multiple choice types, each with three possible responses. The reusable test booklet can be administered on individual as well as on group.

Administration: The subjects are reminded to complete the test at a brisk pace. Majority of the subjects take about 45 to 60 minutes to complete the test.

Each answer is scored with 0, 1 or 2 points except for the Factor B answers for which 0 is scored for incorrect and 1 is scored for correct response. The score of each item contributes to only one factor i.e. 'G'. The total test can be hand scored with a stencil key or machine scored. The new scores are converted to stencil score and then compared with the norm. A profile of personality traits as measured by this test can also be drawn.

Personality Differential

This scale is used to measure self -concept of students and adults.

Description: The test consists of a test booklet and manual. The Personality Differential (PD) scale is based on semantic differential technique. There are total 34 concept forms, which takes about 40-50 minutes to respond. The PD can be administered on individual as well as on group. It is always better to repeat instructions and give illustrations before the subject starts scoring. The subject is to put a tick on a seven point scale for each step. To put more than one tick mark on a single scale, is not allowed.

Administration: The book is supplied to the subject. Instructions are given in an elaborate way. After the completion of the test, booklets are collected. Hand scoring is done as per instructions in the manual. Norm tables are available for interpretation.

Thematic Apperception Test (TAT)

Thematic Apperception Test was originally introduced by Morgan and Murray in 1935 in Harvard Psychological Clinic. The Indian adaptation of the test was later made available through the efforts of Indian Psychologists. This test is used to study the aspects of personality like conflicts, attitude, level of aspiration etc. The test result also reveals the psychodynamics of interpersonal relationship. The test can be administered on all, irrespective of age, educational level, gender, social status etc.

Description: The original TAT devised by Murray consisted of 32 cards in which one card was blank. Presently, revised editions (Indian) of the test is used which generally consists of 12 cards, each card has a picture depicting a situation. On the basis of the figures and the nature of contents, four cards have male figures, four cards have female figures and four contains both the sexes. The situations in the cards relate to the pleasant and unpleasant experiences, stresses and conflicts, interpersonal relationship, frustrations, attitude to self and others.

Administration: One card at a time is shown to the subject. He is asked to observe the card and prepare a story describing what has led to the event shown in the picture, what is presently happening, what the characters in the figure are feeling and thinking and what would be the outcome of the story.

After the story of the first card is completed by the subject, the next card is shown and the respondent is asked to proceed as before. The scoring and interpretation of the stories are done following the guidelines given in the manual.

Rorschach Ink Blot Test

The Rorschach's Ink Blot Test is used to find out the personality structure of the individual. The test was first devised and used by Hermann Rorschach, a Swiss Psychiatrist in 1911. The test can be administered on adolescents and adults.

Description: The test consists of ten symmetrical ink blot pictures impressions, each with nonspecific figures. The production of such figure is done by putting a few large ink blots on a piece of paper and then folding the paper. Thus the ink is spread and gives nonspecific figures. Every figure is to fulfill certain general and specific requirements. Out of these ten figures (one each in single card) five are coloured. All these cards are arranged in a particular order and numbered.

Administration: The subject is given one card at a time. Before showing the card the following instruction is given in the beginning:

> 'People see all sorts of things in these inkblot pictures: now tell me what you see, what it might be for you. What it makes you think of'?'

The subject generally holds the card for some time, turns it about as much as he likes and gives his response. An attempt is made to get at least one answer for every card. Suggestions of any form are avoided. Answers are noted down as long as they are given by the subject. The interpretation of the answers reveals subjects' general personality structure, like the way s/he deals with the inner drives, his introversive and extroversive tendencies, and so on.

Concept of Emotional Intelligence

Emotions are sources of motivation. They drive the individual to action by adding excitement. But for this the individual should have control over emotions i.e. the individual should have emotional maturity.

According to Wlater D. Smitson (1974) emotional maturity is a process in which the personality continually strives for greater sense of emotional health, both intra-physically and intra-personally. There are several criteria which reflects the emotional maturity of the individual. Bernard (1954) has stated some characteristic of mature emotional behaviour. These are as follows:

- Inhibition of direct expression of negative emotions
- Cultivation of positive, up building emotions
- Development of higher tolerance for disagreeable circumstances
- Increasing satisfaction from socially approved responses
- Increasing dependence of actions
- Ability to make a choice and not board about other choices
- Freedom from unreasonable fear
- Understanding and act in accordance with limitations
- Awareness of the ability and achievement of others
- Ability to be recognised without feeling disgraced
- Ability to carry victory and prestige with grace
- Ability to delay the gratification of impulses
- The enjoyment of daily living.

Causes of Lack of Emotional Stability

The major predisposing cause of emotional instability is the feeling of insecurity and uncertainty. Insecurity and uncertainty are the results of several social factors. If certain social factors which lead to emotional instability are either controlled or changed then it is possible to bring emotional maturity. Several social factors have been identified in this connection. These include unfavourable family relationship, conflict with family and friends, situations in which the individual feels inadequate, social expectations of more mature behaviour, adjustment to work/academic environment, and career problems.

Emotional conflicts, if not properly handled by the individual may lead to emotional out- burst. Emotional conflict produces tension, anxiety and stress within the individual. Mental conflict is a painful mental state in which opposing or contrary wishes, thoughts and needs are ranged against each other by pulling the individual in opposite direction. The individual loses control over his emotions.

Erick Fromm, one of the great thinkers of our time observed the evils of present society and modernisation. Due to complicated environment we are apt to lose control over our emotions. Fromm gave four postulates dealing with the general conditions of human existence. These are based on understanding of oneself which have bearing on emotional maturity. These postulates are as follows:

1. We are suffering and we are aware that we are.
2. We recognise the origin of our ill being.
3. We recognise that there is a way of overcoming our ill being.
4. We accept that in order to overcome our ill being we must follow certain directives for living and change our present practice of life.

Emotional Intelligence

Fulfillment of emotional needs helps the individual to become emotionally mature. Further, emotional maturity contributes towards emotional intelligence (EI). EI refers to an assessment of affective domain skills, capabilities and competencies that influence a person's ability to succeed in coping up with environmental demands and pressures.

EI includes empathy, self-control, self-awareness, pragmatic sensitivity to the situations persistence and self-motivation.

It has been found that self-awareness is the corner stone of emotional intelligence. It reflects the ability of a person to be able to know the reasons for his emotional response, thus improving his chances of handling it in an appropriate manner.

Emotional intelligence constitutes one of the important dimensions of affective domain. Moderate to high level of EI empower the individual in:

- Self-awareness
- Self-control
- Solving intrapersonal conflicts
- Self- motivation
- Decision making and
- Dealing with deviant workplace behaviour.

Methods of Fostering Emotional Intelligence

To develop emotional intelligence the individual should have control over his emotions. Several steps can be followed by the individual to have emotional control. Once control over emotions has been achieved, the individual automatically becomes emotionally mature. Emotional Maturity is the core component of Emotional Intelligence. The following steps can be taken by the individual to foster emotional intelligence.

- Developing self-confidence
- Eradicating personal inadequacy
- Developing competencies and skills in human relations

- Developing logic and application of reasons
- Developing realistic attitude
- Developing philosophy of life
- Use of Relaxation Strategies
- Practice of Meditation.

Auto Vincent (1998) VP, Human Resources of Mahindra Ford, Chennai observed that emotional intelligence is inherent in Indians. This may be because of our strong family ties. He has suggested only combining this inherited potential with the western concept of EI to arrive at the correct balance.

Bibliography

Adams, Donald and W. Chapman. (1998). Education and National Development in Asia: Trends and Issues, *International Journal of Educational Research, 29(7): 581-602.*

Ahlstrom, G. (1982). *Engineers and Industrial Growth,* London: Groom Helm.

Albett, Jonathan and Ivar-Andrė Slengesol. (2000). 'Education in Crisis: The Impact and Lessons of the East Asian Financial Shock.1997-1999' Washington DC: World Bank, Human Development Network.

Anastasi, A., & Urbina, S. (1997). *Psychological Testing* (7th Ed.). Upper Saddle River, NJ: Prentice-Hall.

Arons, A. B. (1997). *Teaching Introductory Physics.* USA, John Wiley & Sons, Inc.

Arthur, C. (1993). *Why Graduates Won't Wear Science,* New Scientist, March 27.

Astolfi, J. P.(1992). L'école pour apprendre: Paris, ESF.

Augustine, N. (1994). *Engineering Education for a Changing World,* ASEE

Aulich, Sen. T.G. (Chair), (1990). *Priorities for Reform in Higher Education, Report of the Senate Standing Committee on Employment, Education and Training,* Canberra: Australian Government Publishing Service.

Backer, Gary S. (1964). Human Capital, New York: National Bureau of Economic Research.

Banles Ed. Frank (1994). *Teaching Technology.* London: Routledge.

Basu, Aparna (1972). *Essays in History of Indian Education.* New Delhi: Concept Publication.

Bell, B. (2005). Pedagogies developed in the Learning in Science Projects and related theses, *International Journal of Science Education,* v. 27, p. 159-182.

Best, J. W. & Khan, J. V. (1990). *Research in Education.* New Delhi: PHI.

Betrand A. & Cebula J. P. (1980). *Tests, Measurement and Evaluation – A Developmental Approach.* Addison – Philippines: Wesley Publishing Company.

Bloom, B. S. (ed). (1985). *Developing Talent in Young People.* New York: Ballantine Books.

Bloom, B. S., Hasting, T. J., & Madaus, G. F. (1971). *Handbook on Formative and Summative Evaluation of Student Learning.* New York: McGraw Hill.

Bloom, Benjamin B. (Ed.). (1956). *Taxonomy of Educational Objectives: the classification of educational goals, by a committee of college and university examiners* 1st Ed. New York: Longman, Green.

Bloom, Benjamin S. (1956). *Taxonomy of Educational Objectives.* Boston: Allyn and Bacon.

Bloom, Benjamin S. (1980). *All Our Children Learning.* New York: McGraw-Hill.

Bogantes, B. (1993). La cooperación en el enfoque centrado en la persona. En *La cooperación en los grupos: Un modelo de trabajo centrado en la persona.* (pp. 44-65). Universidad Iberoamericana, Ciudad de México.

Bohart, A. (2000). Carl Rogers' Helping System: Journey and Substance. *British Journal of Guidance & Counselling, 28* (2), 297.

Bong, M. & Skaalvik, E. M. (2003). Academic self-concept and self-efficacy: How different are they really. *Educational Psychology Review, 15* (19), 1-40.

Bouchard, T. J., & Segal, N. L.: Environment and IQ. In B.B. Wolman (Ed.). (1985). *Handbook of Intelligence: Theories, Measurements, and Applications* (pp. 391-464). New York: John Wiley

Bowring, Philip. (2000). 'East Asia's Revival of hope', International Herald Tribune (January), Reprinted in '*The Asian Age*', 10th January, p.18.

Braham, J.(1992). *The Silence of the Nerds?* Machine Design, Volume 64, No. 17, p.77.

Brown George & Hutton N. (1997). *Explanation & Explaining.* Macmillan Education

Carnoy, Martin (ed). (1995): *International Encyclopedia of Economics of Education.* Oxford: Pargamon.

Carr, H.E. (1964). *Studies in Revolution,* New York: Grossett and Dunlap.

Clegg, Victoria L. and William E. Cashin. (1986). Improving Multiple-Choice Tests. Idea Paper 16, Center for Faculty Evaluation and Development, Kansas State University.

Cohen, L.& L. Manion (1983). *A Guide to Teaching Practice.* London: Methuen.

Cravino, J. P.(2004). Ensino da Física Geral nas Universidades Públicas Portuguesas e sua Relação com o Insucesso Escolar - Caracterização do Problema e Desenho, Implementação e Avaliação de uma Intervenção Didáctica: Vila Real, Universidade de Trás-os-Montes e Alto Douro.

Crouch, C., and Mazur, E. (2001). Peer Instruction: Ten Years of Experience and Result: Am. J. Phys., V. 69, p. 970-7.

Crow, L. D. & Crow, A. (1973). *Educational Psychology.* New Delhi: Eurasia Publishing House.

Crow, L.D. & Crow, A. (1962). *An Introduction to Guidance*. New Delhi. Eurasia Publishing House.

Crow, L.D. & Crow, A. (1973). *Educational Psychology*. New Delhi: Eurasia Publishing House.

Daniels, M., Devlin, B., & Roeder, K.(1997). Of genes and IQ. In B. Devlin, S. E. Fienberg., & K. Roeder (pp. 45-70). *Intelligence, Genes, and Success: Scientists respond to The Bell Curve*. New York: Springer.

David Merrill, M. (1997). *Instructional Design: Readings*. New York: Prentice-Hall.

Davis, Barbara Gross (1993). *Tools for Teaching*. San Francisco: Jossey-Bass.

Department of Employment, Education and Training (2005). *Selected Higher Education Statistics 2004*, DEET, Canberra: AGPS.

Department of Employment, Education, Training and Youth Affairs (1998). *Selected Higher Education Statistics 1997,* DEETYA, Canberra: AGPS

Department of Labour and National Service (1973). *Survey of the Australian Engineering Profession-1971,* Canberra: Australian Government Printing Service.

Devlin, B., Fienberg, S. E., Resnick, D. P., & Roeder, K. (Eds.) (1997). *Intelligence, Genes, and Success: Scientists respond to The Bell Curve*. New York: Springer.

Diedrich, G. (2000). *Private Communication,* Hamburg, Germany, July.

Edward de Bono (2000). *New Thinking for the New Millennium.* Renguin Books.

Ellington, Henry & Percival, Fred (1984). *A Handbook of Educational Technology.* Kogan Page.

Engle, R. A., and Conant, F. R. (2002). Guiding Principles for Fostering Productive Disciplinary Engagement: Explaining an Emergent Argument in a Community of Learners Classroom: *Cognition and Instruction*, V. 20, p. 399-483.

Erickson, Bette LaSere and Diane Weltner Strummer(1991). Teaching College Freshmen San Francisco: Jossey-Bass.

Eysenck, H.(1971). *Race, Intelligence and Education*. London: Maurice Temple Smith.

Felder, R. M. (1995).We never said it would Be Easy: *Chem. Engr. Education*, V. 29, pp. 32-33.

Felder, R. M. (1997). Beating the Numbers Game: Effective Teaching in Large Classes, ASEE Annual Conference: Milwaukee, WI.

Felder, R. M. (2004). Teaching engineering at a research university: problems and possibilities: *Educación Química*, v. 15, p. 40-42.

Felder, R. M. (2007). Research on Teaching and Learning Enginnering, in Lecture, A. o. C. E. A., editor, Department of Chemical and Biological Engineering, University of Missouri-Rolla.

Felder, R. M., and Brent, R. (1999). How to Improve Teaching Quality: *Quality Management Journal*, v. 6, p. 9-21.

Felder, R. M., and Brent, R. (2007). Cooperative Learning, in Mabrouck, P. A., editor, Active Learning: Models from the Analytical Sciences: Washington, DC: American Chemical Society, ACS Symposium Series 970.

Feldman, D. H. (1985). *Nature's Gambit: Child Prodigies and the Development of Human Potential.* New York: Basic Books.

Ferster, C. B. & Skinner, B. F. (1957). *Schedules of Reinforcement.* New York: Appleton-Century-Crofts.

Findley, W. G., (Ed.). (1963). The Impact and Improvement of School Testing Programmes. The Sixty Second Yearbook of the National Society for the Study of Education, Part II, Chicago University of Chicago Press

Fuhrman, Miriam. (1996). Developing Good Multiple-Choice Tests and Test Questions. *Journal of Geoscience Education* 44; pp 379-384.

Gabbard, G. O. (Ed), (1989). Sexual exploitation in professional relationships. Washington D.C.: American Psychiatric Press.

Garrett, H, E (1958). *Statistics in Psychology and Education.* New York: Longmans.

Gijlers, H., and Jong, T. D. (2005). The relation between Prior Knowledge and Students' Collaborative Discovery Learning Process: *J. of Research in Science Teaching*, v. 42, p. 264-282.

Glaser R. (Ed.) (1962). *Training Research and Education.* New York: Columbia University Press.

Glaser R. (Ed.). (1965). Teaching machines and programmed learning II: data and directions. Washington D.C.: National Education Association.

Glaser R. (Ed.). (1978). *Research and Development and School Change.* New York: Wiley.

Glaser R. (Ed.). (1983). Cognitive and Motivational Aspects of Instruction: selected International Congress papers. Amsterdam: Elsevier.

Glaser R. (Ed.). (2000). Advances in Instructional Psychology: *Educational Design And Cognitive Science.* Volumes 1–5. Mahwah, N.J. Lawrence Erlbaum and Associates.

Gordon, G. (2000). Comparability of postgraduate academic qualification: Some issues, challenges and experiences: *Higher Education*, v. 40, p. 377-388.

Gorsky, P., Caspi, A., and Trumper, R. (2006). Campus-based university students' use of dialogue: *Studies in Higher Education*, v. 31, p. 71-87.

Gronlund, N. (1993). *How to make achievement tests and assessments.* New York: Allyn and Bacon.

Grounlund, N.E. & Linn, R. L. (1995). *Measurement & Evaluation in Teaching*, New York: Macmillan Pub. Co.

Guay, F., Vallerand, R. J., & Blanchard, C. (2000). On the assessment of situational intrinsic and extrinsic motivation: The situational motivation scale (SIMS). *Motivation and Emotion, 24* (3), 175-213.

Guilford, J. P. (1965). *Fundamental Statistics in Psychology and Education.* New York: McGraw Hill.

Guthrie E.R. (1935). *The Psychology of Learning.* New York: Harper & Row

Hake, R. (1998). Interactive-engagement vs traditional methods: A six-thousand-student survey of mechanics test data for introductory physics courses: Am. J. Phys., v. 66, p. 64-74.

Hampton, S. E., and Reiser, R. A. (2004). Effects of a theory-based feedback and consultation process on instruction and learning in college classrooms: *Research in Science Education*, v. 45, p. 497-527.

Haq, M. S. (1975). *Education and Development Strategy in South and South East Asia*, Honolulu: East-west Centre.

Harper, A.E. (Jr) & Harper, E.S.(1985). *Preparing Objective Examinations*, Printice Hall of India Pvt. Ltd.

Heller, P., R.Keith, and Anderson, S. (1992). Teaching problem solving through cooperative grouping. Part1: Group versus individual problem solving: Am. J. of Phys., v. 60, p. 627-636.

Hendriks, P. G. & Van Snippenburg, L. B. (2002). Measuring motivations for media exposure: A thesis. *Quality and Quantity, 36* (3), 259-276.

Herrnstein, R. J., & Muray, C. (1994). *The bell curve.* New York: The Free Press.

Hohn, R.L. (1995). *Classroom Learning & Teaching.* Longman Publishers.

Howe, M. J. A.(1997). *IQ in Question: The truth about intelligence.* London: Sage.

Hoyle, Eric. (1969). *The Role of the Teacher.* New York: Routledge & Kegan Paul.

Hudson, L. (1975). *Human Beings*, London: Cape.

Hull, Clark (1952). A History of Psychology in Autobiography. Worcester. MA: Clark University Press.

Jacobs, Lucy Cheser & Clinton I. Chase (1992). *Developing and Using Tests Effectively: A Guide for Faculty.* San Francisco: Jossey-Bass.

Jakobeit, Cord. (1999). The World Bank and Human Development, *Development and Cooperation,* No.6 (Nov/Dec): 4 -5.

Jensen, A. R. (1969). How much can we boost IQ and scholastic achievement? *Harvard Educational Review*, 39, 1-123.

Johnston, C. (1994). *Profession moves to convert conservatism to social relevance,* Campus Review, November 24-30, p.13.

Kearney, M. (2004). Classroom Use of Multimedia-Supported Predict-Observe-Explain Tasks in a Social Constructivist Learning Environment: *Research in Science Education*, v. 34, p. 427-453.

Keeves, J. P. (Ed.). (1997). *Educational Research, Methodology and Measurement: An International Hand book.* Oxford: Pargamon Press.

Ketteridge, Steve & Stephanie Marshall. (1999). *A Hand book for Teaching and Learning in Higher Education.* New Delhi: Crest Publishing House.

Khan, A. R. (1998). The Impact of Globalization on South Asia and Growth and Poverty in East and South East Asia in the Era of Globalization, in A. S. Bhalla (ed.), *Globalization Growth and Marginalization.* pp. 103-124 and 125-148. London: Macmillan.

Kline, P.(1991). Intelligence: The Psychometric View. London: Routledge.

Koen, V.B. (1984). *Toward a Definition of the Engineering Method,* Engineering Education, Vol 75, 3, Pp. 150-158, Washington, DC: American Society for Engineering Education (ASEE).

Köhler, Wolfgang (1925). The mentality of apes, transl. from the 2nd German edition by Ella Winter. London: Kegan, Trench and New York: Harcourt, Brace and World.

Köhler, Wolfgang (1929). *Gestalt Psychology.* New York: Liveright. London: Bell 1930. A heavily revised translation into German, Psychologische Probleme, was published in 1933 by Springer, Berlin.

Köhler, Wolfgang (1938). *The Place of Value in a World of Facts.* New York: Liveright. Norton.

Köhler, Wolfgang (1940). *Dynamics in Psychology.* New York: Liveright.

Köhler, Wolfgang (1947). *Gestalt Psychology: an introduction to new concepts in modern psychology.* New York: Liveright.

Köhler, Wolfgang (1969). *The task of Gestalt psychology.* Princeton University Press.

Köhler, Wolfgang (1971). Henle, Mary (ed). The selected papers of Wolfgang Köhler. New York: Liveright.

Larson, M.S. (1979). *The Rise of Professionalism: A Sociological Analysis,* Berkeley, CA: University of California Press.

Lewin K. (1943). Defining the 'Field at a Given Time'. *Psychological Review.* 50: 292-310.

Lewin, K. (1946). Action Research and Minority Problems. *J Soc. Issues* 2(4): 34-46.

Lewin, K.; Lippitt, R.; White, R.K. (1939). Patterns of aggressive behavior in experimentally created social climates. *Journal of Social Psychology* 10: 271-301.

Liungman, C.G. (1975). *What is IQ? Intelligence, Heredity and Environment.* London: Gordon Cremonesi.

Locke, R.R. (1984). *The End of the Practical Man: Higher Education and the Institutionalisation of Entrepreneurial Performance in Germany, France and Great Britain-1880 to 1940,* in McKay, J. (ed), Industrial Development And The Social Fabric, London: JAI Press Inc., Volume 7.

Lopes, J. B.(2004). Aprender e Ensinar Física: Textos Universitários de Ciências Sociais e Humanas: Lisboa, Fundação Calouste Gulbenkian, 430 p.

Loren. W. Anderson & David. R. Krathwohl (2001). *Taxonomy for Learning, Teaching and Assessing—A Revision of Bloom's Taxonomy of Educational Objectives.* Longman.

Lyotard, F.J.(1984). *The Postmodern Condition:A Report on Knowledge.* Minneapolis: University of Minnesota Press.

Mager, R.F. & Pipe, P. (1997). Analyzing Performance Problems: Or, You Really Oughta Wanna—How to Figure out Why People Aren't Doing What They Should Be, and What to do About It (3rd Ed.). Atlanta, GA: The Center for Effective Performance Inc.

Mager, R.F. (1973). Measuring Instructional Intent Or, Got a Match?. Atlanta, GA: The Center for Effective Performance Inc.

Mager, R.F. (1983). Troubleshooting the Troubleshooting Course, or, Debug D'Bugs. Atlanta, GA: The Center for Effective Performance Inc.

Mager, R.F. (1984). Developing Attitude toward Learning (2nd Ed.). Atlanta, GA: The Center for Effective Performance Inc.

Mager, R.F. (1986). How to Write a Book. Atlanta, GA: The Center for Effective Performance Inc.

Mager, R.F. (1997). Goal Analysis: How to Clarify Your Goals So You Can Actually Achieve Them (3rd Ed.). Atlanta, GA: The Center for Effective Performance Inc.

Mager, R.F. (1997). How to Turn Learners on... Without Turning Them Off: Ways to Ignite Interest in Learning (3rd Ed.). Atlanta, GA: The Center for Effective Performance Inc.

Mager, R.F. (1997). Making Instruction Work: Or Skill bloomers: A Step-By-Step Guide to Designing and Developing Instruction That Works (2nd Ed.). Atlanta, GA: The Center for Effective Performance Inc.

Mager, R.F. (1997). Measuring Instructional Results. (3rd Ed.). Atlanta, GA: The Center for Effective Performance Inc.

Mager, R.F. (1997). Preparing Instructional Objectives: A Critical Tool in the Development of Effective Instruction (3rd Ed.). Atlanta, GA: The Center for Effective Performance Inc.

Mager, R.F. (1999). What Every Manager Should Know About Training: An Insider's Guide to Getting Your Money's Worth From Training (2nd Ed.). Atlanta, GA: The Center for Effective Performance Inc.

Mager, R.F. (2014). Making Schools Work. Carefree, AZ: Mager Associates, Inc.

Mager, Robert F. (1997). Preparing Instructional Objectives a critical tool in the development of Effective Instruction (3rd Ed.). Atlanta, Ga.: Center for Effective Performance.

Mann, R.C.(1919). *The American Spirit in Education,* US Bureau of Education Bulletin, No. 30 (1919) p.50.

Manolakes, L. A.: Cognitive Ability, Environmental Factors, and Crime: Predicting Frequent Criminal Activity. In B. Devlin, S.E. Fienberg. & K. Roeder (pp. 235-255). *Intelligence, Genes, and Success: Scientists respond to The Bell Curve.* New York: Springer.

Mayer, J. D. & Cobb, C. D. (2000). Educational policy on emotional intelligence: Does it make sense? *Educational Psychology Review, 12* (2), 163-183.

Mazumder, Tapas. (1998). Economics of Indian Education: The Emerging Policy, and Finance' *Asian Development Review, 15(2): 86-130.*

Mazur, E. (1997). *Peer Instruction, a user's manual.* New Jersey, Prentice Hall, 253 p.

Mc. Morris, R. S. (1967): *Educational and Psychological Measurement.* Oxford & IBH , Calcutta.

McGregor, D. (1960). *The Human Side of Enterprise,* New York: McGraw-Hill.

McKeachie, Wilbert (1994). *Teaching Tips: Strategies, Research, and Theory for College and University* Teachers (9th Ed.) Lexington, Mass: D.C. Heath and Company.

Meltzer, D. E., and Manivannan, K. (2002). Transforming the lecture-hall environment: The fully interactive physics lecture: *American Journal of Physics*, v. 70, p. 639-654.

Merrill, D. C., Reiser, B. J., Ranney, M. & Trafton, J. G. (1992). Effective Tutoring Techniques: A Comparison of Human Tutors and Intelligent Tutoring Systems. Journal of the Learning Sciences2 (3): 277.

Merrill, D., Reiser, B., Merrill, S. & Landes, S. (1995). Tutoring: Guided Learning by Doing. Cognition and Instruction 13 (3): 315.

Miller, Harry G., Reed G. Williams, and Thomas M Haldyna (1978). Beyond Facts: Objective Ways to Measure Thinking Englewood Cliffs: Educational Technology Publications.

Miner, J. B. (2005). Organizational Behavior: Behavior 1: Essential Theories of Motivation and Leadership. Armonk: M.E. Sharpe.

Natarajan, V. (1976). Towards Better Questions. New Delhi: Association of Indian Universities.

Neumann, K., and Welzel, M. (2007). A new lab work course for physics students: Devices, Methods and Research Projects: Eur. J. Physics, v. 28, p. 61-69.

Noble, F.D. (1984). *The Forces of Production: A Social History of Industrial Automation,* New York: Alfred. E. Knopf.

Norman M. Goble & J.F.Porter (1977). The Changing Role of the Teacher. Paris: UNESCO.

Novak, G. M., Patterson, E. T., Gavrin, A. D., and Christian, W. (1999). *Just-in-time teaching: blending Active Learning with web technology*: NJ, Prentice Hall, Upper Saddle River.

Palmer, S. and Szymanska, K. (1994). How to avoid being exploited in counselling and psychotherapy. *Counselling*, Journal of the British Association for Counselling, 5, 1, 24.

Palmer, S. and Szymanska, K. (1994). Referral guidance for participants attending stress management training courses. *Stress News*, Journal of the International Stress Management Association, 5, 4, 10- 11.

Papanek, Gustav. (1988). The New Asian capitalism: An Economic Portrait, cit in P.L.Berger and H.H.M. Hsiao (eds), *In Search of an Asian development Model,* pp 27-80. Brunswick: Transaction Books.

Paul. D. Eggen *et al.* (1979). *Strategies for Teachers*. New York: Prentice Hall.

Paulsen, M.B., & Wells, C.T.(1998). *Domain differences in the epistemological beliefs of college students,* Research in Higher Education, 39(4), pp.365-384.

Pavlov, I. P. (1927). *Conditioned Reflexes*. Oxford: Oxford Univ. Press.

Payne, D. A. & Mc. Morris, R. S. (1967). *Educational and Psychological Measurement*. Calcutta: Oxford & IBH.

Pearson, P.H. (1974). Conceptualizing and measuring openness to experience in the context of psychotherapy. En D. A. Wexler & L. North Rice (Eds.), *Innovations in client-centered therapy* (pp. 139-170). New York: John Wiley & Sons, Inc.

Peel, E. A.(1956). *The Psychological Basis of Education*. London: Oliver and Boyd.

Pope, K.S. (1990). Therapist -Patient Sexual Involvement: A Review of the Research. *Clinical Psychology Review*, 10, 477-490.

Ramsden, P. (1987). Improving Teaching and Learning in Higher Education: the case for a relational perspective: *Studies in Higher Education*, v. 12, p. 275-286.

Ramsden, P. (1991). A Performance Indicator of Teaching Quality in Higher Education: The Course Experience Questionnaire: *Studies in Higher Education*, v. 16, p. 129-150.

Razik, Taher A. (1972). System Approach to Teacher Training and Curriculum Development- The case of Developing Countries. Paris: UNESCO.

Redish, E. F. (1994). The implications of cognitive studies for teaching physics: Am. J. of Phys., v. 62, p. 796-803.

Redish, E. F. (2003). *Teaching Physics with the Physics Suite*. USA, John Wiley & Sons, Inc., 216 p.

Redish, E., and Steinberg, R. (1999). Teaching Physics: Figuring Out What Works: *Physics Today*, v. 52, p. 24-30.

Reynolds, M. C. (ed.) (1990). *Knowledge Base for the Beginning Teachers*, Pargamon Press, Oxford.

Romiszowski, A. J. (1981). *Designing instructional systems: Decision making in course planning and curriculum design*. New York: Kogan Page.

Romiszowski, A.J. (1984). *Producing Instructional Systems*. London: Kogan Page.

Romiszowski, A.J. (Ed.). (1997). A Systems Approach to Education & Training. New York: Kogan page.

Roy, R. (2002). Information Based Instruction (IBI) and Future. *Jour. of NEIES*, IX (I): pp. 150-158. Shillong.

Roy, R. (2007). Ethno-Pedagogy: *Education of Tribes, Teachers' Training and Juxtaposition of Status*. New Delhi: Shipra Publications.

Roy, R. (Ed.). (2008). *Beyond Curriculum, Pedagogy and Teachers' Training for* Environmental Education. New Delhi: Shipra Publications

Roy, R. (Ed.). (2009). Engineering Education: *Perspectives, Issues and Concerns*. New Delhi: Shipra Publications.

Roy, R. (Ed.). (2009). Women, Education and Development: *Perspectives, Issues and Concerns*. New Delhi: Shipra Publications

Roy, R. (Ed.). (2011). Educational Technology *in Changing Society*. New Delhi: Shipra Publications

Roy, R. (Ed.). (2014). Education and Sustainable Development. New Delhi: Shipra Publications

Roy, R. *et al.* (2004). Education, Technology and development: An Approach, *ISC*, 18(4), 36 – 44.

Roy, R. *et al.* (2004). Technology and Education for Human Resource Development in Asia and Pacific, Cit in Conference Proceedings of International Conference on New Challenges in Technology Education for HRDAP, pp. tp. 114 – 125, Kolkata.

Roy, R. *et al.* (2006). Attitude of the Working Engineers towards Distance Mode of Instruction. *IJOL; 15* (3), 225-235.

Roy, R. et. al. (2004). Interface between Creativity and Education, Cit in Proceedings of National Seminar on Applying Creativity and Systems Thinking For Business Innovation, April, 2004, pp. 67 – 72, Kolkata.

Roy, Rajarshi. (2005). Social Aspects of Educational Researches: Trends and Issues, *ISC*, 19(3), 39 – 46,

Russell, J. (1990). Breaking Boundaries: A research note. *Counselling*, Journal of the British Association for Counselling, 1, 2.

Schultz, Theodore W. (1990). '*Restoring Economic Equilibrium*', Cambridge: Basil Blackwell.

Scott, P. H., Mortimer, E. F., and Aguiar, O. G. (2006). The Tension Between Authoritive and Dialogic Discourse: A Fundamental Characteristic of

Meaning Making Interactions in High School Science Lessons: Science Education, v. 90, p. 605-631.

Sen, Amartya. (2000). *Development as Freedom*. New Delhi: Oxford University Press.

Sing, A. (2002). Monograph on Internal Assessment. New Delhi: AIU-Publication Cell.

Singh, A. K. (1982). *Tests, Measurements and Research Methods in Behavioral Sciences*. New Delhi: Tata McGraw Hill Publishing Company Ltd.

Singh, R.P. (1969). *The Indian Teacher*. New Delhi: National.

Singh, R.S. (1992). *Teachers' Effectiveness in India*. New Delhi: Chugh Pub.

Skinner, B. F. (1953). *Science and Human Behavior*. New York: Macmillan.

Skinner, B. F. (1953). *The Possibility of a Science of Human Behavior*. New York: The Free House.

Skinner, B. F. (1958). *Verbal Behavior*. Acton, MA: Copley Publishing Group.

Skinner, B. F. (1976). *Particulars of my life*: Part 1 of an Autobiography. New York: Kogan page.

Skinner, B. F. (1979). *The Shaping of a Behaviorist*: Part 2 of an Autobiography New York: Kogan page.

Skinner, B. F. (1983). *A Matter of Consequences*: Part 3 of an Autobiography. New York: Kogan page.

Skinner, B.F. (1938). *Behavior of Organisms*. New York: Appleton-Century-Crofts.

Skinner, C. E. (Ed.) (1958). *Essentials of Educational Psychology*. New Jersey: Prentice-Hall.

Stanley, J. C. & Hopkins, K. D.(1978). *Educational and Psychological Measurement and Evaluation*. New Delhi: Prentice Hall of India Private Limited.

Stephen, J. G. (1995). *Educational Measurement and Testing*. Boston: Allyn and Bacon. Inc.

Sternberg, R. J., & Grigorenko, E. (Eds.) (1997). *Intelligence, Heredity, and Environment*. Cambridge: Cambridge University Press.

Strawbridge, S. (2001). Carl Rogers. *The Psychologist, 14* (4), 182-185.

Streeten, Paul. (1998). 'Globalization: Threat or Opportunity?' *Pakistan Development Review,* 37(4) (Part 1: Winter): pp 51-83.

Taba, Hilda (1962). *Curriculum Development: Theory and Practice*. New York: Harcourt Brace & World.

Taba, Hilda (1967). *Teacher's Handbook for Elementary Social Studies*. Palo Alto, Calif.: Addison-Wesley.

Taiwo, A. A. (1995). *Fundamentals of Classroom Testing*. New Delhi: Vikas Publishing House Pvt. Ltd.

Thorndike, E. L. (1911). *Animal Intelligence: Experimental Studies*. New York: Macmillan.

Tilak, J.B.G. (2001). Education and Development, *Indian Social Science Review,* 3 (2): pp. 219-266.New Delhi.

Tolman, E. C. (1932). *Purposive Behavior in Animals and Men.* New York: Century.

Tolman, E. C. (1938). The Determinants of Behavior at a Choice Point. *Psychological Review*, 45, 1-41.

Tolman, E. C. (1942). *Drives towards war.* New York: Appleton-Century-Crofts.

Tolman, E. C. (1951). Behavior and Psychological Man: essays in motivation and learning. Berkeley: Univ. of California Press.

Tolman, E.C. (1948). Cognitive Maps in Rats and Men. *Psychological Review*, 55, 189-208.

UNDP. 1999-2003. *Human Development Reports*, New York, Oxford University Press.

Van Dalen, D.B. (1999). *Understanding Educational Research: An Introduction.* New York: McGraw-Hill.

Wagner, Robert W. Edgar Dale (1970). Professional Theory into Practice. 9(2).

Watson, J. B. (1928). *Psychological Care of Infant and Child.* New York: W.W. Norton Company.

Watson, J. B., Goldman, R. N., & Warner, M. S. (Eds.). (2002). *Client-centered and experiential psychotherapy in the 21st century: Advances in theory, research and practice.* London: PCCS Books.

Watson, J.B. (1903). *Animal Education*, Chicago: University of Chicago Press.

Watson, J.B. (1925). *Behaviorism.* New York: W.W. Norton & Company Inc.

Weinberg, R.A. (1989). *Intelligence and IQ: Landmark issues and great debates.* American Psychologist, 44, 98-104.

Wertheimer, M. (1938). Gestalt theory. In W. D. Ellis (Ed.), *A source book of Gestalt psychology* (pp. 1–11). London, England: Routledge & Kegan Paul.

Wertheimer, M. (1938). The General Theoretical Situation. In W. D. Ellis (Ed.), *A source book of Gestalt psychology* (pp. 12–16). London, England: Routledge & Kegan Paul.

Wertheimer, M. (1938c). Laws of organization in perceptual forms. In W. D. Ellis (Ed.), *A source book of Gestalt psychology* (pp. 71–94). London, England: Routledge & Kegan Paul. (Original work published 1923)

Wertheimer, M. (1945). *Productive thinking.* New York: Harper.

White, R. T., & Gunstone, R. F. (1992). *Probing Understanding.* London: Falmer Press.

Wilenski, H. (1964). *Varieties of Work Experience,* in Borrow, H. (ed) Man in a World of Work, Boston: Houghton-Miffin.

Willam, W& Stephen J.G. (1985). *Educational Measurement and Testing,* Allyn and Bacon Inc, Boston.

William, W. & Stephen, J.G. (1995). *Educational Measurement and Testing.* Boston: Allyn and Bacon Inc.

Wilson, R. (2005). *Projections of Occupations and Qualifications,* DfEE & Institute of Employment Records, Warwick, UK: University of Warwick

Winship, C., & Korenman, S.(1997). Does staying in school make you smarter? The effect of education on IQ in The Bell Curve. In B. Devlin, S.E. Fienberg., & K. Roeder (pp. 215-234). *Intelligence, Genes, and Success: Scientists respond to The Bell Curve.* New York: Springer, 1997.

Ziman, J. (1991). *Reliable Knowledge: An exploration of the grounds for belief in science,* Cambridge: Cambridge University Press.

Index